GETTING A GOVERNMENT JOB:
THE CIVIL SERVICE HANDBOOK

PETERSON'S

A **nelnet** COMPANY

About Peterson's, a Nelnet company

To succeed on your lifelong educational journey, you will need accurate, dependable, and practical tools and resources. That is why Peterson's is everywhere education happens. Because whenever and however you need education content delivered, you can rely on Peterson's to provide the information, know-how, and guidance to help you reach your goals. Tools to match the right students with the right school. It's here. Personalized resources and expert guidance. It's here. Comprehensive and dependable education content—delivered whenever and however you need it. It's all here.

For more information, contact Peterson's, 2000 Lenox Drive, Lawrenceville, NJ 08648; 800-338-3282; or find us on the World Wide Web at www.petersons.com.

© 2009 Peterson's, a Nelnet company

Previous editions © 2001, 2003, 2005

Stephen Clemente, President; Bernadette Webster, Director of Publishing; Therese DeAngelis, Editor; Mark D. Snider, Production Editor; Ray Golaszewski, Manufacturing Manager; Linda M. Williams, Composition Manager; Cara Cantarella, Contributing Editor

ISBN-13: 978-0-7689-2796-2
ISBN-10: 0-7689-2796-X

Printed in the United States of America

10 9 8 7 6 5 4 3 2 1   11 10 09

First Edition

By printing this book on recycled paper (40% post consumer waste) 120 trees were saved.

Contents

Contents

Before You Begin

HOW THIS BOOK IS ORGANIZED

- **Part I** provides an overview of the U.S. government, the advantages and disadvantages of working for the federal government, and questions you should ask yourself to see if a government job is right for you. In addition, we've included information about salary and benefits, job qualifications, training and advancement, opportunities for veterans and students, and advice on finding jobs with state and municipal governments (with sample job announcements).

- **Part II** zeros in on the five fields in the federal government projected to experience the greatest job growth within the next few years: security, protection, compliance, and enforcement; medical and public health; accounting, budget, and business; engineering and sciences; and program management/analysis and administration. We also provide additional information about fields that are expected to experience increased demand. The chapters in Part II supply sample job announcements, outline typical qualifications for particular job categories, and tell you which fields of government work require that you take an exam.

- **Part III** lists some of the basics of conducting an effective and efficient job search. We provide advice on how you can determine what sort of job matches your personal skills, tips for sifting through thousands of job vacancy announcements to locate those that are best for you, and guidance about how to complete forms, present your education and work experience in the best light, and create an effective online resume.

- **Part IV** guides you through writing an outstanding cover letter and pulling together and submitting the various pieces of your application package. We also explain how to follow up on your application, how to prepare when you're called for an interview, and how to negotiate salary.

- **The Appendixes** contain a broad variety of supplemental information, including samples of resumes appropriate for the high-growth fields covered in Part II, a list of federal employment Web sites you can use in your job search, an overview of the types of government jobs that require you to pass an exam, and a glossary of common hiring terminology.

YOU'RE WELL ON YOUR WAY TO SUCCESS

The world of civil service employment offers an enormous array of opportunities and advantages. Your decision to use our book will give you an important advantage;

the information we've presented will help you get a head start on making sense of the sometimes confusing and complex process of finding a civil service job.

GIVE US YOUR FEEDBACK

Peterson's publishes a full line of civil service resources to help guide you through the hiring process. Peterson's publications can be found at your local bookstore, library, and college guidance office, and you can access us online at www.petersons.com.

We welcome any comments or suggestions you may have about this publication and invite you to complete our online survey at www.petersons.com/booksurvey. Or you can fill out the survey at the back of this book, tear it out, and mail it to us at:

Publishing Department
Peterson's, a Nelnet company
2000 Lenox Drive
Lawrenceville, NJ 08648

Your feedback will help us make your career and education dreams possible.

PART I
GETTING STARTED

The U.S. Government in Review

chapter 1

OVERVIEW

- **Where the jobs are: federal civilian employment**
- **Is a government job right for you?**
- **Comparing public-sector and private-sector employment**
- **It's up to you**
- **Summing it up**

The U.S. government is the nation's largest employer. About one in every six employed people in the United States is in some form of civilian government service. State and local governments employ five out of six public service workers; the remainder work for the federal government.

Over the next several years, the federal government projects that it will hire an additional 193,000 employees, primarily in five "mission critical" fields:

1. Security, protection, compliance, and enforcement
2. Medical and public health
3. Accounting, budget, and business
4. Engineering and sciences
5. Program management/analysis and administration

These positions encompass myriad professional fields and will be filled by government agencies across the United States and throughout the world.

WHERE THE JOBS ARE: FEDERAL CIVILIAN EMPLOYMENT

The federal government employs nearly 3 million civilian workers in the United States on a full-time basis, including postal employees. Although most federal departments and agencies are headquartered in the Washington, D.C., area, nine out of ten federal jobs are located outside the nation's capital.

Although many government employees work in large cities—for example, Norfolk-Virginia Beach, VA; Baltimore, MD; and Philadelphia, PA, have the highest number of federal workers—some federal employees work in small towns or in remote, isolated places such as lighthouses and forest ranger stations. And federal jobs exist around the world. In fact, approximately 90,000 federal employees work outside the United States, mostly in embassies or defense installations.

Many federal occupations parallel those in the private sector, including accounting, computer programming, and health care. Other types of employment opportunities are unique to the federal government, such as regulatory inspectors, Foreign Service officers, and Internal Revenue agents. More than 100 agencies and bureaus exist within the federal government, and each has specific employment needs.

Although numerous opportunities are available within the executive, legislative, and judicial branches of the federal government, the executive branch employs the majority of federal workers. Composed of the Office of the President, the cabinet departments, and about 100 independent agencies, commissions, and boards, the executive branch is responsible for a wide range of activities: It administers federal laws, conducts international relations, conserves natural resources, treats and rehabilitates disabled veterans, delivers the mail, conducts scientific research, maintains the flow of supplies to the Armed Forces, and oversees programs to promote the health and welfare of the people of the United States.

The Department of Defense, which includes the Army, Navy, Air Force, Marine Corps, and noncombat agencies such as the National Security Agency and the Defense Intelligence Agency, is the largest department within the executive branch. It employs about 35 percent of all civilian workers. Another 25 percent of federal workers are employed by the U.S. Postal Service, an independent agency. Other federal jobs are distributed among other departments, including the Department of Veterans Affairs, the Department of Homeland Security (DHS), and the Department of the Treasury.

Sixty-five agencies within the executive branch operate independently and do not fall under the jurisdiction of the larger departments. They include the Central Intelligence Agency (CIA), the Federal Communications Commission (FCC), the Federal Trade Commission (FTC), the Social Security Administration, the National Aeronautics and Space Administration (NASA), and the Environmental Protection Agency (EPA). Although these agencies account for fewer than 200,000 federal jobs, it's a good idea to keep them in mind when searching for public service employment.

Federal civilian employment is also available in the legislative branch of the federal government. This branch includes Congress, the Government Printing Office, the General Accounting Office, and the Library of Congress. The judicial branch, the smallest federal government employer, hires people for jobs within the U.S. court system.

White-Collar Government Occupations

Because of its wide range of responsibilities, the federal government employs white-collar workers in many occupational fields. ("White-collar" is an informal term that describes both salaried professionals and educated workers who perform semiprofessional tasks in office, administrative, and sales settings.) White-collar jobs account for about 90 percent of all federal civilian jobs. As the United States continues to shift from a manufacturing to a knowledge-based economy, the need will increase for professional workers with technical expertise and those with superb reasoning, communication, collaboration, and problem-solving skills. Government professional fields with the highest projected number of new hires through 2016 include information technology (IT), mathematics, health care, education, and library science.

Management, Business, and Finance

According to the Bureau of Labor Statistics (BLS), one-third of all federal employees work in management, business, and finance. Upper-level managers are responsible for directing the activities of government agencies, while midlevel managers supervise various programs and projects. Because they are responsible for overseeing the executive branch, senators and legislators are also categorized as white-collar management.

The General Accounting Office (GAO), Internal Revenue Service (IRS), and the Department of the Treasury employ accounting experts and budget administrators, and the demand for workers in this field is expected to increase significantly to include more than 20,000 new hires in the next few years. Accountants and auditors analyze financial reports and investigate government spending and inefficiencies. Additional business experts work in purchasing, cataloging, storage, and supply distribution—often on a large scale, given the size of the federal government. Most of these jobs are in the Department of Defense, and they include managerial and administrative positions, such as supply management officers, purchasing officers, and inventory management specialists, as well as large numbers of specialized clerical positions.

Professionals

About one-third of white-collar federal workers are categorized as professional workers, including lawyers, doctors, computer experts, scientists, and engineers. The majority of employees in this group work in the life sciences, physical sciences, and social sciences. For example, biologists determine the effectiveness of new medications, geologists predict hurricanes, and forest technicians help prevent forest fires in national parks.

The federal government—mostly in the Departments of Agriculture and the Interior—employs about 50,000 biological and agricultural science workers. Many of these employees work in forestry and soil conservation; others administer farm assistance programs. The Departments of Defense, Commerce, and the Interior typically employ physical scientists. Chemists, physicists, meteorologists, and cartographers can find work within the federal government, as can physical science technicians, meteorological technicians, and cartography technicians. Federal job opportunities for engineers and scientists will continue to expand over the next few years, with more than 17,000 new hires. Prospects for IT specialists are also expected to rise, with more than 11,000 new hires projected over the next 10 years.

Approximately 80,000 federal employees are nurses, surgeons, and physicians who work in hospitals or in medical, dental, and public health occupations. The federal government also employs dieticians, technologists, and physical therapists. Technician and aide jobs with the U.S. government include medical technicians, medical laboratory aides, and dental assistants. Health-care employees work primarily for the Veterans Administration (VA), although some work for the Department of Defense or the Department of Health and Human Services. Hiring projections within the medical and public health fields are very good—more than 35,000 health-care workers are projected to be hired by the federal government over the next several years.

Economists and other social scientists work for the U.S. government, as do psychologists and social workers (who work primarily for the Veterans Administration). Foreign affairs and international relations specialists typically find employment at the Department of State. Most social insurance administrators working for the federal government are employed by the Department of Health and Human Services.

Federal positions in law include professional positions such as attorneys and paralegals, as well as administrative positions like passport examiners and tax law specialists. The U.S. government hires claims examiners.

Many federal government departments require the expertise of engineers to construct bridges, develop computer systems, and design spacecraft. The Department of Defense employs experts in electronics, surveying, and drafting. Computer software engineers and computer network administrators write computer programs, analyze data, and ensure that computer systems run smoothly.

Professional mathematicians, statisticians, mathematics technicians, and statistical clerks are employed by the U.S. government, primarily with the Departments of Defense, Agriculture, Commerce, and Health and Human Services.

Office and Administrative Support

Nearly 15 percent of all federal jobs are in office and administrative support. Employees in these occupations assist management with administrative duties. General clerical workers, such as information and record clerks, secretaries, and administrative assistants, are employed in all federal departments and agencies. Office machine operators, stenographers, clerk-typists, mail and file clerks, telephone operators, and those in computer-related occupations are categorized as office support personnel. However, data compiled by the BLS indicate that the number of administrative support jobs in the federal government is declining as automated office procedures continue to replace duties once performed by clerical workers.

Other public service workers perform administrative work related to private business and industry. For example, they arrange and monitor contracts with the private sector and purchase goods and services needed by the federal government. These occupations include contract and procurement specialists, production control specialists, and IRS officers.

Service Workers

Eight percent of federal employees work in service occupations, including officers at federal prisons, criminal investigators, and health regulatory inspectors. These employees are generally hired by the Department of Justice (DOJ) or the Department of Agriculture (USDA). Service jobs are primarily filled by local and state governments, who hire firefighters, police officers, and state prison guards.

Many new positions with the federal government are linked to the establishment of the DHS, which was established by the Department of Homeland Security Act of 2002 in the aftermath of the September 11, 2001, terrorist attacks. In 2007, the number of federal workers hired for compliance and enforcement jobs increased fourfold, from 6,760 to 27,243. Continued hiring in this "mission-critical" field is expected as a result of expanded border security, customs, and immigration activities initiated by the Department of Homeland Security.

White-Collar Job Requirements

Entrance requirements for white-collar jobs vary widely. Some require that applicants have high school diplomas; others require an undergraduate or graduate degree. Although an advanced degree in a specified field is necessary in some professional occupations, such as physicians and lawyers, many others merely require some combination of education and experience, such as that of office clerk.

Entrants into administrative and managerial occupations with the federal government usually are not required to have knowledge of a specialized field. However, they must demonstrate potential by having earned a degree from a four-year college or significant and comparable job experience. New federal employees in these occupations usually begin as trainees and learn their duties on the job. Typical entry-level management positions include budget analysts, claims examiners, purchasing specialists, administrative assistants, and personnel specialists.

Technician, clerical, and aide-assistant occupations in the U.S. government include entry-level positions for applicants with a high school education or the equivalent. For many of these positions, no previous experience or training is required. Entry-level positions filled at the trainee level include engineering technicians, supply clerks, clerk-typists, and nursing assistants. Individuals who have junior college or technical school training or with specialized skills may enter these occupations at higher levels.

Blue-Collar Occupations

A blue-collar worker can be described as a member of the working class who typically performs manual labor and who earns an hourly wage rather than an annual or other type of salary. Blue-collar workers are distinguished from those in the service sector and from white-collar workers (who do not perform manual labor). Blue-collar occupations—such as construction, labor, and janitorial—provide full-time employment for nearly 300,000 federal workers. The Department of Defense employs about three-fourths of these workers in naval shipyards; arsenals and Army depots; construction sites; and harbor, flood control, irrigation, and reclamation projects. Other blue-collar positions are with the VA, the U.S. Postal Service, the General Services Administration, the Department of the Interior, and the Tennessee Valley Authority (TVA).

Skilled Laborers

Skilled laborers make up the largest blue-collar group of federal workers. Many are also employed in machine tool and metal work, motor vehicle operation, warehousing, and food preparation and service. The federal government employs blue-collar workers for maintenance and repair work as well, including electrical and electronic equipment installation and repair and vehicle and industrial equipment maintenance and repair. All these jobs require a range of skill levels, and most are comparable to occupations in the private sector.

Although the federal government employs blue-collar workers in many different fields, about fifty percent are concentrated in a small number of occupations. The largest group—skilled mechanics—perform in air-conditioning, aircraft, automobile, truck, electronics, sheet metal, and general maintenance mechanics. A great number of crafts-people are employed with the federal government as painters, pipefitters, carpenters, electricians, and machinists. About the same number are warehouse workers, truck drivers, and general laborers. Some blue-collar workers are employed with the U.S. government as janitors and food service workers.

Those who have had training in a skilled trade may apply for positions with the federal government at the journey level (the level of skill above that of an apprentice and below that of a master in the skilled trades). People with no previous training may apply for appointment to one of several apprenticeship programs. These generally last four years, during which trainees receive classroom and on-the-job training. After completing an apprenticeship, a federal worker is eligible for a position at the journey level. Many of these positions require little or no prior training or experience, including janitors, maintenance workers, messengers, and many others.

IS A GOVERNMENT JOB RIGHT FOR YOU?

Trying to get a job with the federal government is like trying to ride an elephant: It can be a safe and rather comfortable ride, and once you're on the elephant, it's not easy to fall off. But getting *on* the elephant? Now, that's another story.

To a job seeker, the federal government can seem overwhelmingly large—and as slow and ponderous as an elephant in the way it responds. This will become apparent to you when you see the amount of information you're asked to provide when applying for a position—and in the time it takes for the agency or department to respond to your application. Some job announcements remain open for several months and applications are not reviewed until after the closing date passes.

According to www.USAJOBS.gov, the federal government's official job Web site, most federal agencies contact potential candidates from 15 to 30 days after receiving their applications. It's not like sending your resume in response to an ad in the Sunday paper or on other job search Web sites. In fact, many people find the process of applying for a government job too complicated and time consuming, so they give up on the whole idea. This is unfortunate, however, because in spite of the complexity of applying for a position, there are real advantages to a civil service career, as we'll soon discuss. In fact, you may even decide that the best possible position for you is in the federal government.

With any job, you need to consider the advantages and disadvantages of taking the position—and each one's relative importance. Not every "pro" equals every "con." For example, for a particular job you're considering applying for, you may be able to name five advantages and only one disadvantage. But if that single disadvantage is an obstacle you're unable to overcome—say, the job requires relocating and you absolutely can't move—then it outweighs any number of advantages.

Other disadvantages may not be stumbling blocks so much as they are tradeoffs. This is especially true when contemplating a public service position. In addition to the obvious pros and cons of a job, keep in mind the intangibles. A career with the federal government brings with it a certain mindset, almost a lifestyle. For people who see this lifestyle as bringing peace of mind, this will be an advantage; for those who see it as repetitive or tedious, it will be a drawback.

Advantages of a Government Job

Let's examine some commonly accepted advantages of working for the federal government or for a state or local government.

The U.S. Government Is America's Largest Employer

Nearly 3 million civilian Americans work for the U.S. government. That's a lot of people—and a lot of jobs. With enormous size comes enormous diversity. Almost every imaginable occupation has a place in the federal government, from special agents and politicians to auto mechanics, pipefitters, and carpenters. There's room for satellite watchers and map readers, secretaries and file clerks, accountants and auditors, purchasing agents and contract administrators, scientists and medical doctors, teachers and law enforcement officers.

Not only does the federal government offer a wide range of occupational choices, but it also allows employees to combine their skills and education with their interests. For example, an engineering major might work for the Department of Transportation designing electrical equipment to help ensure safe air travel; a chemist might perform analytical chemistry for the Department of Agriculture to help solve problems affecting America's farms. Almost anyone can find a position that matches his or her educational background, skill set, and personal interests.

The Government Is Always Hiring

Roughly 10 percent of all currently filled federal jobs will become vacant in any given year. This is the result of turnover—attrition from retirement and promotions, as lower-grade employees apply for positions that higher-grade employees have vacated. According to the Office of Personnel Management (OPM), about 40 percent of the current federal work force will retire by 2016, creating a significant number of job vacancies.

What about the current economic crisis? Politicians may announce publicly that they're in favor of reducing the federal government, but the fact is that because of attrition, the government must always hire more workers, even during so-called hiring freezes and reorganizations. Additionally, the recession that began in late 2007 has actually spawned new government hiring programs, namely through the American Recovery and Reinvestment Act of 2009 (ARRA). In an effort to jump start the American economy, President Barack Obama signed the act into law in early 2009. The Recovery Act (sometimes informally called the economic stimulus plan) includes provisions for creating energy independence, modernizing health care and health-care records, improving education, rebuilding the nation's infrastructure, offering tax relief, and protecting those in economic need. Job seekers looking for federal recovery–related jobs may access these listings through www.USAJOBS.gov, or through a new government Web site that offers Recovery-related jobs, career planning, and information on the many kinds of financial opportunities offered by the U.S. government: FedBizOpps.gov.

A Government Job Is a Secure Job

Although getting a government job can prove to be a challenge, once you're "on the elephant," it's likely that no one will be able to get you off until you're good and ready. In other words, you can stay or leave according to your own inclination. Reductions in Force (RIFs) happen infrequently, and when they do, most government agencies faced with downsizing or restructuring achieve their goals through early retirements and by attrition (not filling the jobs left vacant by those who have taken other jobs or retired). Through the Voluntary Separation Payment Authority, federal agencies can offer optional retirement to employees who choose to separate by voluntary resignation, or they can offer early retirement incentive payments of up to $25,000.

A Government Job Provides Opportunities for Advancement and Growth

Once you're hired for a position with the federal government, you'll find that you have opportunities to move up or to move laterally in your field—or to change fields entirely. If you perform well, advancement is almost guaranteed, because good work is generally rewarded. For example, in the BLS, employees are eligible to advance to the next grade (and the next salary bracket) after one year of service. If you begin at the GS-5 level and perform your work effectively, you can advance to a GS-12 position within four years.

Many government agencies also offer fast track programs for even speedier advancement in your field. The security of a government position allows you to make fairly reliable long-term career plans. In most cases, you'll know just what you need to do to earn a promotion—and a raise to the next-higher pay grade.

A Government Job Is a Career in Public Service

Working for the government can provide a level of satisfaction that other careers can't offer. You are a public servant in the best sense. By example, consider the work and responsibilities of these important federal agencies:

- Federal Emergency Management Administration (FEMA)
- Federal Aviation Administration (FAA)
- Federal Bureau of Investigation (FBI)
- Small Business Administration (SBA)
- Centers for Disease Control and Prevention (CDC)
- National Institutes of Health (NIH)

Each of these agencies—and every one of their employees—is contributing to the health and welfare of the American people. Working for the federal government allows you to help solve problems that affect all Americans. Many employees of such agencies are midcareer professionals who have enjoyed success in private-sector careers but who want to give something back to their community or their country.

A Government Job Offers Opportunities for Advanced Professional Training

Not everyone who is hired by a government agency is prepared to begin working productively on their first day or to effectively handle an increase in job responsibility. In response to this need, federal and state agencies ensure that their employees are fully trained by offering multiple training and educational opportunities. These opportunities may include full or partial tuition reimbursement, or time off—sometimes with pay—to complete the programs. Some federal agencies will reimburse up to $10,000 per year of employees' student loans; others will cover the cost of graduate school should employees decide to pursue an advanced degree related to their work. Educational, training, and development opportunities offered by the federal government are *major* benefits, enabling employees to perform their jobs better and prepare for future promotions.

The Government Hires People at All Stages of Career Development

This is an important point. You may be a high school graduate who has virtually no work experience, or you may be a college student or recent graduate. You may be a midcareer worker seeking to find a new field, or you may be a veteran who is separating or retiring from the U.S. military. You may have a Ph.D. or you have earned your GED certificate. No matter where you are in your education or career, the government will have open positions for which you can apply.

The Federal Government Values Diversity

The federal government strives to be a model for workplace diversity, and it actively encourages minorities and candidates with disabilities to consider public service employment. To this end, the government offers fellowship and internship programs to recruit new employees and maintain a diverse workforce. Currently, about 17.6 percent of the federal government's workers are African American, 7.6 percent are Hispanic, 5.2 percent are Asian/Pacific Islanders, and 1.9 percent are Native Americans. As of 2007, about 1 percent of federal workers were classified as having disabilities.

Federal Jobs Offer Competitive Pay, Flexible Schedules, and Good Benefits

On average, salaries in the federal government are competitive with those in the private sector. Pay increases are regular and predictable, and they may be rapid for those who possess exceptional skills and a strong education.

For employees who care for children or other family members, the work-life balance offered by many government agencies can be an appealing benefit. Job sharing, flexible work schedules, telecommuting options, elder-care resources, employee assistance programs, and on-site child care centers are available to many civil service workers, especially at larger facilities. Moreover, federal benefits are competitive with those in the private sector: they include health insurance, retirement benefits, and vacation time, as well as travel subsidies for those who travel to and from work using public transportation.

Disadvantages of a Government Job

Of course, anyone seeking to work for the federal government needs to consider the drawbacks as well as the advantages of such a position.

You Work for a Bureaucracy

The government is a bureaucracy—an organization with standardized procedures that guide most or all processes and one that holds to a formal division of powers. Everything you do must be approved through a fairly rigid chain of command, and every action you take must have a precedent. Your employment is regulated by preexisting guidelines and procedures outlined in a personnel manual. These regulations protect you from being unfairly fired and help ensure that your position will not be eliminated.

However, such rules also require regular adherence to standards that may seem outdated or unreasonable to certain types of workers. A bureaucracy the size of the U.S. government changes slowly. Many of its regulations and requirements were established long ago, and they may still remain in force even though the situations they addressed may have changed.

All is not lost, though. According to a recent OPM publication, "Modernizing Merit: OPM's Guiding Principles for Service Transformation," the federal government recognizes that problems have been created by layers of bureaucracy within its civilian workforce. It admits that standardized rules and regulations established to encourage fairness and equal treatment among federal workers have, at times, fostered an environment of mediocrity and rigidity. The OPM is doing its part to eradicate this one-size-fits-all frame of mind by allowing government agencies more autonomy and flexibility in hiring and personnel decisions.

The Government Favors Rule Followers Over Risk Takers

A bureaucracy by nature favors rule followers. This makes perfect sense. If you're not the type to strictly adhere to long-established rules, however, this fact can challenge your patience and persistence. If you're the kind of person who sees what needs to be done, wants to do it, and is accustomed to doing it on your own, you may find this aspect of civil service difficult to bear. What you may view as a case of taking initiative may be viewed by superiors as unreasonable risk taking: After all, you're acting without precedent and without approval. You may believe you are being a self starter, but in the eyes of a bureaucracy you may look like a loose cannon.

Change in Most Government Agencies is a Slow Process

It is a general rule that as an organization grows, it tends to become less nimble. This sometimes results in resistance to change. Although the federal government is initiating organizational adjustments designed to give individual agencies more independence, this may take some time in an organization as large as the federal government, where a huge conglomerate of agencies and departments are all subject to regulation by the legislative and executive branches. These agencies may have huge budgets, but they are not fully independent. They are intended to execute "the will of the people," as expressed by Congress and the executive branch.

Incompetence Is More Easily Hidden in a Large Organization

The larger the organization, the more easily it can carry employees who simply go through the motions of doing their jobs but who actually accomplish little. These individuals rely heavily on being "covered" by those who are dedicated to their careers.

Although most government coworkers will be just as diligent as you are, you may find yourself carrying the weight for other, less motivated, employees. And because all federal workers benefit from job security, you may find that these coworkers will be working with you for quite a while.

It May Be Difficult to Leave a Department Once You're Hired

At some point in your civil service career, you may decide to transfer to another position or agency. Be forewarned that receiving a transfer within the federal government can be cumbersome. Every personnel-related action in the federal government involves a great deal of paperwork and may take months to process. You may be lucky and have your transfer approved right away—or you may have to wait until someone in the department for which you'd like to work decides to retire or is promoted, thereby creating a vacancy.

Even if you are eligible for transfer to another agency or position, this does not guarantee the transfer. Individual agencies select a pool of qualified candidates for open positions at their own discretion. Consider, too, that federal employees must wait at least three months after being hired before applying for transfers involving a different geographic area, higher pay scale, or new line of work.

Government Agencies Are Subject to Intense Political Pressures

Government agencies need to take into account many constituencies and audiences when making decisions. The political and/or public pressures governing a given situation may cloud facts and logic and make what would be a relatively straightforward decision in the public sector an extremely complex and difficult decision in a government agency.

A Federal Government Position May Require You to Travel or Relocate

Federal agencies and departments administer programs throughout the United States and overseas. Agencies need many people to ensure that these programs are operating properly and that field offices are successfully performing their assigned duties. Occasionally, a civil service worker may be asked to relocate to accept a position—and this may be difficult or untenable for you.

If travel or relocation is required, this will usually be stated under "conditions of employment" on a vacancy announcement. Sometimes a particular position is available in a variety of locations; in such cases, applicants are asked to indicate their geographic preferences when they apply. A vacancy may even state that "failure to specify a geographic preference on your application will result in a rating of ineligible."

The news is not all bad, though. Employees who must relocate to take a job are paid an incentive—usually about 25 percent of their annual salary.

You May Have to Work Harder for Less Pay Than You Expect

Many people have the mistaken idea that working for the federal government is easy. They may be under the impression that there is very little to do, ample opportunity for paid vacations and holidays, and unbelievable benefits. This is a myth—and the truth can come as quite a shock.

Government employees, for the most part, work very hard. And while their salaries and benefits are very good, they are not the highest-paid workers in the country. If you're motivated by money alone and want to reach extreme professional heights very quickly, public service may not be for you.

COMPARING PUBLIC-SECTOR AND PRIVATE-SECTOR EMPLOYMENT

It's useful to compare how a civil service career, with all its advantages and disadvantages, compares with private-sector work.

Job Security

Do you wake up every morning worrying about whether you will have a job after today? Do you anxiously listen to news reports about economic downturns and corporate takeovers? With the deep economic recession of the past few years, job security has become a scarce commodity in the private sector—in fact, most traditionally accepted ideas about job security no longer hold true. Even the terminology has changed: "laying off" has become "downsizing"—as if changing the language might disguise the nightmare of losing one's job.

As a rule, in the private sector, job security no longer exists. Even a Fortune 500 company can be acquired by another company unexpectedly or may suffer huge financial losses. Cutting payroll is one of the easiest methods for companies to show a temporary economic gain.

The federal government, by contrast, doesn't have to show evidence of profit to stockholders every three months, and no one is trying to buy out the Department of Agriculture. For this reason, job security is one of the largest advantages of working for the government. With a career in public service, your worries about basic economic survival are greatly diminished—though of course not completely extinguished—and you will likely have greater peace of mind over where your career is headed.

Discrimination

No one likes to talk openly about discrimination, such as sexism or racism, in the workplace. However, the truth is that it exists both in the private and public sectors. Because the process of hiring and promoting government employees is ruled by precedent and regulations and is less vulnerable to individual likes and dislikes, there is often less chance of experiencing discrimination.

This is particularly true regarding age. In the private sector, youth is often prized more than experience because it's believed that younger workers have more energy and enthusiasm and that they have the most current applicable knowledge because they are more recently graduated from school. Younger workers on the whole may also be willing to accept lower pay than workers with more experience. Consequently, a more mature worker may find it difficult to find a new position in the private sector.

In the federal government, however, unless a job has specific physical requirements that limit the type of worker needed, positions are graded in terms of salary, not by age of the employee. For example, a federal agency may have a GS-13 position to fill for an accountant. Anyone with the requisite education and experience is eligible to apply, no matter how old he or she is. If you are hired for the position and you are 37, you won't be paid any more or less than someone who is 53 and is hired for the same position, as long as you both fully qualify for the job.

This means that many older workers with 10 or 20 years of job experience in the private sector can begin a full second career in government. Veterans who have completed a full 20-year career in the military can begin a second career as civil service worker as well. This is much more difficult to do successfully in private-sector work.

Teamwork vs. "Superstars"

Working in a government bureaucracy is not about acting alone. Nor is it about taking chances based on sudden hunches with the hope of taking center stage and getting applauded for your intuition and initiative. Unlike private companies, the federal government has very few employee "superstars." Most government work is not about being an all-star. It's more about building a set of working relationships with other professionals and about using these contacts to advance your organization or agency's agenda.

If you are the type of worker who thrives on attention and recognition, you may want to consider seeking work in the private sector rather than in civil service. On the other hand, if you don't mind working behind the scenes and you don't think it's important who gets the credit as long as the job is done, you may do very well in a government career.

Compensation and Benefits

Do you want to make a lot of money, and make it quickly? If these are your core career goals, working in the private sector may be a better choice.

Top executives in the private sector earn substantially higher salaries than public-sector executives who manage programs of comparable size. Compensation for the government's executive-level employees ranges from $143,500 to $196,700, whereas executives working in the private sector may earn many times that amount. Commissions, stock options, golden parachutes—none of these are available to civil service workers.

IT'S UP TO YOU

There is no easy formula for comparing civil service jobs to those in the private sector, but there are advantages and disadvantages to each. As we've seen, many of the advantages are practical: salary, health-care benefits, vacation, and pension benefits. Conversely, many of the disadvantages may be a matter of workplace politics and dynamics and how these fit with your own personality.

The smart way to make the decision is to be absolutely honest about your specific needs, your family's needs, what motivates you, and even what drives you crazy. Ask yourself these questions, and answer them truthfully:

- How much money is "enough"—that is, what salary range allows you to live comfortably?
- How much job risk will you tolerate?
- How much financial risk can your family tolerate?
- What health-care needs do you and your family have?
- How well do you handle change?
- Do you require constant change or do you prefer routine?
- What type of work environment do you prefer?
- How well do you work with other people?
- Are you comfortable being a team player rather than a star employee?
- How much frustration or dissatisfaction can you tolerate in exchange for job security?

Every person's answers to these questions will vary. It's up to you to choose the career factors that are most important and that make the most sense for you and your family. You'll also have to rely on a certain level of instinct and decide which type of job feels right to you.

SUMMING IT UP

- Many federal occupations parallel those in the private sector, including accounting, computer programming, and health care. Other types of employment opportunities are unique to the federal government, such as regulatory inspectors, Foreign Service officers, Internal Revenue agents.

- White-collar jobs account for about 90 percent of all federal civilian jobs. Government professional fields with the highest projected number of new hires through 2016 include information technology (IT), mathematics, health care, education, and library science.

- Federal job opportunities for engineers and scientists will continue to expand over the next few years, with more than 17,000 new hires. Prospects for IT specialists are also expected to rise with more than 11,000 new hires projected over the next 10 years.

- Nearly 15 percent of all federal jobs are in office and administrative support.

- Entrance requirements for white-collar jobs vary widely. Some require that applicants have high school diplomas; others require an undergraduate or graduate degree.

- Blue-collar occupations, construction, labor, janitorial, provide full-time employment for nearly 300,000 federal workers.

Working for the Government: Federal, State, and Local

chapter 2

OVERVIEW

- Understanding how U.S. government hiring works
- General job categories and programs available at the federal level
- Government pay: the general schedule and the federal wage system
- Government job benefits
- Government work schedules and conditions
- How to qualify for a government job
- Training and advancement opportunities
- Federal student programs, internships, and fellowships
- Job in state and major municipal governments
- Salaries for state, county, and city jobs
- Summing it up

The federal government is so vast and complex that you may have a hard time envisioning yourself as its employee. You're probably familiar with civil service at the local level: Chances are that you know your town's or city's police and fire personnel, at least by sight. You may even be familiar with civil service workers at a county level; for example, you may have served on a jury or toured the county's court or prison system. It's likely that you've visited a county office to renew your vehicle registration or to register to vote. But the federal government may seem remote, immense, and inaccessible.

The federal government has innumerable offices throughout the country—just look in your county phone book to find local listings. The VA, the Social Security Administration, various sites of the Armed Forces, the Justice Department, IRS, the Small Business Administration, the Department of Transportation, and many other federal departments and agencies are likely to have offices close to where you live.

UNDERSTANDING HOW U.S. GOVERNMENT HIRING WORKS

Before you begin looking for a job with the federal government, it's important to familiarize yourself with its system of hiring. For example, you may not know that there are two classes of jobs in the federal government—the competitive service and the excepted service.

Those in the competitive service fall under the jurisdiction of the OPM, and hiring processes for those jobs must adhere to civil service laws passed by Congress. These laws ensure fair and equal treatment for job candidates during the hiring process, and they allow agency officials to consider all qualified applicants based on job-related criteria. In other words, a hiring manager can't hire her cousin without reviewing other applicants—and if her cousin does get hired, he must be the best candidate for the job and meet all qualification requirements.

Excepted service agencies are not subject to these civil service laws, and they do not have to follow the same appointment, pay, and classification rules. In some agencies, specific jobs may be excepted from civil service procedures; in other agencies, such as the FBI and the CIA, all employees work in excepted service positions. All excepted positions must adhere to Veterans' Preference regulations, which will be discussed later in this book.

A federal agency can choose among three groups of candidates when filling a position that falls within the competitive service:

❶ Primarily, candidates come from a list of eligibles administered by the OPM or by an agency under the OPM's direction. Individuals on this list (in rank order) have responded to a vacancy announcement and have met the requirements specified in the announcement.

❷ Agencies may also hire from a list of candidates who are eligible for noncompetitive movement within the competitive service because they are or were serving under career-type appointments in the competitive service.

❸ Federal agencies may also choose from those who qualify for special noncompetitive appointing authority, either by law or executive order. Candidates who qualify for this group include those who are eligible for a Veterans' Readjustment Appointment (VRA), veterans who are disabled by 30 percent or greater, Peace Corps volunteers, and those who are mentally or physically disabled.

Candidates seeking positions for which there exists a severe shortage of workers—including certain medical professions, IT management positions, and Iraqi reconstruction personnel—may also be hired through the federal government's direct-hire authorities.

GENERAL JOB CATEGORIES AND PROGRAMS AVAILABLE AT THE FEDERAL LEVEL

The federal government has an enormous variety of special programs that encompass various hiring situations. Let's review some of the larger occupational groups.

• **Professional occupations.** These are positions that require knowledge of a field, that is usually gained through education or training equivalent to a bachelor's degree or higher, with major study in or pertinent to the specialized field. About one-third of the federal workforce are employed in professional positions. These include engineers, computer scientists, health professionals, lawyers, biologists, and chemists.

- **Management, business, and financial occupations.** These positions usually require progressively responsible experience and include upper-level managers who oversee programs and agencies and middle-level managers who administer certain aspects of these programs. Other employees in these positions oversee contracts with the private sector and purchase goods and services needed by the government. They include contract specialists, budget analysts, purchasing officers, claims examiners, product control specialists, accountants, auditors, and IRS officers.

- **Investigative and law enforcement occupations.** Several government agencies employ police officers and investigators in positions ranging from border patrols to intelligence operatives. These agencies include the Department of Justice, Department of State, Department of the Treasury, the U.S. Postal Service, U.S. Customs and Border Protection, the FBI, and the Department of Homeland Security.

- **Technical occupations.** These positions typically involve support work in a nonroutine professional or administrative field. Examples of technical occupations include computer programmer, telecommunications specialist, and electronics technician.

- **Clerical occupations.** Clerical workers are typically hired for structured work in support of office, business, or fiscal operations. Positions include clerk-typists, mail clerks, and file clerks, among hundreds of others classified as clerical.

- **Skilled trades.** Skilled tradespeople perform manual work that usually requires a journeyman status. Skilled trade positions include plumber, HVAC technician, electrician, carpenter, and machinist.

- **Manual labor and mechanical positions.** Most people don't realize that the U.S. government is the country's largest employer of manual labor and mechanical workers. Positions classified as labor and mechanical include mobile equipment operator, mechanic, machine tool worker, metalworker, maintenance and repair worker, food preparer, and food server.

- **Unskilled positions.** Thousands of positions in government service are open to people who have no formal skills or have only minimal training or experience. These positions include housekeeping aide, janitor, laundry worker, and mess attendant.

Part-Time Programs and Other Nontraditional Arrangements

Part-time positions—16 to 32 hours per week—are available in agencies throughout the federal government. Flex time, job sharing, telecommuting, and nontraditional workday and workweek scheduling are also available for certain positions. Part-time workers are eligible for benefits as well, including health and life insurance, retirement, and vacation or sick leave on a prorated basis. For specific information about these positions, check with the personnel office at your local government agency.

A variety of student programs, internships and fellowships are offered through the federal government. We'll discuss them in greater detail at the end of this section. If you are a student or the parent of a student and are interested in a specific department or field, contact the agency in which you're interested. You can find additional information for students at the U.S. government's e-Scholar site, www.studentjobs.gov.

Volunteer Programs

Volunteer programs are unpaid work opportunities that allow students and prospective workers to explore federal occupations and gain valuable experience at the same time. Most recently, the Obama administration has issued a call to all Americans to participate in our country's economic recovery and renewal, and numerous opportunities are available for those who want to become involved. Check with the agency for which you're interested in volunteering to find out what's available, or visit www.serve.gov for more information.

Veterans Programs

U.S. military veterans are entitled to special consideration in the federal hiring process. In some cases, veterans are entitled to positions that are not open to the general public. In other cases, veterans may qualify for extra points on their exam scores, which gives them a competitive advantage over other applicants. The Veterans' Employment Coordinator at your agency of interest can provide additional information.

Programs for People with Disabilities

If you are seeking a government job and have a disability, contact the Selective Placement Coordinator at the agency in which you're interested. You can find out about special placement assistance that's available for candidates with physical, cognitive, or emotional disabilities. By law, the federal government—and private-sector businesses—must make "reasonable workplace accommodations" for workers with disabilities. This means that the employer may adjust the duties of the job, the location in which it's performed, or the methods by which it's performed. To qualify for this program, applicants with disabilities must provide two documents: a proof of disability and a certification of job readiness (a statement describing how the candidate will be able to fulfill his or her duties with reasonable accommodation).

Programs for Residents Outside the Continental United States

Alaska, Guam, Hawaii, Puerto Rico, and the U.S. Virgin Islands offer limited federal employment possibilities. Most positions in these areas are filled through competitive service announcements, and local residents receive first consideration for employment in their own region. Foreign nationals, U.S. citizens living abroad, and dependents of citizens employed or stationed out of the country may also be hired for employment overseas.

GOVERNMENT PAY: THE GENERAL SCHEDULE AND THE FEDERAL WAGE SYSTEM

All civil service jobs vary in expectations, requirements, and salary, but the federal government's pay classification system provides a good general idea of pay scale. The following is an example of pay scales on the General Schedule, which is used for most white-collar federal employees. The General Schedule establishes federal pay rates based on salary surveys for similar nonfederal jobs in a given location. Hourly wages for blue-collar workers are determined by the Federal Wage System; they originate from recommendations by the Federal Prevailing Rate Advisory Committee, which comprises management and labor unions. The committee surveys nonfederal pay for similar jobs in the same location, then advises the Director of the OPM regarding pay policy.

GENERAL SCHEDULE
(Range of Salaries)
Effective January 1, 2009

GS Rating	Low	High
1	$17,540	$21,944
2	19,721	24,815
3	21,517	27,970
4	24,156	31,401
5	27,026	35,135
6	30,125	39,161
7	33,477	43,521
8	37,075	48,199
9	40,949	53,234
10	45,095	58,622
11	49,544	64,403
12	59,383	77,194
13	70,615	91,801
14	83,445	108,483
15	98,156	127,604

The General Schedule includes 15 grades of pay for white-collar and service positions, each defined according to work difficulty, responsibility, and qualifications required. Each pay grade is made up of 10 steps. Advancement from steps 1 through 3 in each grade is scheduled after each 52 weeks of service; through steps 4, 5, and 6 after each 104 weeks of service; and through steps 7, 8, and 9 after each 156 weeks of service. At step 2 of each grade, compensation is based on the average going rate for private-sector employees performing the same job. This means that although the first step of each pay grade may fall below the *average* pay rate for an area, it still falls within the *range* of what an actual private-sector job might pay. At step 5 within each grade, however, civil service employees are paid 12 percent above the average private-sector rate—one of the advantages of moving through the ranks of federal employment.

Advancement to higher grades generally depends on ability, work performance, and the availability of job openings at higher levels. Most agencies fill vacancies by promoting their own employees whenever possible. Promotions are based on increased responsibility, experience, and skill.

It is not always necessary to move to a new job to reach a higher pay grade. Sometimes an employee's work assignment changes a great deal in the ordinary course of business to the point where a position classifier determines whether the job should be moved to a higher grade because of increased difficulty or responsibility.

Most employees receive within-grade pay increases at one-, two-, or three-year intervals if their work is acceptable. (Some managers and supervisors receive increases based on job performance rather than time spent in a particular grade.) Within-grade increases may also be given to recognize an employee's high-quality performance.

The law requires that government salaries, at least on the federal level, be comparable to their private-sector counterparts. Government pay for white-collar workers is determined by comparisons to salaries in the private sector. Federal workers also receive locality pay, which may add as much as 30 percent to an employee's base salary. Each January, an across-the-board increase in both the General Schedule and the locality pay is enacted to ensure that federal salaries are in line with private-sector salaries.

Most blue-collar federal workers are paid according to the Federal Wage System. Under this system, craft, service, and manual workers earn hourly wages based on local prevailing rates paid by private employers for similar work. As a result, the federal government wage rate for an occupation varies by locality.

The government's commitment to meeting the local wage scale allows federal workers not only to earn salaries or hourly wages comparable to those in the private sector but also to enjoy the benefits and security of a government job.

GOVERNMENT JOB BENEFITS

Federal health care, life insurance, vacation, sick leave, and retirement benefits are another important aspect of employee compensation. Conversely, to stay competitive, many private-sector companies have been forced to trim benefits packages, and many no longer offer some or all of these benefits to employees. Because of the most recent economic recession, benefits in the private sector are now more vulnerable than those offered by the federal government—and in some cases they may not exist at all. With health-care costs rising and health insurance premiums skyrocketing just as quickly, a strong benefits package is one of the most important advantages of working for the federal government.

In addition, civil service retirement plans are very good—and they're guaranteed. Federal workers participate in the Federal Employees Retirement System (FERS), a plan that not only includes Social Security but also a pension plan and a Thrift Savings Plan that allows employees to make government-matched tax-deferred contributions to retirement accounts. Private-sector plans, on the other hand, are susceptible to fluctuations in the overall economy and may not be available when workers retire. As the stock market rises and falls, private-sector pension plans may crumble under administrative costs and poor investments. Additionally, compensation in the private sector tends to favor executives in both salaries and benefits, whereas the government offers the same benefits package to all workers regardless of their pay grade. Comprehensive benefits, combined with job security, are often the deciding factor when people consider federal employment.

As a quick example of these differences, take a look at the number of paid holidays a company might offer in comparison with federal holidays.

Federal Holidays

New Year's Day	Labor Day
Martin Luther King Jr. Day	Columbus Day
Washington's Birthday	Veterans Day
Memorial Day	Thanksgiving Day
Independence Day	Christmas Day

In private-sector jobs, paid holidays vary widely. For example, one Fortune 500 company gives employees 12 paid holidays, of which six are national holidays and three are paid holidays decided on by the employee's local branch. The remaining three days are personal holidays, chosen by the employee. By contrast, a large national retail chain offers only the six paid national holidays each year and is open for two of those six days—Memorial Day and Labor Day. So even though an employee will be paid for these holidays, he or she may have to work.

GOVERNMENT BENEFITS AT A GLANCE

Type of Benefit	Who Is Eligible	Available Options

Health:
 	
Federal Employees Health Benefits (FEHB)
	Federal employees, federal retirees, and their survivors.
	
	Coverage may include self only, or family coverage for employee, spouse, and eligible dependent children.
		• Managed Fee for Service Plans
		
		• Point of Service (PPO) options
		
		• Health Maintenance Organizations (HMOs)
		
		  1. High-Deductible Health Plans
		
		  2. Consumer-Driven Health Plans

Retirement: Federal Employees Retirement System (FERS)	Almost all federal employees hired after 1984 are automatically covered.	FERS is a three-tiered retirement plan: 1. Social Security benefits for those 62 and retired 2. Basic Benefits Plan (financed by the government with a small employee contribution) 3. Thrift Savings Plan (tax-deferred retirement savings and investment plan; similar to 401(k) plans)
Life: The Federal Employees' Group Life Insurance Program (FEGLI)	Federal employees and retirees, many family members.	Basic Insurance (automatic unless employee opts out) and three Optional Insurance selections

Long-Term Care: Federal Long Term Care Insurance Program (FLTCIP)	All employees who are eligible for the FEHB.	Employees pay premiums based on age and other benefits selected. Premiums are paid through payroll deduction, automatic bank withdrawal, or direct bill.

GOVERNMENT WORK SCHEDULES AND CONDITIONS

The majority of federal government employees work a standard 40-hour week. Most work eight hours a day, five days a week, Monday through Friday, although some agencies allow flexible or compressed work schedules. Employees who are required to work overtime may receive premium rates for the additional time or compensatory time off. Annual earnings for most full-time federal workers are not affected by seasonal factors.

Federal employees earn 13 days of vacation each year during their first three years of service; 20 days each year for the next 12 years; and 26 vacation days per year after 15 years of service. In addition, workers who are members of military reserve organizations receive up to 15 days of paid military leave annually for training purposes. Although federal layoffs (RIFs) are uncommon, all federal workers who are laid off are entitled to severance pay or unemployment compensation similar to what is provided for employees in private industry.

HOW TO QUALIFY FOR A GOVERNMENT JOB

How many times have you seen a job advertisement request a certain number of years of experience or a college degree? Such qualifications are required for most private-sector jobs. With government jobs, however, the process of qualifying is much more flexible. Often, a vacancy announcement will indicate the number of years of experience that can be substituted for a certain number of years of college education, sometimes even for a college degree.

Because it is a public-sector employer paying salaries with public funds, the government has made a point—supported by laws and legislation—of protecting the rights and supporting the career aspirations of all its workers. As a result, many government positions at lower grade levels (GS-2 or GS-3) require only a high school diploma or as little as three months of work experience. For jobs at the GS-7 level or higher, applicants must have some specialized experience closely related to what is required to perform the duties of the position. Those who have a bachelor's degree often qualify for positions in a number of fields because on-the-job training is provided. Other positions, usually involving research, scientific, or professional work, require a particular academic degree. Candidates who have earned a master's degree may start at the GS-9 level, and those with Ph.D.'s may start at GS-11 positions.

It's possible to qualify for many government jobs that might be out of your reach in the private sector. The key, of course, is in how well you present your qualifications. Later in this book, we'll help you learn how to submit a successful application for a federal position.

The Merit System

More than 90 percent of jobs in the federal government fall under the merit system. The Civil Service Act, passed by Congress in 1978 and administered by the OPM, ensures that federal employees are hired based on fair recruitment and individual merit. It provides for competitive examinations to determine the best candidate for each job and the selection of new employees from among the most qualified applicants.

Some federal jobs are exempt from civil service requirements, either by law or by action of the OPM, but most of these positions are covered by the separate merit systems of other agencies, such as the Foreign Service of the Department of State, the FBI, the Nuclear Regulatory Commission (NRC), and the TVA.

Age Requirements

Along with education, experience, and skill requirements, civil service jobs come with some general age requirements. There is no maximum age limit for federal employment. The usual minimum age limit is 18, but high school graduates as young as 16 may apply for certain jobs. If you are younger than 18 and out of school but you have not earned a high school diploma, you can still be hired provided you have been out of school for at least three months (not counting summer vacation), you successfully complete a formal training program, and you ask school authorities to sign a form (provided by the hiring agency) approving your preference for work instead of additional schooling.

Some positions, particularly law enforcement and firefighting positions, may have set age limits because of the physical requirements of the job. Be sure to review each job announcement carefully before applying.

Physical Requirements

To be hired by the federal government, you must be physically able to perform the duties of your position, and you must be emotionally and mentally stable. This does not mean, however, that a physical disability will automatically disqualify you. As long as you can perform the position's work requirements efficiently without posing a hazard to yourself or to others, the federal government by law is required to make reasonable workplace accommodations. Some positions, such as border patrol agent, law enforcement officer, and firefighter, may be filled only by those who are in topnotch physical condition. In such cases, the physical requirements are clearly stated in the job announcement.

Special Considerations for Veterans

If you are a veteran of the U.S. Armed Forces, you may be eligible for Veterans' Preference, which could give you an edge in the civil service hiring process. Veterans' Preference may increase your exam score by either 5 or 10 points, depending on your eligibility. In some cases, it may also enable you to submit certain job applications after the closing date for the civil service exam.

To qualify for Veterans' Preference in general, you must meet certain criteria. First, you must have received an honorable or general discharge. Second, unless you are a disabled veteran, your rank must be lower than major or lieutenant commander when you retire. Finally, if your service was with the National Guard or Army Reserve for training purposes, you do not qualify for preference.

Five-Point Preference

If you are eligible to claim Veterans' Preference, indicate this on your application or resume. If you meet the general criteria outlined above and you have passed the civil service exam, you may have an additional 5 points added to your exam score. To gain the five points, you must meet at least one of the following conditions:

- You served between 12/7/1941 and 7/1/1955.
- You served for more than 180 consecutive days from 1/31/1955 through 10/15/1976.
- You served for more than 180 consecutive days between 9/11/2001 and the ending date for Operation Iraqi Freedom (as declared by Presidential proclamation or law).
- You served during the Gulf War from 8/2/1990 through 1/2/1992.
- You served in a military campaign for which a campaign medal has been authorized.

Ten-Point Preference

You may have 10 points added to your passing exam score if you qualify under any of the following conditions:

- You are a veteran with a service-connected disability.
- You are a veteran who is receiving compensation, disability benefits, or a pension from the military.
- You are a veteran who received a Purple Heart (this qualifies you as a disabled veteran).
- You are the unmarried spouse of a certain veteran who is deceased.
- You are the spouse of a veteran who cannot work because of a service-related disability.
- You are the mother of a veteran who died during service or who is permanently and totally disabled.

To claim a 10-point preference, you must complete form SF-15, Application for 10-Point Veteran Preference. For more information about the Veterans' Preference Program and your eligibility, contact the Veterans Employment Coordinator for the agency at which you are seeking employment.

TRAINING AND ADVANCEMENT OPPORTUNITIES

Most federal employees are also eligible to participate in training programs, tuition assistance or reimbursement, executive management and leadership programs, fellowship programs, seminars, and workshops, all of which are designed to help federal workers develop maximum job proficiency or advance to higher-paying jobs. Training programs may be conducted in government facilities or in private educational facilities at government expense.

If federal employees perform their work satisfactorily, they usually receive periodic step increases within their pay grade. Further advancement to higher grades is competitive, based on merit, and occurs when vacancies arise.

Top managers in the federal government are members of the Senior Executive Service (SES), the highest positions obtainable without nomination by the president and confirmation by the U.S. Senate. Opportunities for these upper-level managerial and supervisory positions are usually located in Washington, D.C., where most federal agencies are headquartered.

FEDERAL STUDENT PROGRAMS, INTERNSHIPS, AND FELLOWSHIPS

The federal government has a number of programs in place specifically designed to provide employment for students.

- **The Student Education Employment Program** is designed to provide students with federal job experience. Students must be enrolled at least half-time in a high school, technical or vocational school, college, or graduate program. This program has two components:

  1. The Student Temporary Educational Program (STEP) offers temporary internships for students lasting either throughout the summer or for as long as the employee is a student. The work need not be related to your academic field.

  2. The Student Career Experience Program (SCEP) is a federal employment opportunity program for undergraduate and graduate students. It offers government employment that is directly related to your course of study and is arranged in partnership with your college or university. Positions in this program are paid, they count toward academic credit, and they can lead to permanent employment upon graduation.

For more information on the Student Education Employment Program, visit www.opm.gov/employ/students/intro.asp.

- **The Federal Career Intern Program** offers professional experience to talented undergraduate and graduate students through entry-level positions with federal agencies. These programs are designed to increase the pool of qualified candidates in a particular occupational area. Examples of internship programs are the Hispanic Association of Colleges and Universities' (HACU's) National Internship Program (HNIP) and the Presidential Management Fellows (PMF) Program.

- **The Presidential Management Fellows (PMF) Program** provides fellowships to outstanding students who have completed graduate programs. Fellows commit to two-year full-time positions and receive extensive training in a variety of assignments. Students must apply for fellowships in early fall and be nominated by their college or university. If completed successfully, these fellowships can lead to a permanent job with the federal government. If you are interested in this program, contact the agency for which you'd like to work, or visit www.opm.gov/careerintern for more detailed information.

JOBS IN STATE AND MAJOR MUNICIPAL GOVERNMENTS

As with federal employment, nearly every kind of job available in the private sector is also available in state and local employment. State and local governments provide a large and expanding source of job opportunities in a variety of occupational fields. About 15 million people work for state and local government agencies throughout the United States; nearly three-quarters of these employees work in local governments such as counties, municipalities, towns, and school districts. State and local government workers help provide essential services to the public, including education, health care, transportation, utilities, courts, and public safety.

Job distribution for state and local government positions differs greatly from federal government service. Defense, international relations and commerce, immigration, and mail delivery are virtually nonexistent in state and local governments. In contrast, state and local governments provide jobs in education, health, social services, transportation, construction, and sanitation.

Educational Services

Educational services comprise the majority of jobs in state and local government. Employees in this field work in public schools, colleges, and various extension services, and about one-half of all education workers are teachers of some sort. School systems, colleges, and universities also employ administrative personnel, librarians, guidance counselors, nurses, dieticians, clerks, and maintenance workers. Job prospects in educational services are favorable, because the number of those retiring is expected to increase within the next few years.

Health Services

The second-largest field of state and local government employment is health services. Almost 1.4 million people are employed in health services and hospital work, including physicians, nurses, medical laboratory technicians, dieticians, kitchen and laundry workers, and hospital attendants. Social services make up another aspect of health and welfare. As the need for welfare and human services increases, so do opportunities for social workers and their affiliated administrative and support staff.

Government Control/Financial Activities

Another 1 million state and local government employees work in general governmental control and financial activities. These include chief executives and staff members; legislative representatives; people employed in the administration of justice, tax enforcement, and other financial work; and those in general administration. Lawyers, judges, court officers, city managers, property assessors, budget analysts, stenographers, and clerks help state and local governments carry out these important functions.

Streets and Highways

More than 500,000 people work in highway construction and maintenance. Road construction and maintenance are major concerns for local and state governments—building and improving roads improves safety and efficiency within a community. Positions in this group include civil engineers, surveyors, equipment operators, truck drivers, concrete finishers, carpenters, construction workers, and snow removers. Toll collectors are considered state or county employees unless they have been contracted by private firms. Mass transportation within municipalities and between the cities and their outlying suburbs is also the province of local government. Maintaining roadbeds, signaling systems, and vehicles (as well as staffing these vehicles) requires a large and varied workforce.

Police and Fire Protection Services

More than 1 million people work in police and fire departments throughout the United States. With police officers and detectives, local fire and police departments require support staff, including administrative, clerical, maintenance, and custodial personnel. Local governments employ all of the nation's 287,000 nonvolunteer firefighters, many of whom work part-time.

Clerical, Administrative, Maintenance, and Custodial Work

Many local and state government workers perform clerical, administrative, maintenance, or custodial work. These positions include word processors, secretaries, data processors, computer specialists, office managers, fiscal and budget administrators, bookkeepers, accountants, carpenters, painters, plumbers, security guards, and janitors.

Residents of a particular state or locality typically fill positions in their state and local governments because most positions have residency requirements. Exceptions are generally made for people with skills that are in high demand.

Other State and Local Government Occupations

Other state and local government work can be found in local water and electric utilities, transportation, natural resources, public welfare, parks and recreation, sanitation, corrections, local libraries, sewage disposal, and housing and urban renewal. These fields require diverse experience and include economists, social workers, all types of engineers, electricians, pipefitters, clerks, foresters, and bus drivers.

SALARIES FOR STATE, COUNTY, AND CITY JOBS

Salaries for state and local government employees vary widely, depending on occupation and locality. Salaries vary from state to state and even within states because of differences in both the general wage level and the cost of living for various localities. Similar to the private sector, supervisory and managerial personnel earn more than other workers.

Some state and local government positions are filled through a type of civil service exam; other professional positions, such as city managers and regional planners, require a college degree. State and local government workers have the same protections as federal government workers: They cannot be refused employment because of their race; they cannot be denied promotion because someone else made a greater political contribution; and they cannot be fired because the boss's son needed a job. Nearly every group of employees has some sort of union or organization, and rates of membership are relatively high. State and local government employees often receive employer-provided benefits, including health and life insurance and retirement plans.

Local and state employees who work in professional, financial, administrative, or office positions usually work a standard 40-hour week. Other positions may include irregular work schedules. Firefighters, for example, may work 50 consecutive hours preceded by several days off; subway operators may work split shifts to accommodate morning and evening rush hours.

Federal workers receive the same base salary and benefits no matter where they work in the United States. A GS-11 in Seattle, WA, receives the same as a GS-11 in Miami, FL, except for differences in pay locality. However, each state operates independently. Take a look at the following chart, which compares starting salaries for 17 job titles in five states. The information was taken from actual job announcements for state, county, and city jobs.

STATE, COUNTY, AND CITY GOVERNMENT JOBS: STARTING SALARIES

	California	Florida	Illinois	New York	Texas
Accountant/Auditor	$54,192	$61,200	$52,560	$59,430	$52,560
Air Traffic Controller	$130,650	$111,870	$128,710	$122,650	$111,910
Civil Engineer	$75,504	$65,582	$74,600	$74,600	$74,640
Computer Systems Analyst	$72,468	$65,728	$75,500	$75,500	$77,100
Corrections Officer	$53,000	$42,390	$38,800	$38,380	$51,130
Court, Municipal, & License Clerk	$36,800	$36,400	$39,590	$37,130	$39,590
Financial Analyst	$70,620	$69,282	$73,150	$73,150	$73,510
Firefighter	$53,730	$45,520	$44,260	$41,920	$48,220
IT Specialist	$66,780	$70,000	$69,740	$69,740	$66,380
Maintenance & Repair Worker	$34,467	$21,880	$37,240	$33,710	$37,240
Police Officer	$56,880	$51,320	$51,410	$51,410	$58,180
Police, Fire, & Ambulance Dispatcher	$40,956	$37,010	$35,390	$38,970	$33,670
Probation Officer	$45,650	$42,390	$45,910	$45,910	$42,250
Registered Nurse	$74,868	$61,290	$62,450	$62,450	$74,460
Surveyor	$61,660	$56,880	$62,510	$66,580	$71,660
Transportation Security Officer	$41,840	$35,930	$39,360	$38,100	$30,800
Word Processor/Typist	$37,776	$28,450	$37,890	$31,390	$31,210

Finding Out About Job Openings

When positions must be filled, government agencies publish job or examination announcements. Each announcement lists everything you need to know about a particular government job, including qualification requirements, salary, duties, and location. If an exam is required, the announcement also tells you when and where to file for the exam, which application forms you must complete, and where to obtain the forms. If the first page of the announcement states "No Closing Date," this means that applications are accepted until all open positions are filled. Otherwise, most job announcements provide a specific deadline for filing an application, and no applications mailed past this date will be considered.

Study the job announcement carefully. It will answer many of your questions and help you decide if you are interested in the position and are qualified for it. Precise duties are described in detail, usually under the heading "Description of Work." Make sure that you meet all the educational, experience, and special requirements listed and that the position's responsibilities fall within the range of your experience and ability.

Pay close attention to any section describing the kind of exam that may be administered for the particular position, including the areas covered in the written test and the specific subjects on which questions will be asked. Sometimes sample questions and the method of grading the exam are given. All of this information is invaluable when preparing for an exam. Not all positions require an exam; some positions are filled based on the applicants' education, experience, and past achievements.

Local agencies and municipalities issue regular bulletins or job announcements detailing all the vacant positions for that period. You may find these bulletins or announcements in several locations, including government offices, local libraries, newspapers, and the Internet. One highly valuable source for employment information online is the U.S. Department of Labor's Employment Standards Administration (www.dol.gov/esa/contacts/state_of.htm), which provides state labor contact information, including Web site addresses.

Another option is to contact the human resources or personnel departments of local government agencies that interest you. Look in the phone book under the government pages (sometimes called the Blue Pages) to find listings for city, county, and state offices and local branches of national agencies. For example, the public works department, recycling department, recreation department, and housing authority might be listed at the city level; the human services department, private industry council, senior citizens' centers, and cultural and historic affairs department at the county level; and the environmental protection department, lottery division, commerce and economic growth commission, and consumer affairs division at the state level. Although not every one of these departments may be in your city, county, or state, the phone book (which is also available online) will direct you to dozens of other local agencies.

State government openings are listed on each state's Web site. These listings provide details about available positions, qualification requirements, location, salary and benefits, and application procedures. In addition, some state sites will connect you to county or city sites that post other employment opportunities.

OFFICIAL STATE WEB SITES

Alabama	www.alabama.gov
Alaska	www.ak.gov
Arizona	www.az.gov
Arkansas	www.arkansas.gov
California	www.ca.gov
Colorado	www.colorado.gov
Connecticut	www.ct.gov
Delaware	www.delaware.gov
District of Columbia	www.dc.gov
North Dakota	www.nd.gov
Florida	www.fl.gov
Georgia	www.ga.gov
Hawaii	www.hawaii.gov
Idaho	www.accessidaho.org
Illinois	www.illinois.gov
Indiana	www.in.gov
Iowa	www.iowa.gov
Kansas	www.kansas.gov
Kentucky	www.kentucky.gov
Louisiana	www.louisiana.gov
Maine	www.maine.gov
Maryland	www.maryland.gov
Massachusetts	www.mass.gov
Michigan	www.michigan.gov
Minnesota	www.state.mn.us
Mississippi	www.ms.gov
Missouri	www.mo.gov
Montana	www.mt.gov
Nebraska	www.nebraska.gov
Nevada	www.nv.gov
New Hampshire	www.nh.gov
New Jersey	www.state.nj.us
New Mexico	www.newmexico.gov
New York	www.ny.gov
North Carolina	www.nc.gov
Ohio	www.ohio.gov
Oklahoma	www.ok.gov
Oregon	www.oregon.gov
Pennsylvania	www.pa.gov
Rhode Island	www.ri.gov
South Carolina	www.sc.gov
South Dakota	www.sd.gov
Tennessee	www.tn.gov
Texas	www.texasonline.com

Utah	www.utah.gov
Vermont	www.vermont.gov
Virginia	www.virginia.gov
Washington	http://access.wa.gov
West Virginia	www.wv.gov
Wisconsin	www.wisconsin.gov
Wyoming	www.wyoming.gov

Check online or visit your local library to see whether your own city or town has its own Web site.

Give Yourself an Edge When Applying for a State or Local Job

Take advantage of local state and municipal civil service offices by networking with people who can provide more information about employment in the departments in which you're interested. Although any openings must be posted publicly, having advance knowledge of a vacancy will give you more time to prepare your resume and application.

If you decide to call an agency about an available position, ask first about the application procedures—then follow them. Most of these procedures will appear in the job announcement itself, and the announcement will usually provide links for applying online—but be sure to call if you have any questions about what you see in the announcement. If you have applied for a federal job before, don't assume that you can take exactly the same steps to apply this time, or that one state will have precisely the same process for applying as another. The application process throughout state agencies is likely to be similar, but it's always smart to double-check.

As with a federal job application, be as explicit as possible when describing your career achievements on a state or municipal application. Ideally, you're not only trying to change jobs, but you're also applying for a job with a significant pay increase. Explain why you deserve the position and why you are the best person for the job.

Finally, be patient. Because state and local governments operate on a much smaller scale than the federal government, you may expect them to move more quickly in their hiring processes. That's not necessarily the case. Offices requiring civil service exams may take four to six weeks simply to grade exams and rank the applicants. While you're waiting for a response, keep looking for other job vacancies that interest you. Don't get discouraged. If you're unsuccessful at getting one position, try for another. Chances are good that you're still on that agency's list of eligibles and can be considered for the next vacancy.

Sample State and Local Civil Service Job Announcements

Take a look at some of the examples of job announcements that follow. Some require that you take a civil service exam; others do not. Study them carefully to find out where they differ and where they're similar. Find out what each one requires you to submit. The more familiar you become with the job announcement format, the better-prepared you'll be when it's time to apply for the position you want.

AUDITOR ASSOCIATE I
COUNTY OF ALAMEDA

Human Resource Services Department

An Equal Opportunity Employer

1405 Lakeside Drive, Oakland, CA 94612

(510) 650-3958

http://agency.governmentjobs.com/alameda

Invites Applications for the Position of: **AUDITOR ASSOCIATE I**

SALARY

$1,539.75 - $1,821.00 Biweekly; $3,336.13 - $3,945.50 Monthly

ISSUE DATE: 08/05/XX

LAST DATE FOR FILING: 8/31/XX at 5:00 p.m.

Postmarks and Faxes are not accepted.

THE POSITION

Applications must be in the possession of the Human Resource Services Department by 5:00 p.m. on the Last Day for Filing. Postmarks and faxes are not accepted.

EXAMINATION DATE(S): September 28-29, 20XX (Written)

Week of October 26, 20XX (Oral)

Under general supervision and direction, positions in this classification are located in the Auditor-Controller/Clerk-Recorder Agency, and perform routine and moderately difficult and/or technical, clerical work involving the exercise of some independent judgment in following instructions within established policies and procedures. Incumbents of this classification are expected to respond to inquiries from the public or other County departments and may be responsible for maintaining a variety of records and/or monitoring and compiling data from a variety of sources. Positions in this classification may work independently with the supervisor or lead clerk available to answer questions or manage unusual situations. It is flexibly staffed with the higher classification of Auditor Associate II, where the incumbents perform many of the same duties, but have achieved competency and knowledge of the full range of duties at this level and may also be assigned to complete similar, but more complex duties exercising greater independent judgment and discretion. Incumbents are expected to rotate through various units of the Auditor Agency as needed to accommodate employee development, staffing, and training needs of the Agency. An Auditor Associate I is expected to gain experience and demonstrate proficiency which qualifies them to promotion to the higher level of Auditor Associate II within one year of full-time experience. Appointment of the Auditor Associate I level will not be extended beyond one year.

QUALIFIED BILINGUAL PERSONS WHO SPEAK ENGLISH AND ARE ALSO FLUENT IN SPANISH, CHINESE, VIETNAMESE, CAMBODIAN, LAOTIAN, KOREAN, MIEN, TAGALOG, AMHARIC, FARSI, DARI, TIGRIGNA, RUSSIAN, ROMANIAN OR SIGN LANGUAGE ARE ESPECIALLY ENCOURAGED TO APPLY. THERE IS AN ADDITIONAL BI WEEKLY COMPENSATION FOR PERSONS IN POSITIONS DESIGNATED BILINGUAL. Qualified candidates may be tested to demonstrate language proficiency.

PROMOTIONAL OPPORTUNITIES: Auditor Associate I may be flexibly staffed to: Auditor Associate II - $1898.25 - Current Bi-Weekly Maximum

MINIMUM QUALIFICATIONS

EITHER I

EXPERIENCE: The equivalent of two years of full-time experience in the class of Clerk II or in an equivalent or higher level clerical class in Alameda County classified service. (Non-classified includes District Attorney's Office, Hospital Authority, and the Consolidated Courts.)

OR II

EXPERIENCE: The equivalent of two years full-time clerical experience including one year full-time experience performing duties of a complex and technical nature in applying legal statutes and rules requiring expertise and specialized knowledge. (Education from an accredited college or university may be substituted for the required experience on a year for year basis. One year of education shall consist of either 30 semester or 45 quarter units.)

KNOWLEDGE AND ABILITIES

The examination may include, but may not be limited to, the testing of concepts related to:

The knowledge of:

- Business arithmetic.
- Business correspondence, filing and standard office equipment operations.
- Techniques and practices for dealing with individuals from various socioeconomic and ethnic groups both on the telephone and in person and through correspondence (including stressful contact with irate and/or hostile individuals).
- Modern office methods and equipment, including commonly used computer spreadsheet, word processing and centralized financial and personnel/payroll programs, preferably ALCOLINK/HRMS.

And the ability to:

- Establish and maintain effective working relationships with the public including co-workers.
- Prioritize work and coordinate several activities to meet critical deadlines.
- Operate common modern office machines, including calculator, computer, printer, and fax.

- Locate and provide basic analysis of data found in large accounting and payroll systems, such as those maintained by the Auditor Agency.
- Prepare periodic and special accounting and payroll reports.
- Identify and correct errors in a variety of mathematical computations and financial/payroll documents.
- Work independently when given specific instructions.
- Apply rules and regulations to specific cases.
- Communicate effectively orally and in writing.
- Research and correct documents for errors.
- Maintain accurate records.

EXAMINATION COMPONENTS

1 Review of the applications to verify minimum requirements.

2 A written exam weighted at 40% of the final exam score.

3 An oral exam weighted at 60% of the final exam score. (The oral interview may include situational exercises.)

Candidates must attain a qualifying rating on each portion of this examination. We reserve the right to make changes to the announced examination steps.

DEPUTY SHERIFF
Grand County, Utah
In-House and Public Job Opportunity

Job Title: Deputy Sheriff

Department: Sheriff's Office

Location: Grand County Courthouse, XXX E. Center St., Moab, Utah

Reports to: Patrol Supervisor

Classification: Grade 13 (Revised 12/20XX)

Type of Position: Full-time with benefits

Job Status: Non Exempt, Safety Sensitive, On Call, Public Safety

Job Summary

Under the direct supervision of the Patrol Supervisor the Deputy Sheriff performs a variety of entry-level professional and technical law enforcement duties The Deputy Sheriff responds to life and property threatening calls such as robbery, burglary, family disturbance, theft, etc.

Conducts investigation and follow-up investigation on scene and suspects, makes arrest of offenders, writes crime case reports, appears and testifies in court, performs traffic enforcement and routine patrol.

The Deputy Sheriff represents the Sheriff in providing education and other services deemed necessary by the Sheriff to meet the goals of the Sheriff's Office.

The Deputy Sheriff is required to be a Category I Peace Officer according to the Utah State Code. This position is required to work rotating shifts and be on call status including weekends and holidays.

Supervision

Received: Patrol Supervisor

Given: None

Essential Duties

- Assists the Sheriff in all day-to-day operations of the Sheriff's Office. Communicates with all supervisory staff.
- Provides information to the supervisor on complaints that merit further investigation.
- Handles incidents assigned and follows up on assigned complaints as is required.
- Patrols all areas of the County to maintain peace and security.
- Serves criminal and civil process when assigned.
- Investigates traffic accidents and enforces all traffic laws.

Knowledge, Skills & Abilities

Knowledge of:

- Basic office practices including Windows-based PC applications and computers, software and other office equipment.

Skills in:

- Reading, writing, and math.

Ability to:

- Learn and follow the Sheriff's Office and Grand County policy and procedures.
- Follow corrections and law enforcement procedures.
- Communicate verbally and in writing.
- Follow verbal and written instructions.
- Work independently on multiple assignments.
- Use judgment to plan, perform and make decisions on sequence of operations and processes.
- Assess unusual circumstances and adapt to variations in approach in completion of duties.
- Establish and maintain professional relationships with public and staff within the Sheriff's Office and other agencies.
- Recognize and follow the Sheriff's Office chain of command.
- Use tact and self-control when communicating.

Physical Demands

- Effort involves moderately heavy lifting, pushing or pulling, and can involve considerable crouching, stooping, or lying in a prone position.
- Must be able to lift or drag up to 100 pounds.
- High manual dexterity under extreme conditions may be required.
- Effort is exerted intermittently for generally short periods of time.
- Employees are intermittently involved in physically restraining hostile persons.

Working Conditions

- Recurring work conditions exist, which involve a chance of injury or loss of life.
- Contact regularly with inmates, hostile persons, the general public, and employees of other law enforcement agencies.
- Works in office with environmentally controlled temperatures.
- Traveling and operating an automobile is a regular a part of the job.
- Works outside in extreme weather conditions.

Education & Experience

- High school diploma or equivalent.
- Law enforcement experience preferred.

Special Requirements

- Must take and successfully pass Peace Officers Standard Training (P.O.S.T.) pre-entrance exam.
- Successfully complete Peace Officers Standard Training (P.O.S.T) Law Enforcement Academy or be able to pass P.O.S.T. waiver Certification Category I Peace Officer exam.
- Must be 21 years of age.
- Must possess a valid Utah driver's license.
- Successful completion of pre-employment drug screening is required.
- Must successfully pass and maintain all required medical, written, oral and physical agility examinations.
- Must successfully pass and maintain all requirements of background checks.
- Must pass and maintain firearm and non-lethal weapons certifications.
- Required to work rotating shifts and be subject to call-out status including weekends and holidays.
- A 12-month probationary period is a prerequisite to this position.
- Safety sensitive position subject to random drug testing.

OFFICE CLERK - OPT SS2

STATE OF ILLINOIS

An Equal Opportunity Employer

Human Services

http://work.illinois.gov

BID ID #: D-HCD Continuous

JOB TYPE: Full-Time

NUMBER OF VACANCIES: 1

SALARY $2,229.00 - $2,939.00 Monthly

OPENING DATE: 01/04/XX

CLOSING DATE: Continuous

DESCRIPTION OF DUTIES/ESSENTIAL FUNCTIONS:

Under general supervision, verifies the accuracy of authorizations of assistance; posts case status changes to financial control cards; processes authorizations and submits them to Springfield and according to strict time schedule; maintains control on case actions to be taken by casework staff.

MINIMUM REQUIREMENTS

Requires knowledge, skill and mental development equivalent to completion of high school. Requires one year of clerical experience. Requires ability to type accurately at 30 WPM. Requires ability to speak, write and read Spanish.

WORK HOURS & LOCATION/AGENCY CONTACT

Work hours: 8:30 a.m. – 5:00 p.m.
Contact:
Employee Services, HCD
XXX South Grand Avenue East, 3rd floor
Springfield, IL 62762
Current employees will need to complete and submit a bid form and copy of an online application or CMS100 Employment Application to the address listed above.
Non State candidates apply below.

HOW TO APPLY

This position may require a current grade from Central Management Services (CMS), Division of Examining and Counseling, to be deemed qualified and available for employment consideration. For more information, please refer to the Work4Illinois website at Work.Illinois.Gov and select "Application Procedures." Additional information may also be obtained from the Agency Contact listed above or by contacting CMS, Division of Examining and Counseling at Work4Illinois@Illinois.gov.

Additional Documentation for Office Clerk:

Option SS2 - Spanish Speaking/Typing

DISTINGUISHING FEATURES OF WORK:

Under direct supervision, performs clerical filing, document processing and general office support functions; work performed at this level is limited in variety, discretion and independence of action and is controlled by established work methods and procedures; operates common office equipment in fulfilling clerical tasks.

ILLUSTRATIVE EXAMPLES OF WORK:

1. Receives, retrieves, sorts or collates documents, papers and forms in accordance with established methods and procedures for further action or final processing or filing; screens forms for presence of required information and completes and/or codes forms in accordance with established, well defined guidelines; may obtain information for form completion when sources are extremely limited or well defined; utilizes manual or automated files to retrieve, file, complete and/or review documents; records and/or maintains routine logs or reports of information pertaining to filing, data entry and retrieval or record processing activities; copies records in response to routine requests and mails to appropriate destination. Sets up and operates such office equipment as microfilm equipment or copy machines in performance of duties.

2. Receives, sorts and/or processes inter-departmental mail, U.S. postal mail, papers, tapes or other documents; weighs, stamps and/or distributes to appropriate destination; prepares routine records or maintains receipts of postage costs or amount of documents mailed; operates packaging, bursting, and decollating equipment; may transport mail or other documents by automobile.

3. Types lists, labels, cards, form letter blank completions, and envelopes utilizing a typewriter or word processor; exercises limited responsibility for spelling, grammar, punctuation.

4. Follows oral or written instructions, gaining experience and knowledge in and applying evolving automated office equipment and technology to tasks performed.

5. Serves as a relief receptionist, greeting and directing persons, answering phones and taking messages, and providing nontechnical information from clearly defined sources.

6. Performs other duties as required or assigned which are reasonably within the scope of the duties enumerated above.

DESIRABLE REQUIREMENTS:

Education and Experience

- Requires knowledge, skill and mental development equivalent to completion of high school.

Knowledge, Skills and Abilities

- Requires elementary knowledge of office practices and procedures.
- Requires elementary knowledge of grammar, spelling and punctuation.
- Requires working knowledge of alpha-numeric sequencing.
- Requires working knowledge of basic mathematics.
- Requires ability to follow oral or written instructions.
- Requires ability to operate commonly used manual and automated office equipment and perform routine maintenance.
- May require possession of an appropriate valid driver's license.
- May require the skill to type accurately.

In addition to having a written and spoken knowledge of the English language, candidates may be required to speak and write a foreign language at a colloquial skill level in carrying out position duties in conjunction with non-English speaking individuals.

Knowledge tested for Options 1, 2, CH1, MC1, MC2, S1 and S2: Reading Comprehension; Alphabetical Filing; Numeric & Alphanumeric Filing; English Usage; Mathematics; Interpersonal Skills.

Knowledge tested for Option 5, MC5 and S5: Alphabetical Filing; Defensive Driving; Name and Number Checking; Written Instructions.

Tests and Weights: Automated multiple-choice test 100%. Applicants for Options 2, MC2 and S2 will be required to qualify in a typing performance test. The performance test requires the ability to type from copy at a minimum net rate of 30 words per minute.

**NOTE: PER THE PERSONNEL RULES AN APPLICANT SHALL NOT BE PERMITTED TO RETAKE A MULTIPLE–CHOICE AND/OR PERFORMANCE EXAMINATION UNTIL 30 DAYS HAS ELAPSED.

Equipment for performance test: Typing tests are available in the Champaign, Chicago, Marion, Rockford and Springfield test centers.

Length of Eligibility: One year.

NOTE: Salary amounts shown are only to be used as a guide; actual salary will be determined at the time of hire based on current salary plans and/or collective bargaining agreements, if applicable.

APPLICATIONS MAY BE OBTAINED FROM: http://work.illinois.gov

IT PROFESSIONAL IV - 07.921

APPROXIMATE ANNUAL SALARY: $59,194.80 to $88,948.80

PAY GRADE: 41

A Permanent, full time vacancy

Department: Transportation

Division: Administration

Location: Carson, Minden, Gardnerville, Genoa

Open to All Qualified Persons

Applications accepted until recruitment needs are satisfied

Qualified individuals are encouraged to apply immediately. Lists of eligible candidates will be established and hiring may occur early in the recruiting process. Recruitment will close without notice when a sufficient number of applications are received or a hiring decision has been made.

ANNOUNCEMENT NUMBER 9774

Posted 07/31/XX

Direct Inquiries to: R. Thomson

(775) 983-3948

or e-mail xxxxx@dop.nv.gov

The Position

Information Technology (IT) Professionals analyze, develop, implement, maintain, and modify computer operations, systems, networks, databases, applications, and/or information security. Incumbents may perform duties in one or more IT specialization areas depending on the needs of the agency.

This position is located within the Administration Division, Information Services Section in Carson City. This position manages the Research and Development, Host Security and Help Desk sections and associated staff. It provides technical direction on host-based security systems such as Symantec AV, 8e6 content filters, WSUS and other software and patching systems. It also functions as the system administrator for TrackIT, the HelpDesk System in a Client Server environment using Crystal Reports. This position will modify, build, and deploy custom .MSI installer files for the maintenance, silent patching and deployment of Statewide systems and applications. The incumbent provides technical project management, hardware research, development and interoperability of systems for existing, new and emerging technologies in a diverse, complex environment.

NOTE: THE SELECTED CANDIDATE WILL BE RESPONSIBLE FOR THE COST OF HAVING THEIR FINGERPRINTS ROLLED.

To see full Class Specifications visit: http://dop.nv.gov/schematic7.htm

To Qualify

Education and Experience

1) Bachelor's degree from an accredited college or university with major course work in computer science, management information systems, or closely related field and five years of progressively responsible professional IT experience relevant to the duties of the position which may include systems administration, network administration, database administration, applications analysis and development, and/or information security, two years of which were at the advanced journey level or in a supervisory or project management capacity; OR bachelor's degree from an accredited college or university with major course work in computer science, management information systems, or closely related field and five years of progressively responsible professional IT experience which may include systems administration, network administration, database administration, applications analysis and development, and/or information security, relevant to the duties of the position, two years of which were at the journey level in information security; OR two years of relevant experience as an IT Professional III in Nevada State service; OR an equivalent combination of education and experience.

Special Notes

1) Applicants for positions in this series may have a combination of complementary education, experience, knowledge, skills and abilities that qualify for the class level and specialty being recruited.

Special Requirements

1) This position is subject to call-out or call-back.

2) Statewide travel is required.

3) Working evenings, weekends, and/or holidays is required.

4) A pre-employment criminal history check and fingerprinting are required.

Additional Position Experience

1) Experience with Systems Management Applications in a Microsoft environment

2) Experience with Enterprise Antivirus systems in a Microsoft environment

3) Experience with Enterprise Patching and Software Deployment technologies in a Microsoft environment

4) Experience with Enterprise Internet Content Filtering Systems in a Microsoft environment

5) Experience with Microsoft Active Directory - Group Policy Management

6) Experience with administrative scripting using .vbs, .vmi and/or other command languages

Examination

Application Evaluation Exam

The exam will consist of an application evaluation. It is essential that applications include extensively detailed information with time frames regarding education and experience. The most qualified applicants will be contacted by the hiring agency for interview.

GENERAL MECHANIC

Job Details

State University of New York

Application Due By: **8/10/20XX**

Title: General Mechanic

Location:

Rochester Educational Opportunity Center, Business Affairs Office

XXX Andrews St.

Rochester, NY 14604

Regions: 4

Grade: 12

Classification: Civil Service

Work Hours: 5 a.m. to 1:30 p.m.

Work Days: Monday – Friday

Employment Type: Full Time

Appointment Type: Permanent

Jurisdictional Class: Non-Competitive

Bargaining Unit/MC: OSU – CSEA

Duties/Responsibilities: Perform mechanical, electrical, plumbing and building maintenance including troubleshooting and repair of mechanical, electrical and plumbing equipment and building systems. Independently performs a variety of skilled and semi-skilled jobs. Perform scheduled PMs; and keep preventive maintenance and work order request records. Supervise maintenance staff consisting of two cleaners and one janitor.

Working knowledge of methods, material, tools and equipment used in the craft or crafts to which assigned.

Working knowledge of applicable standards and plumbing and electrical code regulations.

Working knowledge of the rules and regulations of the facility governing the activities of state wards under the supervision of the General Mechanic.

Ability to use the tools, machines, equipment and material of the craft or crafts to which assigned.

Ability to train and supervise others.

Ability to plan and layout work and diagnose problems.

Ability to read and interpret plans, diagrams, architectural blueprints and specifications.

Ability to understand and carry out written and oral instructions.

Minimum/Preferred Qualifications:

MINIMUM QUALIFICATIONS:

Four years of full-time experience in a trade under a skilled journey-level position which would provide training equivalent to that given in an apprenticeship program. Apprentice training in a trade or training gained by the completion of technical courses in a trade at a school or institute may be substituted for the above experience on a year-for-year basis.

PREFERRED QUALIFICATIONS:

Candidate must be quality minded, self-motivated, team player, and have the desire to work in a fast-paced environment.

Must possess a valid New York State Driver License.

Excellent time and attendance record.

Demonstrated proficiency in carpentry, electrical and plumbing, and HVAC systems.

Working knowledge of the construction and the safe and efficient operation of boilers, chillers, auxiliary heating, ventilating and air-conditioning equipment.

Asbestos Supervisor Training Certification.

Ability to train and supervise others. Minimum of one year supervisory experience.

NOTE: NY State Preferred list candidates, if applicable, have preference.

Contact Information:

Contact Name: Office of Human Resources

Address: College at Brockport State University of New York

XXX New Campus Dr.

Brockport, NY 14420

Additional Instructions: Please indicate General Mechanic – ROCHESTER on application or cover letter/resume.

The Classified Job Application can be downloaded from the College at Brockport, Human Resources, Classified Vacancies site at: http://www.brockport.edu/hr/vacancies/classified_service.htm

CLINICAL SOCIAL WORKER

Job Information

This Position is Open to All Applicants

The State of Michigan is an Equal Opportunity Employer

Civil Service Rule 2-7 requires that all newly hired state employees submit to and pass a pre-employment drug test prior to their actual appointment.

Hiring Agency: Community Health

Posting No.: 3904-09-030

Date Posted: 8/5/20XX

Deadline for Response: 8/12/20XX

Common Job Title: CSW

Classification Title: CLINICAL SOCIAL WORKER 9 10/P11

Pay Rate: $18.42 - $27.55/hr

Type of Employment: Full-time

Location: BRANCH County, Coldwater, Mich.

Brief Description:

Works as a member of a multi-disciplinary treatment team to provide a full range of mental health services to prisoners at the Lakeland/Crane Correctional Facility Outpatient Mental Health Program. These services include a comprehensive evaluation of all prisoners referred and suspected of mental illness or mental disorders; identification of needed treatment program, provision of and implementation of individualized treatment plans, and monitoring of progress.

Other Information:

This position functions within the security perimeter of a Correctional Facility and treats mentally ill/disordered prisoners from the Department of Corrections.

Education:

Masters Degree in Social Work. Please include a copy of your original college transcripts when applying.

Experience:

Clinical Social Worker 9: No specific type or amount is required.

Clinical Social Worker 10: One year of professional experience providing social casework and treatment services in a clinical setting equivalent to a Clinical Social Worker 9.

Clinical Social Worker P11: Two years of professional experience providing social casework and treatment services in a clinical setting equivalent to a Clinical Social Worker, including one year equivalent to a Clinical Social Worker 10.

Two years of professional experience as a Clinical Social Worker preferred.

Other Requirements:

PLEASE INCLUDE POSTING NUMBER 3904-09-030 IN ALL CORRESPONDENCE. Failure to do so will not guarantee that your application will be attached to the correct recruitment file. Current employees, please include your employee ID number and the name and location of the position you are applying for. Registration as a social worker by the Michigan Board of Examiners of Social Workers will be required at the time of appointment.

Union: United Auto Workers

How To Apply:

Submit a cover letter stating the position and location you are applying for, a copy of your licensure, a copy of original college transcripts and a resume that includes month and year of job experience to:

M. Smithson

Huron Valley Correctional Complex

XXXX Bemis Road

Ypsilanti, MI 48197

or fax to 555-435-4059

FAILURE TO SUPPLY ALL OF THE REQUIRED DOCUMENTS WILL RESULT IN THE INABILITY TO PROCESS YOUR APPLICATION.

PLEASE NOTE THE FOLLOWING WHEN APPLYING FOR VACANCIES: Your application for any job does not guarantee that you will be contacted by the department for further consideration.

If you are a veteran, surviving spouse of a veteran, or spouse of a disabled veteran, please indicate this information at the top of your resume when you submit it to us.

Click here to obtain more information about Veterans' Preference.

Applicants with a disability who may need an accommodation to participate in the interview process should make such an accommodation request at the time they are contacted by a department representative to schedule an interview.

HIGH SCHOOL SCIENCE TEACHER

Job Posting ID: 6099683

Employer Posting No: MVA-060209

Closing Date: Aug 07, 20XX

Requires Supervisory Experience: No

Openings Filled: 0 of 1

Public Transportation: No

Job Site Address: MCALLEN, Texas 78501

Veterans Only: No

Recovery Act Job: No

Green Job: No

Job Description

The Science teacher provides students with appropriate educational activities and experiences that enable them to fulfill their potential for intellectual, emotional, physical and social growth. He or she helps students develop the skills necessary to be productive members of society. The teacher is also responsible for maintaining classroom discipline, documenting attendance and monitoring the academic progress of each student assigned to his or her classroom.

Job Requirements

Occupation:

Secondary School Teachers, Except Special and Vocational Education

Certification: No

Experience / Education: 1 yrs 0 mos and Bachelors Degree

Preferred Skills:

Skill Description

Experience

1. Assigns lessons and corrects homework.

Less than 1 year

2. Confers with students, parents, and school counselors to resolve behavioral and academic problems.

Less than 1 year

3. Develops and administers tests.

Less than 1 year

4. Evaluates, records, and reports student progress.

1 to 2 years

5. Instructs students, using various teaching methods, such as lecture and demonstration.

1 to 2 years

6. Keeps attendance records.

Less than 1 year

7. Maintains discipline in classroom.

1 to 2 years

8. Participates in faculty and professional meetings, educational conferences, and teacher training workshops.

1 to 2 years

9. Performs advisory duties, such as sponsoring student organizations or clubs, helping students select courses, and counseling students with problems.

1 to 2 years

10. Prepares course outlines and objectives according to curriculum guidelines or state and local requirements.

1 to 2 years

11. Selects, stores, orders, issues, and inventories classroom equipment, materials, and supplies.

1 to 2 years

12. Uses audiovisual aids and other materials to supplement presentations.

1 to 2 years

Workweek and Pay Details

Minimum Pay: $30,000.00 / Year

Maximum Pay: $41,798.00 / Year

Workweek: Full Time - 30 hours or more per week

Duration: Regular

Shift: Days (First)

Benefits:

1. Medical/Health Insurance Plan

2. Other Insurance Plans

3. Other Paid Leave

4. Retirement Plan

5. Sick Leave

6. Vacation Leave

Additional Workweek Details: Teachers work 187 days per year with winter, spring and summer breaks.

Additional Pay Details: The Mid-Valley Academy is a public open enrollment charter school and a TRS eligible employer.

Language Skills:

English

Spanish

Additional Details:

Driver's License Type: Class C - Standard Driver's License

License State: Texas

WATER RESOURCES ENGINEER

Portland, Oregon

Job Listing 612012

Application Deadline: Open Until Filled

Date Posted: 08/06/20XX

Computer Skills: N/A

Occupational Skills: Required

Job Title: Principal Water Resources Engineer Urs36758

Hours Worked Per Week: 40

Shift: Day Shift

Duration of Job: Full Time, more than 6 months

How to Apply: The employer has requested that WorkSource Oregon pre-screen all applicants for this position. Please contact your local WorkSource Oregon office if you wish to apply for this job.

Job Summary:

REQUIREMENTS:

* Bachelor Degree in Civil/Water Resources Engineering

* Registered Professional Engineer

* 10 years technical water resources experience

* 5 years managerial / supervisory experience

* Proficiency in hydrologic and hydraulic analyses

* Knowledge of NPDES (Stormwater), TMDL, and other relevant regulations and policies

* Ability to plan for regulations and requirements/or design projects that effectively address multiple regulatory objectives and incorporate sustainability and/or green design principles

JOB DUTIES:

* Market and win water resource projects

* Supervise staff

* Serve as a key member of Business Line management team

* Manage multiple water resources projects

* Serve as high level coordinator/communicator among projects' clients and staff

* Assist junior staff and provide high-level service to clients

Job Classification: Civil Engineers

Licenses/Certifications Required: Engineers, Registered Professional

Compensation/Salary: Depending on Experience

Experience Required: At least 10 years

Education Required: Bachelors

Minimum Age: N/A

Gender: N/A

SUMMING IT UP

- There are two classes of jobs in the federal government—the competitive service and the excepted service.

- Those in the competitive service fall under the jurisdiction of the OPM, and hiring processes for those jobs must adhere to civil service laws passed by Congress.

- Excepted service agencies are not subject to the civil service laws, and they do not have to follow the same appointment, pay, and classification rules.

- Volunteer programs are unpaid work opportunities that allow students and prospective workers to explore federal occupations and gain valuable experience at the same time.

- U.S. Military veterans are entitled to special consideration in the federal hiring process. Veterans are entitled to positions that are not open to the general public.

- If you are seeking a government job and have a disability, contact Selective Placement Coordinator at the agency in which you're interested.

- Most federal employees are eligible to participate in training programs, tuition assistance or reimbursement, executive management and leadership programs, fellowship programs, seminars, and workshops, all of which are designed to help federal workers develop maximum job proficiency.

PART II

WHERE THE JOBS ARE

The Top Five High-Growth Government Fields

chapter 3

OVERVIEW

- Security, protection, compliance, and enforcement
- Medical and public health
- Accounting, budget, and business
- Engineering and sciences
- Program management/analysis and administration
- Summing it up

Some trends in the general population are creating a more favorable climate for people seeking jobs, especially in the federal government. As America's population ages, the largest segment of the country's working population—the baby boomers—are beginning to retire. This means that the workforce will gradually be reduced. In fact, the OPM—the federal government's central human resource agency—projects that by 2016, 40 percent of all current federal employees will be retired. Increasing federal government turnover also means that agencies will have to hire many new employees to fill vacancies.

A good percentage of the jobs lost to retirement will be in the private sector and in state and local governments as well. This will create intense competition for professional and technical talent, especially in the fields of science, engineering, health care, and IT. It is expected that in many of these fields, the demand over the next several years for skilled professional employees will be significantly greater than the available pool of talent.

To address the government's growing future need for skilled employees, the OPM and many individual federal agencies have stepped up their efforts to promote and publicize the rewarding and challenging opportunities of government employment. Agencies are also making efforts to streamline their processes to reduce the lengthy hiring process and are improving assessment practices to ensure they find the most appropriate people for the openings they have. Increasingly, agencies are also using incentives such as recruitment bonuses and student loan repayments to attract top-quality candidates.

Although the positions available in the federal government include almost every conceivable type of job—with positions in more than 2,000 categories—in the near future, the majority of the government's new employees will be hired to fill positions in five key areas:

1 Security, Protection, Compliance, and Enforcement

2 Medical and Public Health

③ Accounting, Budget, and Business

④ Engineering and Sciences

⑤ Program Management/Analysis and Administration

SECURITY, PROTECTION, COMPLIANCE, AND ENFORCEMENT

The single largest field in which government hiring is expected to increase dramatically is in security, protection, compliance, and enforcement, according to the 2007 Partnership for Public Service report entitled "Where the Jobs Are—Mission Critical Opportunities for America." The projected increase in hiring is linked primarily to expanded customs, border security, and immigration activities by the Department of Homeland Security. Occupations in this category include:

- criminal and noncriminal investigators
- inspectors
- police officers
- security and prison guards
- park rangers
- transportation safety officers (airport screeners)
- customs and border patrol officers
- immigration agents
- import specialists
- intelligence analysts
- international relations and foreign affairs specialists
- security administration personnel

The National Security Agency (NSA) and the CIA are recruiting a new breed of intelligence staff—namely, officers and analysts, including those who are fluent in Arabic, Farsi, and other Middle East languages.

The Department of Homeland Security is also seeking to increase personnel in these areas. The Department of Justice is expected to hire additional criminal investigators for FBI and corrections officers for the federal prison system. The Department of Defense (DOD), the Department of Homeland Security, the Department of Justice, the NRC, and the Department of the Treasury also plan to hire more intelligence analysts, especially those who are proficient in foreign languages.

In addition to the Departments of Homeland Security and Justice, 10 other agencies report plans to fill additional compliance and enforcement positions. These agencies oversee and administer laws that affect U.S. employers, workplaces, and workers. They enforce labor laws and environmental regulations and they work to prevent waste, fraud, and abuse in government programs.

These agencies and organizations are expected to see the most significant job growth in the security and protection field:

- Department of Agriculture
  - Agricultural Commodity Grading
  - Consumer Safety Inspection
  - Food Inspection
- Department of Commerce
  - General Compliance
- Department of Defense
  - Foreign Affairs
  - Intelligence Analysis
  - International Relations
  - Security Administration
- Department of Education
  - Criminal Investigation
- Department of Energy
  - Environmental Protection
  - Safety and Health Management
- Department of Homeland Security
  - Adjudication Officer
  - Air Interdiction (includes pilots/agents)
  - Asylum Officer
  - Border Patrol Agent
  - Contact Representative
  - Criminal Investigation
  - Customs and Border Protection Officer
  - General Investigation
  - Immigration Agent/Information Officer
  - Import Specialist
  - Intelligence Analysis
  - Police Officer
  - Security Administration
  - Transportation Security Officer
- Department of Housing and Urban Development
  - Equal Opportunity Compliance
- Department of Interior
  - Park Ranger

- Department of Justice
  - Compliance Inspection Support
  - Correctional Officer
  - Criminal Investigation
  - General Inspection and Investigation
  - Intelligence Analysis
  - Security Administration
- Department of the Treasury
  - Intelligence Analysis
- Department of Veterans Affairs
  - Police Officer
- Nuclear Regulatory Commission
- Office of Personnel Management
  - Personnel Security Specialist

MEDICAL AND PUBLIC HEALTH

Currently, the VA drives the demand in this occupational area to staff its network of hospitals. DOD and the Department of Health and Human Services (HHS) also project they will be hiring in this field.

Medical and public health occupations in the federal government include:

- consumer safety specialists
- dieticians and nutritionists
- doctors
- industrial hygienists
- medical technicians
- nurses
- nursing assistants
- occupational therapists
- occupational and rehabilitation therapists
- pharmacists
- radiologists

These agencies and organizations are expected to see the most significant job growth in the security and protection field:

- Department of Agriculture
  - Consumer Safety
  - Dietician/Nutritionist
- Department of Defense
  - Nurse

- o Pharmacist
- o Physician
- Department of Energy
  - o Industrial Hygiene
- Department of Health and Human Services
  - o Consumer Safety
  - o General Health Science
  - o Health Insurance
  - o Nurse
  - o Physician
  - o Program Management
  - o Social Science
- Department of Labor
  - o Industrial Hygiene
- Department of Veterans Affairs
  - o Diagnostic Radiology Technologist
  - o Medical Records Technician
  - o Medical Technology
  - o Nursing Assistant
  - o Pharmacist
  - o Physician
  - o Practical Nurse (LPN/VN)
  - o Registered Nurse

ACCOUNTING, BUDGET, AND BUSINESS

The number of accounting, budget, and business positions open in the federal government is increasing at least in part because of the growing demand for contracting specialists. Accounting, budget, and business occupations in the federal government include:

- accountants
- auditors
- budget and financial analysts
- financial managers/administrators
- revenue agents
- tax specialists
- property managers
- trade specialists

- loan specialists
- realty specialists

In the Department of the Treasury, the IRS is driving hiring in this occupational category as it continues to hire revenue agents and tax examiners to step up enforcement activities. DOD anticipates hiring contracting specialists, and the General Services Administration (GSA) is also expected to hire more contracting professionals to oversee the government's procurement of goods and services. Additionally, the Securities and Exchange Commission (SEC), the Federal Deposit Insurance Corporation (FDIC), the DHS, and NASA all plan to add employees in all categories of this occupational area.

These agencies and organizations are expected to see the most significant job growth in the accounting, budget, and business field:

- Department of Agriculture
  - General Business and Industry
  - Loan Specialist
- Department of Commerce
  - General Business and Industry
- Department of Defense
  - Contracting
- Department of Education
  - Accounting
  - Auditing
  - Financial Management
  - Loan Analysis
- Department of Energy
  - Budget Analysis
  - Contracting
  - Financial Analysis
- Department of Homeland Security
  - Contracting
- Department of Housing and Urban Development
  - Business and Industry Analysis
  - Contracting
  - Financial Analysis
  - Property Appraisal
- Department of Interior
  - Realty Management
- Department of Labor
- Department of Transportation
  - Financial Management

- Department of Treasury
  o Accounting
  o Internal Revenue Agent
  o Procurement
  o Tax Examining
- Environmental Protection Agency
  o Contract/Grant Specialist
- Federal Deposit Insurance Corporation
  o Financial Institution Examiner
- General Services Administration
  o Acquisition
  o Financial Management
  o Realty Management
- Government Accountability Office
  o Auditing
- National Aeronautics and Space Administration
  o Contracting
  o Financial Management
- Securities and Exchange Commission
  o Accounting
- Small Business Administration
  o General Business and Industry
  o Loan Specialists

ENGINEERING AND SCIENCES

DOD, the NRC, NASA, and the Departments of Transportation and Energy will continue to generate demand for engineers and scientists in a broad range of disciplines. Engineering and science occupations in the federal government include:

- engineering
- architecture
- microbiology
- ecology
- zoology
- physiology
- entomology
- toxicology
- botany
- plant pathology and physiology
- horticulture
- genetics
- soil science/conservation
- forestry
- fish and wildlife
- animal science
- ranger
- irrigation system operations
- physics
- chemistry
- astronomy
- geology
- oceanography
- food/textile/forest products technology

- land surveying
- veterinary medical sciences

DOD will hire engineers in various disciplines over the next three years, and the bulk of its demand will be for electrical and general engineers. NRC expects to hire consistently in these fields—primarily engineers and physical scientists—in anticipation of increased applications for new nuclear reactors.

The threat of bioterrorism is also driving the demand for scientists. The Department of Agriculture and DHS expect to hire new employees in the biological sciences and agricultural science, respectively. According to the BLS, the federal government will account for more than 20 percent of all new U.S. jobs in the biological sciences.

These agencies and organizations are expected to see the most significant job growth in the accounting, budget, and business field:

- Broadcasting Board of Governors
- Department of Agriculture
  - Biological Technician/Specialist
  - Forestry Technician/Specialist
  - Soil Conservation Technician/Specialist
  - Soil Science
  - Veterinarian
- Department of Commerce
  - Chemistry
  - Electrical Engineering
  - Fishery Biology
  - General Physical Science
  - Hydrology
  - Meteorology
  - Physics
- Department of Defense
  - Civil Engineering
  - Computer Engineering
  - Electronics Engineering
  - General Engineering
- Department of Energy
  - General, Electrical, and Nuclear Engineering
- Department of Health and Human Services
  - Chemistry
  - General Biology
  - General Physical Sciences
  - Microbiology

- Department of Homeland Security
  - Agriculture Science
  - Chemistry
  - Microbiology
  - Physics
- Department of Housing and Urban Development
  - Construction Analysis
  - General Engineering
- Department of Interior
  - Civil Engineering
  - General Biology
  - Geology
  - Hydrology
  - Wildlife Biology
- Department of Labor
  - Mining Engineering
- Department of Transportation
  - Scientist
- Environmental Protection Agency
  - Biology
  - Environmental Engineering
  - Environmental Science
  - Toxicology
- Federal Communications Commission
- National Aeronautics and Space Administration
  - Aerospace Engineering
  - Computer Engineering
  - Electronics Engineering
  - General Engineering
  - Materials Engineering
  - Physical Science
  - Space Science
- National Science Foundation
  - Program Director
- Nuclear Regulatory Commission
  - Engineering
  - Physical Science

PROGRAM MANAGEMENT/ANALYSIS AND ADMINISTRATION

This broad category includes program managers, skilled analysts who monitor program operations, and administrative staff. Program management/analysis and administration occupations in the federal government include:

- human resources
- equal employment opportunity
- telecommunications
- clerical support

Most of the available positions in this field will be project management and program analysis. For example, the GAO, the federal agency charged by Congress with evaluating the effectiveness of government operations, expects most of its new hires to be auditing analysts over the next several years. Almost all of the agencies surveyed for the report indicated they will hire management and program analysts, with the highest demand at DOJ, DHS, GSA, HHS, and the Department of Transportation.

These agencies and organizations are expected to see the most significant job growth in the program management/analysis and administration field:

- Broadcasting Board of Governors
- Department of Agriculture
  - General Administration Management
  - Management and Program Analysis
- Department of Commerce
- Department of Defense
  - Logistics Management
- Department of Education
  - Equal Opportunity
  - Human Resources
  - Management/Program Analysis
- Department of Energy
  - Human Resources
- Department of Health and Human Services
  - Public Health
- Department of Homeland Security
  - Human Resources
  - Management and Program Analysis
  - Telecommunications
  - Training

- Department of Housing and Urban Development
  - General Administration Management
  - Human Resources
  - Management and Program Analysis
  - Support Clerk/Assistant
- Department of Justice
  - Human Resources
  - Management and Program Analysis
  - Miscellaneous Administration
  - Support Clerk/Assistant
- Department of Labor
  - Grants Management
  - Human Resources
- Department of Transportation
  - Program Management
- Department of Treasury
  - Human Resources
- Department of Veterans Affairs
  - Human Resources
- Environmental Protection Agency
  - General Administrative Management
  - Management and Program Analysis
- General Services Administration
  - Policy and Program Management
- Government Accountability Office
  - Analyst
- National Aeronautics and Space Administration
  - General Administrative Management
  - Human Resources
- National Archives and Records Administration
  - Management and Program Analysis
  - Secretary
- National Labor Relations Board
  - Labor-Management Relations Examiner
- National Science Foundation
  - Administrative Manager

- o Program Assistant
- o Science Assistant
- Office of Personnel Management
  - o General Administration/Program Management
  - o Human Resources
  - o Management and Program Analysis
- Small Business Administration
  - o Human Resources
- Social Security Administration
  - o Human Resources

SUMMING IT UP

- To address the government's growing future need for skilled employees, the OPM and many individual federal agencies have stepped up their efforts to promote and publicize the rewarding and challenging opportunities of government employment.

- The single largest field in which government hiring is expected to increase dramatically is in security, protection, compliance, and enforcement.

- The majority of the government's new employees will be hired to fill positions in five key areas: security, protection, compliance, and enforcement; medical and public health; accounting, budget, and business; engineering and sciences; and program management/analysis and administration.

Other Government Fields With Increasing Job Demand

chapter 4

OVERVIEW

- **The federal aviation administration**
- **Department of State and U.S. Agency for International Development (USAID)**
- **The U.S. patent and trademark office**
- **The Department of Homeland Security**
- **More government agencies and organizations that are hiring**
- **Summing it up**

In addition to the five highest-growth government fields we reviewed in the previous chapter, several other federal departments are expected to see increasing demand for employees:

- the Federal Aviation Administration (FAA)
- the Department of State and the U.S. Agency for International Development
- the Patent and Trademark Office
- the Department of Homeland Security

In this chapter, we'll provide an overview of the varieties of jobs available in these high-demand fields, the qualifications required to secure a position, and the agencies or organizations in which these positions are available. You'll also have a chance to review examples of actual vacancy announcements for some of these positions.

THE FEDERAL AVIATION ADMINISTRATION

The FAA, as part of the Department of Transportation, operates the largest aviation system in the world. It is responsible for the safety and certification of aircraft and pilots, around-the-clock operation of the nation's air traffic control system, and the regulation of U.S. commercial space transportation. As is the case with so many agencies, the FAA is facing a wave of retirements and is making great efforts to hire new employees to replace those leaving. Employment opportunities at the FAA include:

- air traffic controllers
- airway transportation systems specialists/electronic technicians
- aviation safety inspectors
- computer specialists
- engineers

The FAA also hires the following:

- accountants and budget analysts
- administrative officers
- air traffic assistants
- attorneys
- audio visual producers
- biological science technicians
- cartographic technicians
- contracting specialists
- engineering draftspeople
- health aides and technicians
- human resource management specialists
- logistics specialists
- management analysts
- managers
- medical technicians
- meteorological technicians
- packagers
- paralegals
- physicians/nurses
- program analysts
- psychology aides and technicians
- safety technicians
- scientific researchers
- social science aides and technicians
- statistical assistants
- trade specialists
- writers and editors

In addition, the FAA Executive System (FAES) employs individuals in the top echelons of senior management. This system comprises three groups:

❶ **Officers.** These workers are assistant and associate administrators who report directly to the FAA administrator and provide corporate strategic vision and leadership. They are expected to foster alliances with industry and governments at all levels and ensure integration of priorities, programs, and resources to meet the FAA's mission and goals.

❷ **Executives.** Executives lead the FAA staff organizations and programs. Employees in this group make up the first level of corporate leadership and provide the link between the administrator's officers and the operational program staff.

Responsibilities include establishing business plans, setting measurable outcomes, and adjusting resources within the organizations to which they are assigned.

3 **Senior professionals.** Senior professionals provide world-class expertise, research, and development in unique scientific and technical subject matter areas. They occasionally supervise groups of subordinate technical employees.

Air Traffic Controllers

Air traffic controllers are by far the largest and most visible group of FAA employees. Becoming an air traffic controller takes extensive skill and preparation, but the FAA has systems in place that support applicants and workers through the process. The agency also provides extensive internships and programs for high school and college students, including Collegiate Training Initiatives, summer employment programs, and year-round employment programs. For information, go to www.faa.gov/about/office_org/headquarters_offices/ahr/jobs_careers/student_programs.

To become an air traffic controller, you must complete an FAA-approved education program; pass a preemployment test; receive a school recommendation; meet the basic qualification requirements in accordance with federal law; and achieve a qualifying score on the FAA-authorized preemployment test. Candidates must also pass a medical exam, undergo drug screening, and obtain a security clearance before they can be hired.

The FAA has stepped up its hiring efforts to ensure uninterrupted air traffic operations. The agency's Web site (www.faa.gov) has an abundance of information for job seekers. Vacancies and hiring locations are listed, along with required forms and details about what you need to do to find a job at the FAA.

DEPARTMENT OF STATE AND U.S. AGENCY FOR INTERNATIONAL DEVELOPMENT (USAID)

According to its mission, the Department of State "creates a more secure, democratic and prosperous world for the benefit of the American people and the international community [and] conducts the nation's foreign affairs and diplomatic initiatives; oversees the Nation's embassies and consulates; issues passports; monitors U.S. interests abroad; and represents the U.S. before international organizations." Headquartered in Washington, D.C., the Department of State also has 250 consulates and embassies worldwide. Within the United States, its highest concentrations of employees are in D.C., New York, South Carolina, Florida, and California.

In addition to the expected demand for foreign service employees, the State Department also expects to see job growth in information management and security occupations. For the civil service, job growth is expected in the passport/visa specialist occupation as a result of the newly enacted Western Hemisphere Travel Initiative, which requires U.S. and Canadian travelers to present a passport or other document that denotes identity and citizenship when entering the United States. It is a result of the Intelligence Reform and Terrorism Prevention Act of 2004 (IRTPA).

The Department of State and USAID plan to continue expanding recruitment of foreign service officers and career staff to enhance diplomatic and reconstruction efforts. It's anticipated that foreign service officers for consular, information management, and security activities will be hired in increasing numbers. A significant number of new employees will be needed to handle the growing demand for passports and visas as well as to support contracting, financial management, and analytical activities.

Additionally, USAID will hire foreign service officers and civil service personnel at entry-level and midlevel positions. Those recruited for the civil service recruitment will fill positions in contracting, health sciences, financial management, human resources, and management and program analysis.

If you have a gift for language or numbers, the Department of State may offer excellent job opportunities. It is targeting its hiring efforts to attract individuals with expertise in foreign languages (especially Arabic, Chinese, and Farsi) and economics. To attract talented new employees, the Department of State has increased its presence at business and other professional schools, and it is working to develop more effective marketing and advertising campaigns in an effort to better acquaint potential applicants with the varied positions available.

The department has added incentives for applicants by offering recruitment bonuses and student loan repayment assistance. To find out more about working for the Department of State, visit www.state.gov/careers.

About USAID

USAID is an independent federal government agency that receives overall foreign policy guidance from the Secretary of State. It has been the primary U.S. agency helping countries that are recovering from disaster and trying to eliminate poverty and reform government. To that end, USAID supports long-term economic growth and U.S. foreign policy objectives by assisting with economic growth, agriculture, and trade; global health; and democracy, conflict prevention, and humanitarian assistance.

USAID provides assistance in sub-Saharan Africa, Asia, Latin America and the Caribbean, Europe and Eurasia, and the Middle East. Although it is headquartered in Washington, USAID's strength lies in its field offices worldwide. The agency works closely with private organizations, indigenous groups, universities, American businesses, international agencies, foreign governments, and other U.S. government agencies. It has working relationships with more than 3,500 American companies and more than 300 U.S.-based private voluntary organizations.

Foreign Service Officers and the Junior Officer Program

Foreign Service Officers (FSOs) are at the core of USAID's staff, and they are vital in carrying out USAID's programs. FSOs essentially perform governmental functions, providing an essential link between the agency's goals and the way in which these goals are achieved.

For the foreseeable future, USAID will be recruiting new FSOs through its entry-level Junior Officer Program for the Foreign Service. The Junior Officer Program seeks highly qualified junior professional candidates who are willing to make a long-term career commitment to the Foreign Service and to international development.

Junior Officers begin with formal training followed by rotational, on-the-job, Washington-based training for up to a year. After they complete Washington training, they are assigned to an overseas office, where they receive broad-based training through rotational assignments. The total Junior Officer training plan lasts about three years. Successful candidates will become representatives of USAID and the U.S. government around the world.

New FSOs have five years in which to earn tenure in the Foreign Service. Requirements include foreign language proficiency and successful completion of at least three years with the agency—of which 18 months must be spent on a permanent overseas assignment in a USAID field office. The three-year training program is included in the five-year tenure requirement.

Although USAID is a Department of State organization, applicants to USAID are not required to take the foreign service examination, unlike applicants to the Department of State. The hiring process for FSOs with USAID involves a series of application reviews and screenings, after which preferred applicants are invited, at their own expense, to a personal interview with a technical panel. Candidates are evaluated on their academic credentials, related overseas and/or domestic development professional experience, technical knowledge, and related skills such as management, leadership, and oral and written communication.

The USAID Fellowship Program

Individual fellowships are offered by USAID. Fellowship programs:

- develop a pool of experts devoted to international development assistance
- provide individuals with practical work experience in humanitarian assistance and economic and social development
- benefit the agency by providing research, technical advice, and intellectual stimulus

Fellowships are limited to two years, but extensions or combinations of different fellowships may lengthen fellowships to four years.

The Fellowship Program provides USAID with fresh ideas, renewed energy, and state-of-the-art technical knowledge, which expands the level of expertise normally represented by the agency's U.S. direct-hire employees. Fellowship programs also provide a means by which USAID can increase its outreach to partners, nongovernmental organizations, universities, and other donors. For fellows, these programs are an introduction to development issues and development institutions. They provide visibility in the donor community and may help fellows jump-start a rewarding career.

THE U.S. PATENT AND TRADEMARK OFFICE

Patent and Trademark Office hiring will continue to increase as the organization struggles to address a long-standing backlog of patent applications. The Patent and Trademark Office is a part of the Department of Commerce, which aims to promote "economic growth and security through export growth, sustainable economic development and economic information and analysis."

According to a recent job announcement, a patent examiner reviews patent applications to determine whether they comply with federal laws and regulations and to basic scientific principles. Patent examiners are responsible for:

- scrutinizing patent applications
- determining the scope of protection claimed by the inventor
- researching relevant technologies
- communicating their findings and decisions to patent practitioners and/or inventors

This job is visually demanding, and almost all of a patent examiner's work is performed on a computer. The examiner is required to conduct an extensive review of a large body of technical information that typically includes detailed drawings, three-dimensional mechanical portrayed drawings, or chemical manufacturing process diagrams. To successfully perform the job, an employee must be able to work in a production-oriented environment, efficiently analyze and digest large volumes of scientific information, and make and communicate timely decisions regarding the patentability of an application. Positions are located in the Patent Examining Corps of the U.S. Patent and Trademark Office in Alexandria, VA.

The Department of Commerce participates in the Presidential Classroom Scholars Program, which provides the next generation of civic leaders with academic and leadership development experience in Washington, D.C. High school sophomores, juniors, and seniors in the program observe the federal government at work; witness the development of public policy; and explore the roles of citizens, lawmakers, experts, and businesses in a democracy. To learn more about the Presidential Classroom Scholars Program, visit www.presidentialclassroom.org.

To learn more about the U.S. Patent and Trademark Office, go to www.uspto.gov. To see available positions within the office and at the Department of Commerce, click on the "Careers" tab at www.commerce.gov.

THE DEPARTMENT OF HOMELAND SECURITY

The Department of Homeland Security expects to fill a great number of positions over the next 10 years, especially in contracting and IT at all grade levels. Nationwide, the department's recruitment activities will focus on enhancing border and air security, so the jobs in demand in the Department of Homeland Security will include:

- adjudication officers
- agriculture specialists

- attorneys
- border patrol agents
- criminal investigators
- customs and border patrol officers
- deportation officers
- immigration enforcement agents
- intelligence analysts
- pilots
- transportation security officers (airport screeners)

The Department of Homeland Security has branch offices nationwide and overseas, with concentrations in Texas, California, Florida, D.C., New York, Virginia, Arizona, Illinois, New Jersey, and Georgia. In an effort to raise awareness about its mission, programs, and benefits and to gain the attention of talented job seekers, the department sends representatives and recruiters to college recruitment events, national conferences, and career fairs. It has also partnered with minority-servicing institutions and veterans' organizations in an effort to recruit the highest-quality workers available.

To address its anticipated shortage of intelligence, IT, finance, contracting, and human resource professionals, the Department of Homeland Security has implemented a number of intern and fellowship programs. In addition to participation in the Presidential Management Fellowship described earlier, it also offers the following programs:

- **Acquisition Professional Career Program.** This is a new entry-level program for college graduates that is designed to develop future acquisition leaders for the more than $20 billion worth of goods and services acquired annually in support of the Department's mission—the third-largest procurement budget in the federal government.
- **Honors Fellowship Program.** This is a two-year paid opportunity for exceptional students from the nation's finest graduate programs.
- **Legal Honors Program.** This two-year rotational assignment through various components of the Department provides highly qualified new attorneys and recent law graduates completing judicial clerkships or fellowships with the opportunity to launch their careers at the Department of Homeland Security. The program is aimed at enhancing their skills and providing hands-on experience with some of the most critical and controversial issues facing the United States.
- **Office of Intelligence and Analysis Federal Career Intern Program.** This program offers paid internships in full- or part-time positions. Upon successful completion, interns may be eligible for permanent placement.
- **Pat Roberts Intelligence Scholars Program.** Offered through the Office of Intelligence and Analysis, this program is designed to recruit and train entry-level intelligence professionals.

To further expand recruitment of top candidates, the Department of Homeland Security may offer recruitment bonuses and assistance with student loan payment. For more information about working for the Department of Homeland Security, go to www.dhs.gov/xabout/careers.

MORE GOVERNMENT AGENCIES AND ORGANIZATIONS THAT ARE HIRING

Here is a close-up look at the hiring priorities of federal departments and agencies that have the greatest need for new employees.

Department of Agriculture

Filling highly skilled positions to protect the safety of the nation's food supply and to prepare for and respond to animal-based and human-based pandemics is the focus of the USDA recruitment efforts. Priority hiring at USDA will be in these areas:

- business development
- information technology
- public health
- resource conservation
- scientific and economic research
- veterinary medicine

The headquarters of the USDA is in Washington, D.C., and it has administrative offices in Maryland and Virginia, with additional offices throughout the world. The highest concentrations of USDA employees are in California, D.C., Oregon, Missouri, Texas, Maryland, Colorado, Montana, Louisiana, and Idaho.

The USDA actively participates in job fairs and works with professional organizations to recruit high-potential candidates to fill key occupational areas. The agency has been a lead federal employer in hiring college students with disabilities and in providing internships to Native Americans. The USDA also participates in the Presidential Management Fellows Program, the Career Intern Program, and other student employment programs that provide career opportunities for high-potential candidates. To attract such applicants, the USDA offers recruitment bonuses and student loan payment programs. To find out more about career opportunities with the USDA, go to www.usda.gov/da/employ.

Department of Defense

DOD is the largest federal employer, and it hires both white- and blue-collar workers. It is headquartered at the Pentagon in Arlington, VA, with offices and installations in every state in the United States and in 146 other countries. The department's priority is to fill positions with workers who have critical skills in these areas:

- contracting
- engineering

- IT
- language
- logistics management
- medicine

To offset personnel attrition resulting from retiring employees, DOD has adopted several hiring programs designed to identify and prepare top-quality candidates, including an active student employment program.

- **The National Security Education Program** provides funding opportunities to U.S. students studying world regions critical to American interests, including international relations, languages, and culture. This program is an integral aspect of the department's ability to attract individuals with high levels of language proficiency.

- **The Science, Mathematics and Research for Transformation (SMART) Program** is designed to increase critical science, mathematical, and engineering skills by providing scholarships for students to pursue academic degrees in these disciplines.

- **The Student Training and Academic Recruitment (STAR) Pilot Program** uses students to represent DOD on campus and promote it as a potential employer with many career opportunities.

DOD also offers student loan repayments and recruitment bonuses. The DOD Web sites, www.dod.gov and www.goDefense.com, offer additional information about its programs and career opportunities.

The Department of Energy

The Department of Energy (DOE) recently identified a hiring priority for engineers, financial analysts, and IT specialists for project management (in various occupational specialties), contract management, IT project management, and technical qualifications programs (safety and support at nuclear facilities), all of which support the core work of the agency. Hiring will be at various grade levels throughout the country.

To recruit top students, the DOE Scholar Program introduces students or recent college graduates to the agency's mission and operations. Entry-level and midlevel opportunities are available in a variety of disciplines and facilities nationwide, including:

- accounting and finance
- engineering
- environmental sciences
- information technology
- law
- mathematics
- physical sciences

- physics
- program management
- safety and health
- statistics

The Scholar Program includes paid internships, fellowships, scholarships and research opportunities. To qualify, applicants must have at least a 2.9 (out of 4.0) grade point average.

The DOE is headquartered in Washington, D.C., with high concentrations of employees in Washington State, Oregon, New Mexico, Maryland, Colorado, Tennessee, California, South Carolina, and Idaho. To help attract top-quality candidates, DOE offers student loan repayments and recruitment bonuses. More information about DOE and its programs can be found at www.energy.gov and www.orise.orau.gov/doescholars.

Department of Health and Human Services

HHS "protects the health and welfare of all Americans and provides essential human services; administers Medicare and Medicaid and manages programs that provide financial assistance and services to low-income families; engages in health and social science research; ensures food and drug safety; prevents diseases, including immunization services for emergencies and potential terrorism; and ensures that health information technology is established to ensure a comprehensive medical system."

HHS has its headquarters in Washington, D.C., major subunits in Maryland and Georgia, and regional offices in 10 cities nationwide, including Seattle, Dallas, San Francisco, New York, and Chicago. The highest concentrations of HHS employees are in Maryland, Georgia, Arizona, New Mexico, District of Columbia, Oklahoma, and California.

The future hiring needs of HHS are in response to the country's expanded focus on preventing bioterrorism. As a result, there is increasing demand to fill occupations in the health and scientific fields, specifically for physicians and biologists.

As is the case with many other governmental departments, HHS has made extensive efforts to partner with universities, participate in job fairs, and market career opportunities targeted to attracting scientific and health professionals. HHS uses several employment programs to attract top-quality candidates and future leaders.

- **The Emerging Leaders Program** recruits high-potential employees and provides fast-track development highlighting leadership and business skills. The program hires interns with a variety of backgrounds for effective analysis and execution of HHS programs. Occupational fields recruited for include administration, information technology, public health, biological sciences, and social sciences.

- **The Health Resources and Services Administration Scholars Program** provides another opportunity for high-potential candidates to participate in a

12-month training and development program that may lead to permanent positions upon successful completion.

Web sites available to assist with your exploration of opportunities at HHS are www. hhs.gov and www.hhs.gov/careers.

The Department of Justice

The headquarters of the DOJ are in Washington, D.C., but offices of DOJ components, including the FBI, the Drug Enforcement Agency (DEA), Alcohol, Tobacco and Firearms (ATF), the U.S. Marshals Service, and the Bureau of Prisons are nationwide. The highest concentrations of DOJ employees are in D.C., Illinois, Texas, Georgia, California, Florida, Pennsylvania, New York, Virginia, and Kentucky. Currently, DOJ is actively recruiting for the following occupations:

- administrative support staff
- compliance and law enforcement (criminal investigators, correctional officers, and staff for the Bureau of Prisons)
- intelligence analysts
- legal (attorneys and paralegals)

The main focus of DOJ's hiring efforts is on combating terrorism. Filling foreign language and intelligence analyst and FBI counterterrorism agent positions remains a priority.

The DOJ relies on a variety of recruitment and outreach strategies to effectively target diverse and talented individuals for key occupational areas. The use of automation is also being emphasized in an effort to effectively target recruitment efforts and reduce the time required to hire new employees.

To attract the best talent, the DOJ makes extensive use of pay and recruitment flexibilities. Within the federal government, the DOJ was the leader in the use of the Student Loan Repayment Program. In fiscal years 2005 and 2006, DOJ granted 3,073 student loan repayments totaling more than $27 million. During that same period, the department also provided 750 recruitment incentives totaling more than $6.5 million. To learn how you can find work with the DOJ, visit www.usdoj.gov.

The Department of Transportation

With headquarters in Washington, D.C., and offices nationwide, DOT's highest concentration of employees work in D.C., California, Texas, Oklahoma, Florida, New York, Georgia, Virginia, Illinois, and Washington.

As with other federal agencies, DOT has focused its hiring on filling positions in key occupational areas such as air traffic control. Through the year 2016, the FAA plans to hire and train more than 15,000 air traffic controllers nationwide. For a full listing of the FAA's planned hiring activity by location, check www.faa.gov.

To help in its recruitment and outreach efforts, DOT partners with schools, transportation associations, and special interest organizations. It also participates in the Federal Career Intern Program and student employment programs that provide career opportunities for high-potential candidates. DOT encourages the hiring of veterans and persons with disabilities. To attract the best candidates, the department also provides recruitment bonuses and assists with student loan repayment. For more information, visit www.dot.gov or www.careers.dot.gov.

The Department of the Treasury

The Department of the Treasury is located in Washington, D.C., with offices worldwide and throughout the United States. The highest concentrations of Treasury employees are in Texas, Tennessee, New York, D.C., Pennsylvania, Georgia, Utah, Maryland, and Kentucky.

The Department of Treasury's recruitment priorities are for critical professional and specialized occupations including the following:

- accountants
- attorneys
- economists
- intelligence analysts
- IRS agents
- mission support employees (human resources, IT, procurement)
- tax examining specialists

The department expects its recruiting efforts to be challenging because of the increased competition for a talent pool whose members have numerous other employment options and seek nontraditional work environments. Nonetheless, it is stepping up its hiring efforts by strengthening its collaboration with colleges, universities, and professional organizations. The department has also launched an aggressive and innovative marketing/recruitment campaign, including Web site redesign, a heightened presence at job fairs, the expanded use of intern programs, and targeted recruitment to meet specific staffing needs.

The Department of the Treasury has also developed a diversity strategy that is fully integrated with its workforce and succession planning efforts. The strategy is intended to provide a roadmap for ensuring that a diverse talent pool is available for its needs. To better promote partnership efforts between and among the bureaus, a Diversity Council has been established.

The Department of the Treasury also offers recruitment bonuses and student loan repayments to attract qualified applicants. For additional information about opportunities available with Treasury, go to www.treasury.gov/organization/employment.

The Department of Veterans Affairs

The VA includes employees in more than 300 occupations, and therefore it offers employment opportunities for a broad range of candidates. The VA's mission is to administer programs involving health care, pensions, benefits, and employment to aid U.S. veterans and their families, run the veterans' hospital system, and operate national cemeteries. It runs 155 hospitals, nearly 900 health clinics, and 123 national cemeteries.

It is headquartered in Washington, D.C., with 58 field offices nationwide. Its highest concentrations of employees are in California, Texas, Florida, New York, and Pennsylvania.

The VA plans to focus its recruitment efforts on attracting qualified health-care professionals, claims examiners, and human resources specialists. As is true for many federal agencies, VA anticipates losing a significant percentage of employees to retirement over the next several years, so it is actively working to attract candidates to join its ranks. The agency's academic affiliations across the nation ensure that thousands of undergraduates and graduate students complete their clinical rotations and residencies at its health-care facilities. The department provides numerous financial incentives to qualified health-care employees, including student loan repayment, scholarships for tuition costs and related expenses, and salary replacement to current employees enrolled full-time in an approved education program. The agency has also created the National Veterans Employment Program, dedicated to educating military veterans about employment opportunities within the VA.

You can find more information about opportunities with the VA at www.va.gov/jobs.

The Federal Deposit Insurance Corporation

The FDIC's mission is to maintain the stability and public confidence in the nation's financial system by insuring deposits, examining and supervising financial institutions, and managing receiverships. In cooperation with other state and federal regulatory agencies, the FDIC promotes the safety and soundness of the U.S. financial system and the insured depository institutions by identifying, monitoring, and addressing risks to the deposit insurance fund. The FDIC is centered in Washington, D.C., and Arlington, VA, with satellite offices in Atlanta, Boston, Chicago, Kansas City, San Francisco, New York City, Dallas, and Memphis.

The FDIC's highly skilled and diverse workforce continuously monitors and responds rapidly and successfully to changes in the financial environment. This is especially true with the most recent economic challenges the United States has faced. The agency is actively reshaping its workforce to reflect future workload requirements. Financial examiners are the agency's predominant occupation, and they will continue to be the focal point of recruitment efforts—but the FDIC also recruits for entry-level and experienced professionals with backgrounds in business, finance, computer science, and a host of other specialties ranging from human resources to marketing.

The FDIC has two programs specifically targeted toward providing the agency with top-performing employees:

- **The Corporate Employee Program** prepares the FDIC's workforce for rapid changes in the financial industry and resulting shifts in workload. To achieve this flexibility, employees are encouraged to develop multiple functional proficiencies so they can be rapidly deployed to different mission-critical efforts.

- **The FDIC Legal Division Honors Program** is a two-year program for law school graduates designed to provide selected candidates with a better understanding of the work of the FDIC. Eligible candidates must have a B average or be in the top one-third of their law school class.

The FDIC participates in on-campus professional and diversity events to attract top candidates. Its Web site lists a schedule of career fairs and campuses where it actively recruits. To learn more about the FDIC and its employment opportunities, visit www.fdic.gov/about/jobs/index.html.

General Services Administration

The GSA's stated mission is to help "federal agencies better serve the public by offering, at best value, superior workplaces, expert solutions, acquisition services and management policies." With headquarters in Washington, D.C., it has regional offices in 11 cities nationwide, including Fort Worth, TX; New York City; San Francisco; and Kansas City, MO. The highest concentrations of GSA employees are in Washington, D.C., Virginia, New York, Texas, California, Missouri, Illinois, Georgia, Pennsylvania, and Washington State.

The GSA seeks to recruit individuals who have strong customer service, acquisition, IT, realty, financial management, or project management skills. There is also increasing federal agency demand for GSA services in contracting, technology, and studies/research.

GSA balances its hiring efforts between filling entry-level and midcareer-level positions and has instituted a corporate marketing strategy based on the motto "You can do that here." The GSA's marketing materials highlight the agency's dynamic work and the range of available career opportunities in many geographic locations. GSA offices have forged strong partnerships with colleges and universities, which serve as prime recruitment sources for filling student trainee and intern positions.

To attract job candidates, the GSA offers recruitment bonuses and a student loan repayment program. To learn whether a job with the GSA is right for you, visit www.gsa.gov/GSAjobssearch.

The Government Accountability Office

The GAO supports Congress in meeting its constitutional responsibilities. It also works to improve the performance and ensure the accountability of the federal government. Centered in Washington, D.C., the GAO has offices in Atlanta; Boston;

Chicago; Dallas; Dayton, OH; Denver; Huntsville, AL; Los Angeles; Norfolk, VA; San Francisco; and Seattle.

Over the next several years, the GAO aims to hire more than 600 staff members from a variety of academic disciplines, including:

- accounting
- economics
- engineering
- IT specialists
- law
- public administration
- physical sciences
- social sciences

The GAO expects the majority of its hires to be entry-level analysts and specialists. In addition, it plans to hire upper-level analysts and specialists (e.g., auditors, economists, IT specialists) to address succession planning needs, as well as critical administrative and professional staff (e.g., human capital, information management, budget). Hiring at the GAO is primarily for positions in Washington, D.C., with some openings in GAO field locations.

To attract and retain a highly qualified and diverse workforce, GAO has a robust entry-level recruitment program that includes established relationships with 50 U.S. universities and colleges, a revised online job application form, and fall and spring job announcements to recruit top candidates throughout the year.

GAO also has a comprehensive student intern program. These 10- to 16-week internships enhance the agency's ability to attract high-quality and diverse students for possible permanent employment. The GAO offers incentives such as student loan repayment, recruitment bonuses, and transit benefits to successfully compete for top talent. Its recruitment and outreach efforts include partnerships with professional organizations and associations whose members have been traditionally underrepresented in the federal workforce, such as the American Association of Hispanic CPAs and the Federal Asian Pacific American Council. To learn whether a job with GAO is right for you, visit www.gao.gov.

The National Aeronautics and Space Administration

NASA's main offices are in Washington, D.C., with centers and laboratories in California, Ohio, Maryland, Texas, Florida, Virginia, Alabama, New York, West Virginia, Mississippi, and New Mexico. The highest concentrations of NASA employees are in Texas, Maryland, Alabama, Virginia, California, Florida, and Ohio.

The retirement of NASA's shuttle program represents a major transition in which the administration must transfer the workforce requirements of the shuttle program to the needs of new programs. As you might expect, NASA's current and future primary recruiting efforts will be in science and engineering.

NASA uses electronic recruitment and assessment tools to find top-quality candidates in a timely fashion. The Web site www.nasajobs.gov provides information on career opportunities and a look at NASA's new automated Staffing and Recruitment System (STARS). Key components of NASA's recruitment efforts include advertising in professional journals and Web sites, a presence at nationwide job fairs, on-campus interviews, and partnerships with minority schools and organizations. Given the highly competitive recruiting environment for science and engineering positions, NASA makes extensive use of recruitment bonuses and student loan repayments to entice high-quality candidates. Visit NASA's Web sites at www.nasa.gov and www.nasajobs.nasa.gov to learn more about job opportunities.

The Nuclear Regulatory Commission

The NRC is responsible for regulating the country's civilian use of byproduct, source, and special nuclear materials to ensure adequate public health and safety protection. It is also charged with promoting the common defense and security and protecting the environment. The NRC carries out its mission at its headquarters in Rockville, MD, and at other offices in King of Prussia, PA; Atlanta; Lisle, IL; Arlington, TX; Las Vegas; Chattanooga, TN, and at each regulated nuclear facility throughout the country. The highest concentrations of NRC employees are in Maryland, Pennsylvania, Illinois, Georgia, and Texas.

The NRC plans to hire 400 to 450 people annually for the next several years in technical positions including engineering, physical science, and security analysis. Most will be located in Rockville. The Atlanta office is home to most of the NRC engineers involved in inspecting new reactor construction.

One of the NRC's greatest challenges is to acquire, develop, and sustain a highly skilled and diverse technical workforce. This requires use of innovative recruitment efforts, including college outreach, career paths programs for entry-, mid-, and senior-level positions, and offers of recruitment bonuses and student loan repayments. The career paths programs include special entry-level programs for nuclear safety and legal positions. In addition, the NRC sponsors a Graduate Fellowship Program for those at the master's and Ph.D. levels in technical areas such as engineering, science, and other disciplines critical to NRC's mission. To find out more about jobs with the NRC, go to www.nrc.gov/about-nrc/employment.html.

The Securities and Exchange Commission

The SEC's mission is to protect investors; maintain fair, orderly, and efficient markets; and facilitate capital formation. Headquartered in Washington, D.C., the SEC has satellite offices in New York City; Boston; Philadelphia; Atlanta; Chicago; Denver; Fort Worth, TX; Miami, FL; Salt Lake City; San Francisco; and Los Angeles.

To fulfill its mission, the SEC recruits attorneys, accountants, and securities compliance examiners. Most SEC employees have had previous experience in the securities industry working for law firms, state or federal prosecutors, public accounting firms, or self-regulatory organizations. A small number of positions are filled at entry level. As you might expect, the number and location of job opportunities vary based on workload and case priorities.

To attract high-performing employees, the SEC conducts annual on-campus interviews at law schools nationwide in the late summer and early fall. Additionally, the SEC maintains a presence at most minority bar association annual meetings and many professional conferences for MBAs and accounting organizations.

The SEC has established a number of programs designed to attract top-performing candidates:

- **SEC Advanced Commitment Program.** Approximately 15 to 30 third-year law students and judicial clerks are hired each year as entry-level law clerks through this program.

- **Business Associate Program.** This is a two-year professional opportunity for recent MBA graduates and other business-related master's degree holders; it introduces candidates to securities market regulation and the work of the commission.

- **Summer Honors Internship programs.** The SEC also offers three paid summer internship programs:

  1. a law program for first- and second-year law students

  2. a business program for MBAs and other business-related master's degree holders

  3. a college program for undergraduates in any major

- **Law Student Observer Program.** This volunteer school-year program exposes law students to the work of the commission for one semester.

The SEC offers employees a variety of work/life programs, including telecommuting, supplemental vision and dental benefits, and student loan repayment. To bolster its recruitment efforts, it has also produced an online video, "Make a Difference: Work for the SEC," intended to attract attorneys, accountants, economists, CPAs, and MBAs. To view the video, go to www.sec.gov/about/media.htm. To learn more about SEC programs and whether a job with the commission is right for you, visit www.sec.gov/jobs.htm.

SUMMING IT UP

- The FAA is responsible for the safety and certification of aircraft and pilots, around-the-clock operation of the nation's air traffic control system, and the regulation of U.S. commercial space transportation.

- The FAA has stepped up its hiring efforts to ensure uninterrupted air traffic operations. The agency's Web site (www.faa.gov) has an abundance of information for job seekers.

- The department of Homeland Security expects to fill a great number of positions over the next 10 years, especially in IT at all grade levels.

- To address it's anticipated shortage of intelligence, IT, finance, contracting, and human resource professionals, the Department of Homeland Security has implemented a number of intern and fellowship programs.

PART III
GOVERNMENT JOB SEARCH BASICS

The Federal Job Application System

chapter 5

OVERVIEW

- **Understanding the federal landscape**
- **Searching for vacancy announcements**
- **The anatomy of a federal job announcement: what to look for and how to use it**
- **Summing it up**

UNDERSTANDING THE FEDERAL LANDSCAPE

For today's federal job seekers, it's easier than ever to locate helpful resources that focus on public service employment. Scores of Web sites—official and otherwise—offer unique perspectives on working for the U.S. government and on the wide range of job opportunities available.

A great place to start exploring federal careers is at www.USAJOBS.gov, the official job site of the U.S. government. In addition to an A–Z listing of all federal agencies and links to their Web sites, this resource will help you search for public service employment by occupation, agency, or geographic area. USAJOBS also presents a general overview of all federal agencies and the exciting and diverse career opportunities each has to offer.

The Web site of the Partnership for Public Service (www.makingthedifference. org) offers several tools to help you investigate the array of available federal positions. The site includes discipline-specific guides and matches specific college majors to applicable public service positions. Guides for student programs and internships, information on federal student loan repayment, and descriptions of high-demand jobs are also featured.

Another excellent resource, "Best Places to Work in the Federal Government" (www.bestplacestowork.org), provides rankings from employee engagement surveys. More than 221,000 federal employees from 283 federal agencies participated in these surveys, and the results can help you pinpoint your area or position of interest. Job seekers can match personal profiles to particular government jobs and agencies to find the best potential employment match.

Charged with ensuring a "high-quality and diverse federal workforce," the OPM provides valuable employment information to the public on its Web site (www. opm.gov). The site includes detailed information about a comprehensive range of topics, including the federal job application process, federal hiring trends, salary and benefits information, and student and other programs. Demographic information pertaining to the federal workforce is also available through another OPM Web site, FedScope (www.fedscope.opm.gov). Statistics include current demographic data arranged by state, department, and/or type of position.

Use Your Resources and Get Educated

In addition to researching federal job information online, you should also take advantage of any personal contacts who might be helpful. Talking with someone who has experience with the federal hiring process will provide valuable insights. If you know anyone who works for the federal government or who knows someone who works in a public service position, see whether you can make arrangements to talk with that person about the hiring process. Here are some other ideas for "insider" contacts:

- **Family and friends:** If anyone in your family or circle of friends is a current or former federal employee, he or she might be the best place to start for making agency contacts and for other useful information. Friends or family members may also be able to put you in touch with other people they know who have federal government work experience.

- **Faculty and career services:** Your high school or university professors, staff, alumni, and career services personnel probably have relationships with federal employees or agencies, and they will be willing to put you in touch with those people.

- **Recruitment personnel:** A more direct way to learn about federal employment is to contact a federal recruiter. You can find federal recruiters through Web site searches or the Government Offices pages in your local telephone book.

SEARCHING FOR VACANCY ANNOUNCEMENTS

The federal government is always looking for qualified candidates and tries to ensure that job openings are clearly posted where the highest number of applicants will access them. Here's a list of the best ways to look for openings in the federal agencies and departments.

Direct Contact

If you know which agency or agencies you're interested in working for, you can contact them directly to learn whether they have openings and how to apply for positions. Some agencies allow you to prepare an application to be kept on file for future opportunities; others accept applications only for current or projected openings. Be sure to ask about whether applications are kept on file at your agency of interest.

If a federal agency has an office in your area, find its telephone number under the "Government Pages" section of the telephone book and ask someone in the human resources office about possible job openings. To get you started, an appendix in this book, "Important Contacts and Web Sites," lists phone numbers, addresses, and Web sites for all major federal agencies.

USAJOBS: The Federal Employment Information System

USAJOBS is the best place to go online for federal employment information. Hiring agencies are required to post job openings with the OPM, and www.usajobs.gov is where the OPM makes listings available to job seekers.

In recent years, the federal government has made a concerted effort to streamline what used to be a cumbersome, time-consuming application process. The USAJOBS site is meant to simplify the process of applying for federal positions. More than 33,000 federal job openings worldwide are posted at USAJOBS on any given day, and the site is updated daily. Prospective employees can search for positions by job category, location, or agency, and official forms are listed for downloading. USAJOBS also offers an online resume builder that helps you create a resume you can use to apply for multiple federal jobs, and you can access fact sheets and automated job searches that allow you to create and save your own job search profile (including a prepared resume) online. When job openings fitting your requirements become available, you are notified by e-mail.

USAJOBS also maintains an automated telephone system. Call 703-724-1850, 866-204-2858, or TDD 978-461-8404 to obtain information about federal job vacancy listings and order official government forms. Like other voice response telephone systems, the system functions by using a menu system, so you have to listen to a range of choices before obtaining the relevant information.

State Employment Service Offices

State Employment Service Offices operate in partnership with the Department of Labor's Employment and Training Administration (ETA) to help job seekers find work and assist employers in finding qualified candidates. The ETA administers:

- federal government job training and worker dislocation programs
- federal grants to states for public employment service programs
- unemployment insurance benefits

These services are provided primarily through state and local workforce development systems.

ETA offices are located nationwide. To find the closest one, try looking in the state government pages of your local telephone book under "job service" or "employment" or visit the ETA Web site at www.doleta.gov.

THE ANATOMY OF A FEDERAL JOB ANNOUNCEMENT: WHAT TO LOOK FOR AND HOW TO USE IT

Job announcements in the private sector are usually short and simple. A typical classified ad in the newspaper or online states the name of a company, the responsibilities and duties inherent in the position, minimum job requirements, and company contact information. You send in your cover letter with your resume, and that's it—you've successfully applied for the job. Your resume will likely go to the company's human resources office and, if it passes the initial screening, is forwarded to the department that has an opening.

As you've seen by now, the federal government application process is far more complex. Most federal vacancy announcements are four to eight pages long. The announcement typically includes a detailed description of the position's duties and responsibilities; lists the qualifications, experience, and KSAs (knowledge, skills, and abilities) successful applicants must have; states whether competitive testing is required; explains how applicants will be evaluated; and so on.

The key to being considered for a federal position and surviving the application process begins with understanding the job vacancy announcement. The announcement is filled with details that *must* be addressed on your application or instructions that *must* be followed to keep your resume out of the trash bin. The announcement contains clues that, if you find and understand them, will tell you what additional information should be included with your application to help ensure that you are called in for an interview.

The "Musts"

You must make absolutely certain that you include each of the following items on your application:

- **The job's vacancy announcement number.** You already know that to qualify for a federal job, you must apply for an announced vacancy: a *specific* position with its own vacancy announcement number. This number must be put on your application; otherwise, the screening panel won't know which position you want to be considered for. Without this number, your application is likely to be discounted. The screening panel will *not* sift through all the applications and match them with currently available jobs—it just won't happen.

- **The job's title, job classification series, and grade-level number.** When you refer to the vacancy in your application, in any correspondence or communication, or even in a telephone conversation, you must refer to the position you want by its official job title, job classification series, and grade-level number. For example, Computer Specialist, GS-334-11 means that the job title is "Computer Specialist," its classification series is "334," and its pay-grade level is GS-11 (remember, GS refers to positions covered by the General Schedule; these levels go up to GS-13, 14, and 15, which are management positions. A position ranked SES refers to higher-rated Senior Executive Service positions, which range from SES-1 to SES-5).

- **The application deadline.** Although you do not need to enter the job posting's deadline on your application, you must meet it. Check the announcement carefully for the closing date. Some federal jobs are "open until filled"; others are "continuously open," but these are the exceptions, not the rule. Each government agency is responsible for posting its own job announcements, including application procedures and timelines. Agencies that require hard copies of forms may specify that applications be received or postmarked by the closing date, so be sure to review those instructions carefully. If you submit your application after the closing date, it will not be considered.

- **The application procedure.** Application guidelines will also vary from agency to agency. Many now accept electronic submissions, but some still request hard copies of specific forms or materials. Again, read carefully. Each vacancy announcement is explicit about what is required to apply and to be considered for a position.

The "Shoulds"

Once you have scrutinized a vacancy announcement for specific instructions, check for more subtle hints about what should be included in your application. Watch for language that mirrors the job announcement's language. Federal job announcements are lengthy and detailed, and agencies know exactly what they're looking for in an ideal candidate. Your application's focus, word choices, and tone should echo the job announcement's language. This shows the person hiring that you are exactly the right person for the job. Obviously, you shouldn't quote directly from the announcement or falsify your background, experience, or abilities—but do keep the announcement at hand when crafting your application and resume. Focus on what's important to the hiring agency and address how your education and background match the position's requirements.

The Typical Job Vacancy Announcement

As you complete your application, keep the job vacancy announcement nearby and refer to it often. Let's review the elements of a typical announcement and see how you can use the information provided by the hiring agency to make your application stand out.

- **Hiring Agency:** At the top of the announcement, you will find the name of the agency and the name of the bureau within the agency.

- **Job Announcement Number:** This number is specific to its particular job opening. It is the number you will use in your application and in any correspondence you have regarding your application for this particular position.

- **Job Title:** Job titles for federal positions are very specific. Although a job title may be the same or similar to one in the private sector, job responsibilities may be very different. It's imperative that you read the entire announcement for additional details about the position.

- **Salary Range:** When there are two acceptable grade levels for a particular position, you will find a salary range posted; otherwise, the announcement will list one established salary for the position.

- **Series and Grade:** Beneath the job title will be a combination of letters and numbers. The two letters at the beginning refer to the salary schedule under which the position falls. For example, white-collar jobs fall under the General Schedule (GS). The number that follows these two letters refers to the job classification series, and the final digits refer to the grade level. Grade level is defined by law according to work difficulty, responsibility, and qualifications required.

- **Promotion Potential:** This line lists the highest grade to which a person working in this position may be promoted.

- **Open Period:** These dates specify the time period during which applications will be accepted.

- **Duty Locations:** Federal jobs are located throughout the country and abroad. Each announcement specifies the city, county, and state where the opening or openings are located.

- **Who May Be Considered:** This line tells you whether the job is open to everyone or only to current or former federal employees. In some instances, qualified applicants must have been displaced from other federal jobs.

- **Major Duties:** Here is the "meat" of the announcement, where you find out what your responsibilities are if you're hired for the job. Read this section carefully to determine whether the duties as described are what you really want in a job.

- **Key Requirements:** This section lists the requirements for employment at each grade-level. Much of this relates to your level of education and experience, but it may also specify your previous employment at a lower job grade.

- **Knowledge, Skills, and Abilities (KSAs):** KSAs are defined by the federal government as the attributes required to perform a job, generally demonstrated through qualifying experience, education, or training. In job announcements, KSAs may also be called "evaluation factors," "rating factors," or "job elements." Vacancy announcements generally ask applicants to submit a narrative in a separate document that contains specific responses to each of these KSAs. This means you must address each KSA listed using as much detail as possible.

Occasionally, a vacancy announcement does not require that an applicant include a description of KSAs with the rest of the application. Here's one place where you *shouldn't* follow directions precisely. By all means, include those descriptions. If more than one applicant passes the initial screening, KSAs will be used to rank qualified applicants. An application with no KSAs or inadequate KSAs will fall to the bottom of the list.

- **How You Will Be Evaluated:** This section explains how applications will be considered and evaluated against one another. It may explain how applications are ranked for the position, the most important ranking factors, the interview process, and if previous supervisors will be contacted for references.

- **Pay, Benefits, and Work Schedule:** This section will tell you whether the job is permanent or temporary, full-time or part-time. It will also present the expected work schedule and benefits for the position. Many announcements now post the option for alternative work schedules or telecommuting as part of their benefits packages.

- **How to Apply:** Acceptable types of applications and any specific documentation required are listed here. This section may also include contact information if you have additional questions about the position. Some announcements include a link to the hiring agency's Web site, and you may find further details about the position, complete application instructions, and a full list of items you need to submit. Occasionally, an announcement will state that you can apply online through the specific department or agency's Web site; usually, however, you will be redirected to the www.USAJOBS.gov Web site. Remember—all your information and documentation *must* be submitted by the closing date for you to be considered for a position.

Working With Keywords

As you read each federal job announcement, pay close attention to the language and specific words used. This will provide valuable input on what the hiring agency is seeking in its ideal candidate. Keywords, used repeatedly or emphasized in multiple sections of the job announcement, should also appear in your application materials. Whether the application instructions call for a federal resume, a specific form (such as the OF-612 or the 1203-FX), or answers to a list of KSAs, make sure that you pick up these keywords and use them liberally in your application for the position. Building your application around these keywords will strengthen your submission and grab the hiring manager's attention.

An excellent way to determine which keywords will be most effective in your federal job application is to study a variety of job announcements (and their accompanying lists of questions) for positions similar to the one that interests you. These announcements may be for other jobs related to your target position and even located in diverse geographic areas, as long as they are in your general field of interest. As you study the announcements, note which keywords appear frequently, especially in the "requirements," "skills," and "qualifications" sections. Jot them down and use them freely in your application materials. In your written narrative, be sure to connect them to your own educational background and job experience.

You can convey a great deal of information about your qualifications and skills with just one keyword. For example, if you include the keyword "analyst" on your application, a screening committee might conclude that you have experience gathering data, researching information, and developing new systems. Keywords allow you to highlight your experience, education, skills, and other credentials relevant to your chosen field.

Discovering Your Core Competencies

In your search for the ideal civil service position, you'll undoubtedly notice the staggering array of opportunities available—literally hundreds of different jobs are available within the U.S. government at any one time. You've probably also discovered that with such a wide array of openings, the government may have positions for which you are well suited but that you previously may not have considered. So how do you match up your talents, interests, and abilities with specific civil service jobs?

An excellent place to start is the "Explore Your Career Opportunities" section of the USAJOBS Web site at http://career.usajobs.gov. This very helpful page supplies tools to help you match your work interests and preferences with actual federal job openings, and it includes indispensable sections such as a "Career Interest Guide," "Job Interest Matching," "Specific Job Exploration," and "Match Federal Jobs to Private Sector Jobs."

If you follow the "Career Interest Guide" link, for example, you will be presented with a set of assessment questions that will help you determine your interest level in performing specific sets of tasks. Based on your responses, the program will then offer a list of federal career areas that correlate with your interests, along with the occupations within these areas. Follow the links provided to obtain more detailed information about each position. The process of assessing your core competencies can be enlightening as you choose a career path—and it may also help you contemplate a wider range of federal job areas and occupations.

SUMMING IT UP

- An excellent resource, "Best Places to Work in the Federal Government" provides rankings from employee engagement surveys.

- The federal government is always looking for qualified candidates and tries to ensure that job openings are clearly posted where the highest number of applicants will access them.

- USAJOBS is the best place to go online for federal online employment information.

- The key to being considered for a federal position and surviving the application process begins with understanding the job vacancy announcement. The announcement is filled with details that must be addressed on your application.

Doing Your Research

OVERVIEW

- **Completing federal hiring forms**
- **Preparing a federal resume**
- **Creating winning KSAs**
- **Summing it up**

Once you have decided to apply for a position with the government, you will need to read the job announcement closely for the application directions. These are usually found under the heading "How to Apply," and the instructions vary across agencies. Many times, job seekers are directed to apply for federal positions by following links provided to online application programs.

In addition to your online application, you may be required to mail or fax other requested materials, such as college transcripts, specialized forms, or Veterans' Preference verification. Some agencies still accept hard copies of application materials, and you will be given the option to apply with either a resume or the OF-612 (Optional Application for Federal Employment). The OF-612, accessible at www.opm.gov/forms/pdf, is the federal government's job application form.

Keep a copy of your selected job vacancy announcement with you as you begin the process of developing your application. It's helpful to refer to the announcement as you prepare your application. Depending on the position and the agency involved, you will be completing application forms (online or in print), updating your resume, and/or developing well-thought-out responses to a set of KSAs. Let's look at each of these in turn.

COMPLETING FEDERAL HIRING FORMS

Once you have selected job vacancy announcements, you can begin the process of filling out an application form. Here we'll review the two forms you're likely to be required to complete to apply for a job with the federal government: the OF-612 and the OPM Form 1203-FX.

The OF-612

This form, developed during the mid-1990s, was part of a concerted effort by the OPM to simplify the federal hiring process. The OF-612 is less cluttered visually and is more user-friendly than previous forms, making the application process a little less intimidating for federal job seekers.

chapter 6

However, many applicants think that because the OF-612 form is only two pages long and uses simple language, their responses can be brief. That reasoning makes sense, but it's not true. When the OF-612 poses questions regarding your past work duties and other qualifications, you should provide ample details because this information can distinguish you from other candidates. Don't hesitate to attach additional pages to the application so you have as much room as you need to answer questions fully. As with all federal job applications, you'll do better if you include more information rather than less. Invariably, federal screening panels choose applicants with the strongest application materials. If you keep this in mind, you'll think more like the people who actually have a vote about your application. Their vote is your ticket to a federal job, so try to put yourself in their shoes.

General Information
Optional Application for Federal Employment – OF 612

You may apply for most Federal jobs with a résumé, an Optional Application for Federal Employment (OF 612), or other written format. If your résumé or application does not provide all the information requested on this form and in the job vacancy announcement, you may lose consideration for a job. Type or print clearly in black ink. Help speed the selection process by keeping your application brief and sending only the requested information. If essential to attach additional pages, include your name and job announcement number on each page.

- Information on Federal employment and the latest information about educational and training provisions are available at www.usajobs.gov or via interactive voice response system: (703) 724-1850 or TDD (978) 461-8404.

- Upon request from the employing Federal agency, you must provide documentation or proof that your degree(s) is from a school accredited by an accrediting body recognized by the Secretary, U.S. Department of Education, or that your education meets the other provisions outlined in the OPM Operating Manual. It will be your responsibility to secure the documentation that verifies that you attended and earned your degree(s) from this accredited institution(s) (e.g., official transcript). Federal agencies will verify your documentation.

  For a list of postsecondary educational institutions and programs accredited by accrediting agencies and state approval agencies recognized by the U.S. Secretary of Education, refer to the U.S. Department of Education Office of Postsecondary Education website at http://www.ope.ed.gov/accreditation/.

  For information on Educational and Training Provisions or Requirements, refer to the OPM Operating Manual available at http://www.opm.gov/qualifications/SEC-II/s2-e4.asp.

- If you served on active duty in the United States Military and were discharged or released from active duty in the armed forces under honorable conditions, you may be eligible for veterans' preference. To receive preference, if your service began after October 15, 1976, you must have a Campaign Badge, Expeditionary Medal, or a service-connected disability. Veterans' preference is not a factor for Senior Executive Service jobs or when competition is limited to status candidates (current or former career or career-conditional Federal employees).

- Most Federal jobs require United States citizenship and also that males over age 18 born after December 31, 1959, have registered with the Selective Service System or have an exemption.

- The law generally prohibits public officials from appointing, promoting, or recommending their relatives.

- Federal annuitants (military and civilian) may have their salaries or annuities reduced. Every employee must pay any valid delinquent debt or the agency may garnish their salary.

- Send your application to the office announcing the vacancy. If you have questions, contact the office identified in the announcement.

How to Apply

1. **Review** the listing of current vacancies.
2. **Decide** which jobs, pay range, and locations interest you.
3. **Follow instructions** provided in the vacancy announcement including any additional forms that are required.
   - You may apply for most jobs with a resume, this form, or any other written format; **all applications must include the information requested in the vacancy announcement as well as information required for all applications for Federal employment** (see below):
   - The USAJOBS website features an online résumé builder. This is a free service that allows you to create a résumé, submit it electronically (for some vacancy announcements), and save it online for use in the future.

Certain information is required to evaluate your qualifications and determine if you meet legal requirements for Federal employment. If your resume or application does not include all the required information as specified below, the agency may not consider you for the vacancy. Help speed the selection process - submit a concise resume' or application and send only the required material.

Information required for all applications for Federal employment:

Job Vacancy Specifics
- Announcement number, title and grade(s) of the job you are applying for

Personal Information
- Full name, mailing address (with zip code) and day and evening phone numbers (with area code) and email address, if applicable
- Social Security Number
- Country of citizenship (most Federal jobs require U.S. citizenship)
- Veterans' preference
- Reinstatement eligibility (for former Federal employees)
- Highest Federal civilian grade held (including job series and dates held)
- Selective Service (if applicable)

Work Experience
- Provide the following information for your paid and volunteer work experience related to the job you are applying for:
  - ▶ job title (include job series and grade if Federal)
  - ▶ duties and accomplishments
  - ▶ employer's name and address
  - ▶ supervisor's name and telephone number - indicate if supervisor may be contacted
  - ▶ starting and ending dates (month and year)
  - ▶ hours per week
  - ▶ salary

U.S. Office of Personnel Management
Previous edition usable

NSN 7540-01-351-9178
50612-101

OF 612
Revised June 2006

Page 1 of 4

How to Apply (continued)

Education

- High School
  - ▶ Name, city, and State (Zip code if known)
  - ▶ Date of diploma or GED
- Colleges or universities
  - ▶ Name, city, and State (Zip code if known)
  - ▶ Majors
  - ▶ Type and year of degrees received. (If no degree, show total credits earned and indicate whether semester or quarter hours.)
- Do not attach a copy of your transcript unless requested
- Do not list degrees received based solely on life experience or obtained from schools with little or no academic standards

Upon request from the employing Federal agency, you must provide documentation or proof that your degree(s) is from a school accredited by an accrediting body recognized by the Secretary, U.S. Department of Education, or that your education meets the other provisions outlined in the OPM Operating Manual. It will be your responsibility to secure the documentation that verifies that you attended and earned your degree(s) from this accredited institution(s) (e.g., official transcript). Federal agencies will verify your documentation.

For a list of postsecondary educational institutions and programs accredited by accrediting agencies and state approval agencies recognized by the U.S. Secretary of Education, refer to the U.S. Department of Education Office of Postsecondary Education website at http://www.ope.ed.gov/accreditation/.

For information on Educational and Training Provisions or Requirements, refer to the OPM Operating Manual available at http://www.opm.gov/qualifications/SEC-II/s2-e4.asp.

Other Education Completed

- School name, city, and State (Zip code if known)
  - ▶ Credits earned and Majors
  - ▶ Type and year of degrees received. (If no degree, show total credits earned and indicate whether semester or quarter hours.)
- Do not list degrees received based solely on life experience or obtained from schools with little or no academic standards

Other Qualifications

- Job-related:
  - ▶ Training (title of course and year)
  - ▶ Skills (e.g., other languages, computer software/hardware, tools, machinery, typing speed, etc.)
  - ▶ Certificates or licenses (current only). Include type of license or certificate, date of latest license, and State or other licensing agency
  - ▶ Honors, awards, and special accomplishments, (e.g., publications, memberships in professional honor societies, leadership activities, public speaking and performance awards) (Give dates but do not send documents unless requested)

Any Other information Specified in the Vacancy Announcement

Privacy Act Statement

The U.S. Office of Personnel Management and other Federal agencies rate applicants for Federal jobs under the authority of sections 1104, 1302, 3301, 3304, 3320, 3361, 3393, and 3394 of title 5 of the United States Code. We need the information requested in this form and in the associated vacancy announcements to evaluate your qualifications. Other laws require us to ask about citizenship, military service, etc. In order to keep your records in order, we request your Social Security Number (SSN) under the authority of Executive Order 9397 which requires the SSN for the purpose of uniform, orderly administration of personnel records. Failure to furnish the requested information may delay or prevent action on your application. We use your SSN to seek information about you from employers, schools, banks, and others who know you. We may use your SSN in studies and computer matching with other Government files. If you do not give us your SSN or any other information requested, we cannot process your application. Also, incomplete addresses and ZIP Codes will slow processing. We may confirm information from your records with prospective nonfederal employers concerning tenure of employment, civil service status, length of service, and date and nature of action for separation as shown on personnel action forms of specifically identified individuals.

Public Burden Statement

We estimate the public reporting burden for this collection will vary from 20 to 240 minutes with an average of 90 minutes per response, including time for reviewing instructions, searching existing data sources, gathering data, and completing and reviewing the information. Send comments regarding the burden statement or any other aspect of the collection of information, including suggestions for reducing this burden to the U.S. Office of Personnel Management (OPM), OPM Forms Officer, Washington, DC 20415-7900. The OMB number, 3206-0219, is currently valid. OPM may not collect this information and you are not required to respond, unless this number is displayed. Do not send completed application forms to this address; follow directions provided in the vacancy announcement(s).

THE FEDERAL GOVERNMENT IS AN EQUAL OPPORTUNITY EMPLOYER

U.S. Office of Personnel Management   NSN 7540-01-351-9178   OF 612
Previous edition usable   50612-101   Revised June 2006

Page 2 of 4

OPTIONAL APPLICATION FOR FEDERAL EMPLOYMENT - OF 612

Form Approved
OMB No. 3206-0219

Section A - Applicant Information

Use Standard State Postal Codes (abbreviations). If outside the United States of America, and you do not have a military address, type or print "OV" in the State field (Block 6c) and fill in the Country field (Block 6e) below, leaving the Zip Code field (Block 6d) blank.

1. Job title in announcement	2. Grade(s) applying for	3. Announcement number
Computer Specialist	**GS-0334-14/15**	**99-63-AP**

4a. Last name	4b. First and middle names	5. Social Security Number
xxxxxx	xxxxxx	000-00-0000

6a. Mailing address	7. Phone numbers (include area code if within the United States of America)
000 Stillwater Place	7a. Daytime **(703) 000-0000**

6b. City	6c. State	6d. Zip Code	7b. Evening
xxxxxx	**MD**	**00000**	(301) 000-0000

6e. Country (if not within the United States of America)

8. Email address (if available)   xxxx@emall.com

Section B - Work Experience

Describe your paid and non-paid work experience related to the job for which you are applying. Do not attach job description.

1. Job title (if Federal, include series and grade)

Computer Specialist, GS-0334-13

2. From (mm/yyyy)	3. To (mm/yyyy)	4. Salary	per	5. Hours per week
08/1996	**Present**	$ **71,565**	year	**40**

6. Employer's name and address	7. Supervisor's name and phone number
Defense Information System Agency (DISA) **00000 xxxxxxxx Square, xxxx, VA 00000**	7a. Name John xxxx 7b. Phone **(703) 000-0000**

8. May we contact your current supervisor?   Yes ☒   No ☐
   If we need to contact your current supervisor before making an offer, we will contact you first.

9. Describe your duties, accomplishments and related skills (if you need to attach additional pages, include your name, address, and job announcement number)

See Attachment

Section C - Additional Work Experience

1. Job title (if Federal, include series and grade)

Telecommunications Specialist, GS-0391-13

2. From (mm/yyyy)	3. To (mm/yyyy)	4. Salary	per	5. Hours per week
05/1995	**08/1996**	$ **63,442**	year	**40**

6. Employer's name and address	7. Supervisor's name and phone number
Space and Naval Warfare (SPAWAR) Systems Command **2451 Crystal Drive, Arlington, VA 22245-5200**	7a. Name CDR 7b. Phone **(703) 000-0000**

8. May we contact your current supervisor?   Yes ☒   No ☐
   If we need to contact your current supervisor before making an offer, we will contact you first.

9. Describe your duties, accomplishments and related skills (if you need to attach additional pages, include your name, address, and job announcement number)

See Attachment

U.S. Office of Personnel Management
Previous edition usable

NSN 7540-01-351-9178
50612-10
Page 3 of 4

OF 612
Revised June 2006

Section D - Education

Upon request from the employing Federal agency, you must provide documentation or proof that your degree(s) is from a school accredited by an accrediting body recognized by the Secretary, U. S. Department of Education, or that your education meets the other provisions outlined in the OPM Operating Manual. It will be your responsibility to secure the documentation that verifies that you attended and earned your degree(s) from this accredited institution(s) (e.g., official transcript). Federal agencies will verify your documentation.

For a list of postsecondary educational institutions and programs accredited by accrediting agencies and state approval agencies recognized by the U.S. Secretary of Education, refer to the U.S. Department of Education Office of Postsecondary Education website at http://www.ope.ed.gov/accreditation/.

For information on Educational and Training Provisions or Requirements, refer to the OPM Operating Manual available at http://www.opm.gov/qualifications/SEC-II/s2-e4.asp.

Do not list degrees received based solely on life experience or obtained from schools with little or no academic standards.

1. Last High School (HS)/GED school. Give the school's name, city, state, ZIP Code (if known), and year diploma or GED received:

Eastern High School, Washington, DC

2. Mark highest level completed: Some HS ☐   HS/GED ☐   Associate ☐   Bachelor ☐   Master ☒   Doctoral ☐

3. Colleges and universities attended.
Do not attach a copy of your transcript unless requested.

3. Name			Total Credits Earned Semester	Total Credits Earned Quarter	Major(s)	Degree (if any), Year Received
3a. Name **University of District of Columbia**					Electronic Technology	A.S., 1979
City **Washington**	State **DC**	Zip Code				
3b. Name **National Lewis University**					Management	B.S., 1995
City **McLean**	State **VA**	Zip Code **22102**				
3c. Name **Eastern Michigan University**					Information Security	M.S., 1997
City **Ypsilanti**	State **MI**	Zip Code **48197**				

Section E - Other Education Completed

Do not list degrees received based solely on life experience or obtained from schools with little or no academic standards.

Section F - Other Qualifications

License or Certificate	Date of Latest License or Certificate	State or Other Licensing Agency
1f.		
2f.		

Section G - Other Qualifications

Job-related training courses (give title and year). Job-related skills (other languages, computer software/hardware, tools, machinery, typing speed, etc.). Job-related honors, awards, and special accomplishments (publications, memberships in professional/honor societies, leadership activities, public speaking, and performance awards). Give dates, but do not send documents unless requested.

See Attachment

Section H - General

1a. Are you a U.S. citizen?   Yes ☒   No ☐ →   1b. If no, give the Country of your citizenship

2a. Do you claim veterans' preference?   Yes ☒   No ☐ → If yes, mark your claim of 5 or 10 points below.

2b. 5 points   ☒ →   Attach your *Report of Separation from Active Duty* (DD 214) or other proof.

2c. 10 points   ☐ →   Attach an *Application for 10-Point Veterans' Preference* (SF 15) and proof required.

3. Check this box if you are an adult male born on or after January 1st 1960, and you registered for Selective Service between the ages of 18 through 25 → ☒

4. Were you ever a Federal civilian employee?   Yes ☒   No ☐ → If yes, list highest civilian grade for the following:

4a. Series **0391/0334**	4b. Grade **13**	4c. From *(mm/yyyy)* **10/1990**	4d. To *(mm/yyyy)* **present**

5a. Are you eligible for reinstatement based on career or career-conditional Federal status?   Yes ☐   No ☒
If requested in the vacancy announcement, attach *Notification of Personnel Action* (SF 50), as proof.

5b. Are you eligible under the ICTAP*?   Yes ☐   No ☐
*ICTAP (Interagency Career Transition Assistance Plan): A participant in this plan is a current or former federal employee displaced from a Federal agency. To be eligible, you must have received a formal notice of separation such as a RIF separation notice. If you are an ICTAP eligible, normally you will be provided priority consideration for vacancies within your commuting area for which you apply and are well qualified.

Section I - Applicant Certification

I certify that, to the best of my knowledge and belief, all of the information on and attached to this application is true, correct, complete, and made in good faith. I understand that false or fraudulent information on or attached to this application may be grounds for not hiring me or for firing me after I begin work, and may be punishable by fine or imprisonment. I understand that any information I give may be investigated.

1a. Signature	1b. Date *(mm/dd/yyyy)*

Previous edition usable
U.S. Office of Personnel Management

NSN 7540-01-351-9178
50612-10
Page 4 of 4

OF 612
Revised June 2006

Attachment Section B

XXXXXX XXXXXX – SSN: 000-00-0000

WORK EXPERIENCE

OVERVIEW

- **Computer Specialist** in the Defense Message System (DMS) Operations Branch on the staff of the DMS Global Service Manager. DMS is a computer-based (X.400/X.500) worldwide Department of Defense-wide Area Network messaging system that will replace the obsolete Automated Digital Network (AUTODIN) now in place. The mission of the Branch is to exercise day-to-day management control of, and provide staff -level operational direction over, deployed elements of the DMS.
- **Personally responsible** for ensuring that reliable, efficient, effective, and economic DMS operations meet the customer's requirements.

KEY ACTIVITIES

Oversee and manage the global system of Regional Operations and Security Centers (ROSC).

RESULT

- Visited ROSC-C to assist in bringing the center to full operational status prior to the start of IOT&E.
- Coordinated the requirements and assessments of the three ROSC to prepare the final format of the Continuity of Operation Plan for the DMS portion of the ROSC's worldwide structure.

Develop policy and directives that provide a framework for processes and procedures in the execution of system implementation as well as operational tasks.

RESULT

- Developed, coordinated, and established the ALLDMSSTA general message in order to establish an electronic means of formally disseminating policy and procedure changes.
- Drawing on program management and cryptologic background, assessed (in concert with D4) the requirements for instituting a viable maintenance management program.

Monitor the implementation of all hardware and software changes/enhancements to the DMS components and infrastructure.

RESULT

- Formally approved all Field Engineering notes for distribution and implementation during IOT&E using newly established software distribution procedures, a process that proved to be highly organized and successful.

Conduct operational performance evaluations and ensure overall compliance with technical criteria to maintain the DMS performance above management thresholds.

Maintain liaison with representative of the Joint Staff, military departments, and other government agencies. Represent the Branch at meetings and conferences with higher echelons.

Obtain, direct, and coordinate necessary technical support when problem resolutions require expertise beyond that of onsite personnel.

RESULT

- Worked closely with the DISA PAC and DISA EUR Regional Service Management staff and WESTHEM Columbus RCC to develop and implement an interim problem-reporting mechanism pending arrival of the DMS Contractor products.

Function as the task monitor for cognizant portions of the DMS that are staffed under contract support and ensure contractor personnel the contract deliverables are in full compliance with requirements as detailed in the contract.

Provide operations input to the implementation design validation process.

Evaluations of Performance:

"A self-starter who uses initiative to research existing activities associated with system and network management tools and capabilities to ensure DMS will be able to readily migrate to a fully integrated system." (from Evaluation, 1996)

Attachment Section C

XXXXXX XXXXXX – SSN: 000-00-0000

WORK EXPERIENCE

OVERVIEW

- **Project Manager** for computer/communications system deployments of the Nova and MMS (Multi-level Mail Server), which were designated as Navy Defense Messaging System components, and provided for the upgrade of automated messaging services while allowing the Navel Telecommunications System to transition from legacy platforms to the Defense Messaging System (DMS) target X.400 and X.500 architecture and components.

KEY ACTIVITIES

Managed and evaluated the execution of contractor performance for acquisition, installation, maintenance, and software support services. Directed and approved contractor efforts in the development of computer-integrated logistics support planning (ILSP) and developed and coordinated site survey and system installation schedules.

RESULT

- Mediated and resolved numerous difficulties, discrepancies, and disagreements between and/or among installation support activities (engineering field activities, contractors, and others).

Provided technical information and direction relative to DMS transitional components that interfaced to host computers.

Reviewed and evaluated computer/communications systems architecture and wiring plans and diagrams. As part of the review process, also developed and submitted detailed wiring schematics and diagrams that described errors and corrections.

RESULT

- Used knowledge of Naval Telecommunication System architecture, interface techniques, and capabilities to provide input to the formulation of a system architecture and connectivity among Navy, Marine, Coast Guard, and other DoD and civil agency components where the object was to provide a seamless transition to the target X.400/X.500 DMS architecture.

Acted as primary liaison with various organizational DMS coordinators in order to ensure timely update of requirements and fielding priorities. Represented the Division at internal or external committees, working groups, and meetings.

RESULT

- Prepared and presented a variety of well-received point papers and briefings to provide information, recommendations, and defense of program positions or actions to be executed.
- Established working relationships across organizational boundaries that were essential to process improvement in the delivery of quality customer service.

Provided administrative management for project implementation tracking and monitoring.

As a member of the Software Configuration Control Board, evaluated and recommended adoption of disapproval of software changes and proposals that were relevant to the Nova, MMS, and related systems.

RESULT

- Made significant contributions to SPAWAR in the economy, efficiency, and service in the implementation of transitional system platforms (Nova, PCMT, GATEGUARD, and MMS).

Evaluations of Performance:

"…a model employee who has proven during this period his value to the organization. He has taken the changes driven by organizational restructuring and realignment in stride and [has] actively promoted the goals and objectives of SPAWAR." (from Evaluation, 1996)

Attachment Section G

XXXXXX XXXXXX – SSN: 000-00-0000

OTHER QUALIFICATIONS

Successfully completed numerous courses on COMSEC and computer equipment and systems. Classes of COMSEC equipment and systems on which trained include general purpose data, voice, specialized tactical, bulk, and broadcast. Specific details will be provided on request.

1) George Washington University
   Fiber-Optic Technology for Communications, 2.16 CEUs   28 June 90
   Application of T-Carrier to Private Networking, 3.60 CEUs   27 Jul. 90
   Data Communication Standards: Interfaces and Protocols for
       Open Systems Network Architectures, 2.6 CEUs   14 Sept. 90

2) Data-Tech Institute
   Intensive Introduction to T1/T3 Networking, 1.50 CEUs   10 Aug. 90

3) Naval Electronic Systems Security Engineering Center
   Contracting Officer's Technical Representative
       (COTR's) Course   23 Aug. 89

4) Office of Personnel Management
   Instructor Training Workshop   14 May 82
   Project Management: Planning, Scheduling, and Control   14 Feb. 92

5) Human Resources Office, NW NMCNCR
   Supervisory Development I   16 May 86
   Supervisory Development II   20 Aug. 86

6) Management Concepts Incorporated
   Statement of Work/Specification Preparation   01 Jul. 87

7) Human Resources Office, Washington, N.Y.
   Managing Conflict   19 Apr. 90
   How to Negotiate   11 May 90
   Value Engineering   06 Aug. 92

8) Naval Computer & Telecommunication Command
   Acquisition Streamlining   15 Mar 91
   Total Quality Leadership Awareness   15 Apr. 92

9) Department of Navy Program Information Center
   Planning, Programming, and Budgeting System
       (PEBS) Course   30 Sept. 92

10) National Defense University, Information Resources
        Management, College Information Engineering   28 May 93

11) Defense Information Systems Agency
    Defense Data Network Seminar   26 Aug. 93

12) Naval Computer & Telecommunication Command
X.400/X.500 DMS/MSP Training (J.G. Van Dyke)   10 Mar. 95

13) National Security Agency
Information Systems Security Engineering Course   12 May 95

AWARDS:

Graduated with honors, B.S. Management, 1995

Honors Student Award, MLS Information Security, 1997

Letter of Appreciation for Technical Professionalism from Commanding Officer NAS Memphis, 1980

Sustained Superior Performance Awards: 1982, 1983

Outstanding Performance Awards: 1992, 1993, 1994, 1995, 1996

OPM Form 1203-FX

To apply for job openings with some federal agencies, you may be asked to complete OPM Form 1203-FX. If you are responding to a position announcement by submitting the 1203-FX form, be sure to read and follow the step-by-step instructions provided by the listing agency as a guide to filling out the required questionnaire. You may find it helpful to print the job announcement and refer to it as you answer the questions. Be sure to double-check your application before submission to ensure you have responded to all questions.

To guide you in completing OPM Form 1203-FX, line-by-line instructions follow.

Social Security Number

Enter your Social Security Number (SSN) in the space indicated. Your SSN is requested under the authority of Public Law 104-134, a law specifying that anyone doing business with the federal government provide this information. Your SSN also uniquely identifies your records from those of other applicants who may have the same name and birth date. As allowed by law or presidential directive, your SSN is used to request information about you from employers, schools, banks, and others who may know you. Providing your SSN is voluntary; however, most listing agencies cannot process your application without it.

Vacancy Identification Number

Enter the Vacancy Identification Number of the job for which you are applying. This number can be found on the position announcement.

Numbered Items

Complete each numbered item as indicated below.

1. Title of Job—Enter the name of the position for which you are applying. Be sure to double-check that you enter the title exactly as it appears on the position announcement.

2. Biographic Data—Enter your contact information. All biographic information is required except for the second part of your ZIP Code (a four-digit number).

3. E-Mail Address—Provide a current e-mail address. Indicate whether you wish to be contacted by e-mail.

4. Work Information—Provide contact information regarding your current employment, if applicable.

5. Employment Availability—Enter information regarding your employment preferences, including full- or part-time hours, temporary or permanent positions, and willingness to travel.

6. Citizenship—Indicate whether you currently maintain U.S. citizenship. (Remember, non-citizens cannot be considered for federal government jobs.)

7. Background Information—Provide background information as requested by the vacancy announcement.

8. Other Information—Indicate your gender and date of birth.

9. Languages—Complete this section as instructed in the vacancy announcement.

10. Lowest Grade—Enter the lowest grade level that you will accept for this position within the established grade-level range.

11. Miscellaneous Information—Leave this section blank, unless otherwise instructed in the vacancy announcement.

12. Special Knowledge—Leave this section blank, unless otherwise instructed in the vacancy announcement.

13. Test Location—Leave this section blank, unless otherwise instructed in the vacancy announcement.

14. Veterans' Preference Claim—If you are not entitled to Veterans' Preference, mark "No preference claimed." For detailed information about Veterans' Preference Qualifications, see the section titled "Special Considerations for Veterans" in Part I, Chapter 2, of this guide.

15. Dates of Active-Duty Military Service—Enter your dates of active-duty military service, if applicable, unless you have claimed derived preference (i.e., widows and spouses of veterans). Use the following date format: (mm/dd/yyyy).

16. Availability Date—Leave this section blank, unless otherwise instructed in the vacancy announcement.

17. Service Computation Date—Leave this section blank, unless otherwise instructed in the vacancy announcement.

18. Other Date Information—Leave this section blank, unless otherwise instructed in the vacancy announcement.

19. Job Preference—Leave this section blank, unless otherwise instructed in the vacancy announcement.

20. Occupational Specialties—Select/enter at least one occupational specialty. The specialty code for a specific position will be provided.

21. Geographic Availability—Select/enter at least one geographic location in which you are interested and will accept employment. The location code for a specific position will be provided.

22. Transition Assistance Plans—Indicate whether you are a surplus or displaced federal employee requesting special priority consideration under the Career Transition Assistance Plan (CTAP) or the Interagency Career Transition Assistance Plan (ICTAP). Note: To receive consideration for CTAP or ICTAP, you must submit the necessary supporting documentation.

23. Job-Related Experience—Leave this section blank, unless otherwise instructed in the vacancy announcement.

24. Personal Background Information—Leave this section blank, unless otherwise instructed in the vacancy announcement.

25. Occupational Questions—Leave this section blank, unless otherwise instructed in the vacancy announcement.

SAMPLE OPM 1203-FX FORM

U.S. Office of Personnel Management
Occupational Questionnaire - OPM Form 1203-FX

Form Approved
OMB No. 3206-0040

51562

Please fill in the following items on each page of this application form. To review the Privacy Act and Public Burden Statements, please refer to the cover page of this form. If this information is not included, we cannot process your application. You must return pages 1 through 6.

Social security number

| 1 | 2 | 3 | – | 1 | 1 | – | 2 | 3 | 4 | 5 |

Vacancy identification number

| 6 | 7 | 8 | 9 | 1 | 2 | 3 | 4 |

Follow the instructions on the vacancy announcement.

- For optimum accuracy, it is recommended that characters be written block style following the examples below.
- Do not write on or outside the boxes.
- Do not use special characters. Use only the characters shown.
- PRINT your responses in the boxes and/or blacken in the appropriate ovals.
- Use black ink. Do not staple this form.
- You may obtain an electronic copy of this form at http://www.opm.gov/forms.

| A | B | C | D | E | F | G | H | I | J | K | L | M | N | O | P | Q | R | S | T | U | V | W | X | Y | Z |

| 0 | 1 | 2 | 3 | 4 | 5 | 6 | 7 | 8 | 9 |

Shade circle like this: ●
Not like this: ⊗ ☑

1. Print title of job applying for   Tax Technician

2. Biographic data

A. First name

| K | a | t | h | r | y | n | | | | | | | | | | | |

B. Middle initial

| S |

C. Last name

| J | o | h | n | s | o | n | | | | | | | | | | | |

D. Street address (house number, street, apartment number, where you want to receive mail)

| 1 | 2 | 3 | | E | a | s | y | | S | t | r | e | e | t | | | | | | | |

E. City

| D | a | l | l | a | s | | | | | | | |

F. State
Use Standard State Postal Codes (abbreviations). If outside the United States of America, and you do not have a military address, print "OV" in State and fill in Country, leaving Zip Code blank.

| T | X |

G. Zip code

| 5 | 5 | 5 | 5 | – | 2 | 7 | 5 | 8 |

+ 4 (optional)

H. Country

| U | S | A | | | | | | | | | | |

I. Telephone number

| 4 | 1 | 8 | 5 | 5 | 5 | 1 | 2 | 1 | 2 | | | | |

J. Contact time

○ Day   ○ Night   ● Either

Use numbers only - no punctuation or spaces. Include area code if within the United States of America.

3. E-Mail address (print your complete e-mail address)
A. Notify me by e-mail:
○ Yes   ○ No   B. kjohnson4567@aol.com

51562

Please fill in the following items on each page of this application form. To review the Privacy Act and Public Burden Statements, please refer to the cover page of this form. If this information is not included, we cannot process your application. You must return pages 1 through 6.

Social security number

| 1 | 2 | 3 | – | 1 | 1 | – | 2 | 3 | 4 | 5 |

Vacancy identification number

| 6 | 7 | 8 | 9 | 1 | 2 | 3 | 4 |

4. Work information (if applicable)

A. Place of employment

| B | a | r | n | e | s | | & | | N | o | b | l | e | | B | o | o | k | s | e | l | l | e | r | s |

B. Work address

| 8 | 9 | | L | a | m | o | n | t | | P | l | a | c | e | | | | | | | | | | | | | |

C. Work city

| D | a | l | l | a | s | | | | | | | | | |

D. Work state Use Standard State Postal Codes (abbreviations). If outside the United States of America, and you do not have a military address, print "OV" in State and fill in Country, leaving Zip Code blank.

| T | X |

E. Work zip code

| 5 | 5 | 5 | 5 | 5 |

+ 4 (optional)

| | | | – | | | | |

F. Work country

| U | S | A | | | | | | | | | | | | | | |

G. Work telephone number

| 4 | 1 | 8 | 5 | 5 | 5 | 1 | 2 | 3 | 4 | | | | |

Extension (if applicable)

| | | | | |

Use numbers only - no punctuation or spaces. Include area code if within the United States of America.

5. Employment availability - Are you available for

A. Full-time employment

     - 40 hours per week?　Y ● 　N ○

B. Part-time employment of

     - 16 or fewer hrs/week?　○ ●

     - 17 to 24 hrs/week?　● ○

     - 25 to 32 hrs/week?　● ○

C. Temporary employment lasting

     - less than 1 month?　○ ●

     - 1 to 4 months?　● ○

     - 5 to 12 months?　● ○

D. Jobs requiring travel away from home for

     - 1 to 5 nights/month?　● ○

     - 6 to 10 nights/month?　● ○

     - 11 plus nights/month?　● ○

E. Other employment questions (see instructions)

	Y	N			Y	N
Question 1.	○	○		Question 4.	○	○
Question 2.	○	○		Question 5.	○	○
Question 3.	○	○		Question 6.	○	○

6. Citizenship

Are you a citizen of the United States of America?

● Yes 　 ○ No

7. Background information

(see vacancy announcement instructions)

	Y	N			Y	N
Question 1.	○	○		Question 4.	○	○
Question 2.	○	○		Question 5.	○	○
Question 3.	○	○		Question 6.	○	○

8. Other information

(see vacancy announcement instructions)

A. Gender　 ○ Male　 ● Female

B. Date of birth (mm/dd/yyyy)

| 0 | 6 | / | 1 | 7 | / | 1 | 9 | 7 | 0 |

51562

Please fill in the following items on each page of this application form. To review the Privacy Act and Public Burden Statements, please refer to the cover page of this form. If this information is not included, we cannot process your application. You must return pages 1 through 6.

Social security number
| 1 | 2 | 3 | – | 1 | 1 | – | 2 | 3 | 4 | 5 |

Vacancy identification number
| 6 | 7 | 8 | 9 | 1 | 2 | 3 | 4 |

9. Languages (see vacancy announcement instructions)

10. Lowest grade

| 0 | 6 |

11. Miscellaneous information

12. Special knowledge

13. Test location

14. Veterans' preference

⦿ No Preference Claimed

○ 5 Points Preference Claimed

10 Point Preference - You must submit a completed Standard Form 15, Application for 10-Point Veterans' Preference.

○ 10 Points Preference Claimed

   (award of a Purple Heart or service-connected disability of less than 10%)

○ 10 Points Compensable Disability Preference Claimed

   (disability rating of at least 10% and less than 30%)

○ 10 Points Other

   (spouse, widow, widower, mother preference claimed)

○ 10 Points Compensable Disability Preference Claimed

   (disability rating of 30% or more)

When entering dates in the following fields, please use the format: mm/dd/yyyy

15. Dates of active duty - military service
   (skip if no veterans' preference is claimed in block 14)

From: | | / | | / | | | |

To: | | / | | / | | | |

16. Availability date

| | / | | / | | | |

17. Service computation date

| | / | | / | | | |

18. Other date

| | / | | / | | | |

19. Job preference (see vacancy announcement instructions)

1○	6○	11○	16○	21○	26○	31○	36○	41○	46○	51○	56○	61○	66○
2○	7○	12○	17○	22○	27○	32○	37○	42○	47○	52○	57○	62○	67○
3○	8○	13○	18○	23○	28○	33○	38○	43○	48○	53○	58○	63○	68○
4○	9○	14○	19○	24○	29○	34○	39○	44○	49○	54○	59○	64○	69○
5○	10○	15○	20○	25○	30○	35○	40○	45○	50○	55○	60○	65○	70○

U.S. Office of Personnel Management   Page 3 of 6   OPM Form 1203-FX
                                                                   Revised August 2002

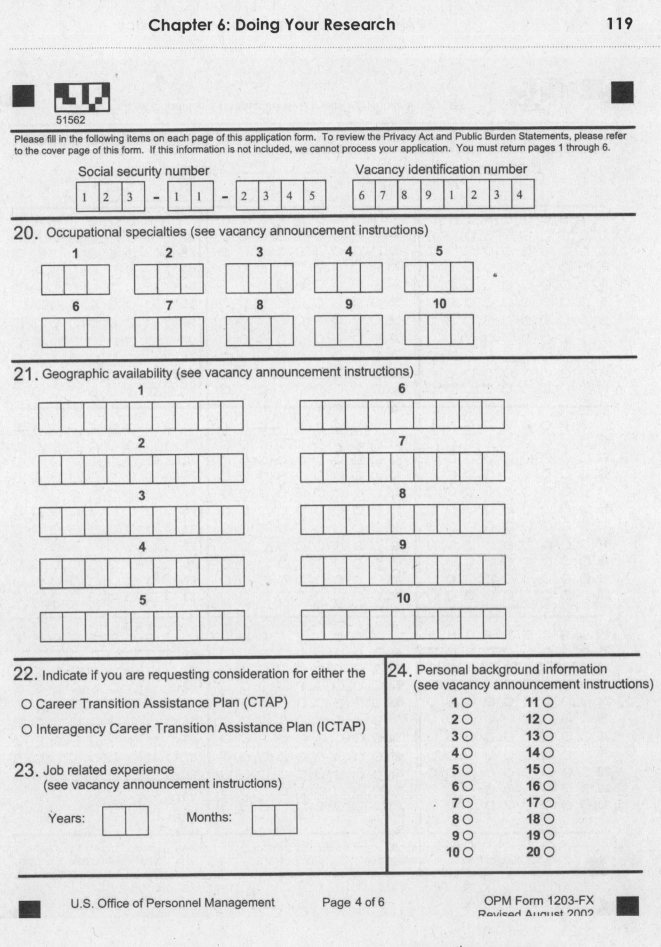

51562

Please fill in the following items on each page of this application form. To review the Privacy Act and Public Burden Statements, please refer to the cover page of this form. If this information is not included, we cannot process your application. You must return pages 1 through 6.

Social security number: 1 2 3 - 1 1 - 2 3 4 5

Vacancy identification number: 6 7 8 9 1 2 3 4

20. Occupational specialties (see vacancy announcement instructions)

1   2   3   4   5

6   7   8   9   10

21. Geographic availability (see vacancy announcement instructions)

1   6

2   7

3   8

4   9

5   10

22. Indicate if you are requesting consideration for either the

○ Career Transition Assistance Plan (CTAP)

○ Interagency Career Transition Assistance Plan (ICTAP)

23. Job related experience
(see vacancy announcement instructions)

Years: ☐☐   Months: ☐☐

24. Personal background information
(see vacancy announcement instructions)

1 ○   11 ○
2 ○   12 ○
3 ○   13 ○
4 ○   14 ○
5 ○   15 ○
6 ○   16 ○
7 ○   17 ○
8 ○   18 ○
9 ○   19 ○
10 ○   20 ○

 51562   **25.** Occupational questions (see vacancy announcement instructions)

Please fill in the following items on each page of this application form. To review the Privacy Act and Public Burden Statements, please refer to the cover page of this form. If this information is not included, we cannot process your application. You must return pages 1 through 6.

Social security number

| 1 | 2 | 3 | – | 1 | 1 | – | 2 | 3 | 4 | 5 |

Vacancy identification number

| 6 | 7 | 8 | 9 | 1 | 2 | 3 | 4 |

	A	B	C	D	E	F	G	H	I
1.	○	○	○	○	○	○	○	○	○
2.	○	○	○	○	○	○	○	○	○
3.	○	○	○	○	○	○	○	○	○
4.	○	○	○	○	○	○	○	○	○
5.	○	○	○	○	○	○	○	○	○
6.	○	○	○	○	○	○	○	○	○
7.	○	○	○	○	○	○	○	○	○
8.	○	○	○	○	○	○	○	○	○
9.	○	○	○	○	○	○	○	○	○
10.	○	○	○	○	○	○	○	○	○

	A	B	C	D	E	F	G	H	I
31.	○	○	○	○	○	○	○	○	○
32.	○	○	○	○	○	○	○	○	○
33.	○	○	○	○	○	○	○	○	○
34.	○	○	○	○	○	○	○	○	○
35.	○	○	○	○	○	○	○	○	○
36.	○	○	○	○	○	○	○	○	○
37.	○	○	○	○	○	○	○	○	○
38.	○	○	○	○	○	○	○	○	○
39.	○	○	○	○	○	○	○	○	○
40.	○	○	○	○	○	○	○	○	○

	A	B	C	D	E	F	G	H	I
61.	○	○	○	○	○	○	○	○	○
62.	○	○	○	○	○	○	○	○	○
63.	○	○	○	○	○	○	○	○	○
64.	○	○	○	○	○	○	○	○	○
65.	○	○	○	○	○	○	○	○	○
66.	○	○	○	○	○	○	○	○	○
67.	○	○	○	○	○	○	○	○	○
68.	○	○	○	○	○	○	○	○	○
69.	○	○	○	○	○	○	○	○	○
70.	○	○	○	○	○	○	○	○	○

	A	B	C	D	E	F	G	H	I
11.	○	○	○	○	○	○	○	○	○
12.	○	○	○	○	○	○	○	○	○
13.	○	○	○	○	○	○	○	○	○
14.	○	○	○	○	○	○	○	○	○
15.	○	○	○	○	○	○	○	○	○
16.	○	○	○	○	○	○	○	○	○
17.	○	○	○	○	○	○	○	○	○
18.	○	○	○	○	○	○	○	○	○
19.	○	○	○	○	○	○	○	○	○
20.	○	○	○	○	○	○	○	○	○

	A	B	C	D	E	F	G	H	I
41.	○	○	○	○	○	○	○	○	○
42.	○	○	○	○	○	○	○	○	○
43.	○	○	○	○	○	○	○	○	○
44.	○	○	○	○	○	○	○	○	○
45.	○	○	○	○	○	○	○	○	○
46.	○	○	○	○	○	○	○	○	○
47.	○	○	○	○	○	○	○	○	○
48.	○	○	○	○	○	○	○	○	○
49.	○	○	○	○	○	○	○	○	○
50.	○	○	○	○	○	○	○	○	○

	A	B	C	D	E	F	G	H	I
71.	○	○	○	○	○	○	○	○	○
72.	○	○	○	○	○	○	○	○	○
73.	○	○	○	○	○	○	○	○	○
74.	○	○	○	○	○	○	○	○	○
75.	○	○	○	○	○	○	○	○	○
76.	○	○	○	○	○	○	○	○	○
77.	○	○	○	○	○	○	○	○	○
78.	○	○	○	○	○	○	○	○	○
79.	○	○	○	○	○	○	○	○	○
80.	○	○	○	○	○	○	○	○	○

	A	B	C	D	E	F	G	H	I
21.	○	○	○	○	○	○	○	○	○
22.	○	○	○	○	○	○	○	○	○
23.	○	○	○	○	○	○	○	○	○
24.	○	○	○	○	○	○	○	○	○
25.	○	○	○	○	○	○	○	○	○
26.	○	○	○	○	○	○	○	○	○
27.	○	○	○	○	○	○	○	○	○
28.	○	○	○	○	○	○	○	○	○
29.	○	○	○	○	○	○	○	○	○
30.	○	○	○	○	○	○	○	○	○

	A	B	C	D	E	F	G	H	I
51.	○	○	○	○	○	○	○	○	○
52.	○	○	○	○	○	○	○	○	○
53.	○	○	○	○	○	○	○	○	○
54.	○	○	○	○	○	○	○	○	○
55.	○	○	○	○	○	○	○	○	○
56.	○	○	○	○	○	○	○	○	○
57.	○	○	○	○	○	○	○	○	○
58.	○	○	○	○	○	○	○	○	○
59.	○	○	○	○	○	○	○	○	○
60.	○	○	○	○	○	○	○	○	○

	A	B	C	D	E	F	G	H	I
81.	○	○	○	○	○	○	○	○	○
82.	○	○	○	○	○	○	○	○	○
83.	○	○	○	○	○	○	○	○	○
84.	○	○	○	○	○	○	○	○	○
85.	○	○	○	○	○	○	○	○	○
86.	○	○	○	○	○	○	○	○	○
87.	○	○	○	○	○	○	○	○	○
88.	○	○	○	○	○	○	○	○	○
89.	○	○	○	○	○	○	○	○	○
90.	○	○	○	○	○	○	○	○	○

51562

25. Occupational questions (continued)

Please fill in the following items on each page of this application form. To review the Privacy Act and Public Burden Statements, please refer to the cover page of this form. If this information is not included, we cannot process your application. You must return pages 1 through 6.

Social security number

| 1 | 2 | 3 | – | 1 | 1 | – | 2 | 3 | 4 | 5 |

Vacancy identification number

| 6 | 7 | 8 | 9 | 1 | 2 | 3 | 4 |

A B C D E F G H I
91. ○ ○ ○ ○ ○ ○ ○ ○ ○
92. ○ ○ ○ ○ ○ ○ ○ ○ ○
93. ○ ○ ○ ○ ○ ○ ○ ○ ○
94. ○ ○ ○ ○ ○ ○ ○ ○ ○
95. ○ ○ ○ ○ ○ ○ ○ ○ ○
96. ○ ○ ○ ○ ○ ○ ○ ○ ○
97. ○ ○ ○ ○ ○ ○ ○ ○ ○
98. ○ ○ ○ ○ ○ ○ ○ ○ ○
99. ○ ○ ○ ○ ○ ○ ○ ○ ○
100. ○ ○ ○ ○ ○ ○ ○ ○ ○

A B C D E F G H I
121. ○ ○ ○ ○ ○ ○ ○ ○ ○
122. ○ ○ ○ ○ ○ ○ ○ ○ ○
123. ○ ○ ○ ○ ○ ○ ○ ○ ○
124. ○ ○ ○ ○ ○ ○ ○ ○ ○
125. ○ ○ ○ ○ ○ ○ ○ ○ ○
126. ○ ○ ○ ○ ○ ○ ○ ○ ○
127. ○ ○ ○ ○ ○ ○ ○ ○ ○
128. ○ ○ ○ ○ ○ ○ ○ ○ ○
129. ○ ○ ○ ○ ○ ○ ○ ○ ○
130. ○ ○ ○ ○ ○ ○ ○ ○ ○

A B C D E F G H I
151. ○ ○ ○ ○ ○ ○ ○ ○ ○
152. ○ ○ ○ ○ ○ ○ ○ ○ ○
153. ○ ○ ○ ○ ○ ○ ○ ○ ○
154. ○ ○ ○ ○ ○ ○ ○ ○ ○
155. ○ ○ ○ ○ ○ ○ ○ ○ ○
156. ○ ○ ○ ○ ○ ○ ○ ○ ○
157. ○ ○ ○ ○ ○ ○ ○ ○ ○
158. ○ ○ ○ ○ ○ ○ ○ ○ ○
159. ○ ○ ○ ○ ○ ○ ○ ○ ○
160. ○ ○ ○ ○ ○ ○ ○ ○ ○

A B C D E F G H I
101. ○ ○ ○ ○ ○ ○ ○ ○ ○
102. ○ ○ ○ ○ ○ ○ ○ ○ ○
103. ○ ○ ○ ○ ○ ○ ○ ○ ○
104. ○ ○ ○ ○ ○ ○ ○ ○ ○
105. ○ ○ ○ ○ ○ ○ ○ ○ ○
106. ○ ○ ○ ○ ○ ○ ○ ○ ○
107. ○ ○ ○ ○ ○ ○ ○ ○ ○
108. ○ ○ ○ ○ ○ ○ ○ ○ ○
109. ○ ○ ○ ○ ○ ○ ○ ○ ○
110. ○ ○ ○ ○ ○ ○ ○ ○ ○

A B C D E F G H I
131. ○ ○ ○ ○ ○ ○ ○ ○ ○
132. ○ ○ ○ ○ ○ ○ ○ ○ ○
133. ○ ○ ○ ○ ○ ○ ○ ○ ○
134. ○ ○ ○ ○ ○ ○ ○ ○ ○
135. ○ ○ ○ ○ ○ ○ ○ ○ ○
136. ○ ○ ○ ○ ○ ○ ○ ○ ○
137. ○ ○ ○ ○ ○ ○ ○ ○ ○
138. ○ ○ ○ ○ ○ ○ ○ ○ ○
139. ○ ○ ○ ○ ○ ○ ○ ○ ○
140. ○ ○ ○ ○ ○ ○ ○ ○ ○

A B C D E F G H I
161. ○ ○ ○ ○ ○ ○ ○ ○ ○
162. ○ ○ ○ ○ ○ ○ ○ ○ ○
163. ○ ○ ○ ○ ○ ○ ○ ○ ○
164. ○ ○ ○ ○ ○ ○ ○ ○ ○
165. ○ ○ ○ ○ ○ ○ ○ ○ ○
166. ○ ○ ○ ○ ○ ○ ○ ○ ○
167. ○ ○ ○ ○ ○ ○ ○ ○ ○
168. ○ ○ ○ ○ ○ ○ ○ ○ ○
169. ○ ○ ○ ○ ○ ○ ○ ○ ○
170. ○ ○ ○ ○ ○ ○ ○ ○ ○

A B C D E F G H I
111. ○ ○ ○ ○ ○ ○ ○ ○ ○
112. ○ ○ ○ ○ ○ ○ ○ ○ ○
113. ○ ○ ○ ○ ○ ○ ○ ○ ○
114. ○ ○ ○ ○ ○ ○ ○ ○ ○
115. ○ ○ ○ ○ ○ ○ ○ ○ ○
116. ○ ○ ○ ○ ○ ○ ○ ○ ○
117. ○ ○ ○ ○ ○ ○ ○ ○ ○
118. ○ ○ ○ ○ ○ ○ ○ ○ ○
119. ○ ○ ○ ○ ○ ○ ○ ○ ○
120. ○ ○ ○ ○ ○ ○ ○ ○ ○

A B C D E F G H I
141. ○ ○ ○ ○ ○ ○ ○ ○ ○
142. ○ ○ ○ ○ ○ ○ ○ ○ ○
143. ○ ○ ○ ○ ○ ○ ○ ○ ○
144. ○ ○ ○ ○ ○ ○ ○ ○ ○
145. ○ ○ ○ ○ ○ ○ ○ ○ ○
146. ○ ○ ○ ○ ○ ○ ○ ○ ○
147. ○ ○ ○ ○ ○ ○ ○ ○ ○
148. ○ ○ ○ ○ ○ ○ ○ ○ ○
149. ○ ○ ○ ○ ○ ○ ○ ○ ○
150. ○ ○ ○ ○ ○ ○ ○ ○ ○

A B C D E F G H I
171. ○ ○ ○ ○ ○ ○ ○ ○ ○
172. ○ ○ ○ ○ ○ ○ ○ ○ ○
173. ○ ○ ○ ○ ○ ○ ○ ○ ○
174. ○ ○ ○ ○ ○ ○ ○ ○ ○
175. ○ ○ ○ ○ ○ ○ ○ ○ ○
176. ○ ○ ○ ○ ○ ○ ○ ○ ○
177. ○ ○ ○ ○ ○ ○ ○ ○ ○
178. ○ ○ ○ ○ ○ ○ ○ ○ ○
179. ○ ○ ○ ○ ○ ○ ○ ○ ○
180. ○ ○ ○ ○ ○ ○ ○ ○ ○

You have now completed the OPM Form 1203-FX. When submitting, **do not** include the cover page. Only submit pages numbered 1 through 6.

Which Form Do I Choose?

On occasion, a hiring agency will state in the job announcement the format that it prefers you use. So, of course, in that instance, you will use the requested form. However, most agencies accept either an official government application form, such as the OF-612 or the 1203-FX, or a resume and will say so in the announcement. Be sure to read the application instructions provided in the job announcement very carefully to make sure you submit the required form and any other necessary materials.

Tips for Filling Out Federal Forms

Filling out the form is half the battle. If you apply for the job, you run the risk of getting rejected. You also may get accepted. If you do not apply for the job, the outcome is clear. So our advice is this: Download the form you've chosen to use or are required to use, and fill it out. See how it looks. Get someone else's opinion. If you are not happy with your responses to the form's questions, keep trying until you are satisfied. Use your previous attempts as outlines to expand wherever possible. Send it in and see what happens. You have given it your best shot.

Follow the application instructions. We cannot stress this strongly enough or too many times. Read the vacancy announcement carefully, and then do what it tells you to do. Take note of whether they want you to use a particular format to apply. If they prefer that you apply online, you should make every effort to do so. Remember that most public libraries make computers with Internet access available to their patrons. Many copy shops also have public computers but charge a fee for this service. You may also be required to submit specialized forms and other supporting materials. If these documents are required, your application cannot be processed without them. Make sure you submit your application and additional materials to the address indicated in the vacancy announcement.

Know your terms. When you're gathering information from the vacancy announcement and adding all the necessary details to your application, you must be familiar with the federal government's hiring terminology. The "Glossary of Civil Service Hiring Terminology," in the Appendixes of this book, has a complete listing of the most common terms you'll encounter and how government agencies use those terms.

PREPARING A FEDERAL RESUME

As an alternative to completing the forms mentioned above, many government agencies will accept a Federal Resume. You will know that sending your resume is an acceptable option if the "How to Apply" section of a vacancy announcement states that you can submit "a resume or OF-612." Don't be misled, however, by the word "resume" on the vacancy announcement. The "resume" you're being asked to submit is a Federal Resume. A Federal Resume is probably the least understood of the job application components because it often gets confused with a private-sector resume.

A Federal Resume includes more specific kinds of information than its private-sector counterpart. If you read the vacancy announcement carefully, you will find a list of details that your resume needs to provide: names and phone numbers of your present and past job supervisors, salaries you earned in these positions, and other information that is typically not included on a private-sector resume.

Unlike a private-sector resume, which often is no more than one or two pages, a Federal Resume can be as long or short as you want it to be. The higher the level of the position you are applying for, the more detailed your Federal Resume should probably be. Federal Resumes that run 6 to 12 pages are acceptable. In the private sector, job candidates would never turn in a 12-page resume unless they were applying for an upper-level academic or research position and had dozens of publications to their credit. An effective Federal Resume provides the hiring agency with a thorough, detailed explanation of your educational background, work history, and other qualifications.

Presenting Your Educational Background and Training

No matter what application format you use to apply for a federal position, you'll want to pay special attention to how you present your educational accomplishments. Relevant experiences you've had as a high school, college, or graduate student will help bolster your credentials and augment your work history to strengthen your application. For example, if you are applying for a position that requires evidence of strong writing skills, you could include work you've done on a college newspaper or contributions you've made to local publications.

As you contemplate your educational background and how it might relate to the federal position for which you are applying, keep the following points in mind:

Internships. One valuable way to gain employment experience while completing your education is through a paid or unpaid internship in your field of interest. Whether it spanned a period of several weeks or an entire semester, if you've completed an internship, it should be featured on your application as a significant educational experience. Employers appreciate the on-the-job experience provided by internships and the initiative and responsibility shown by those who undertake them.

Leadership positions. If you took on a leadership role for a school group or organization, this experience should also be highlighted as part of your educational accomplishments. Examples of leadership positions might include serving as president of a college sorority or fraternity, chairing a student committee, or taking responsibility for an important project or activity. Be sure to not only mention these worthwhile experiences, but also the positive results of your participation—what was achieved as a result of your leadership?

Extracurricular activities. Your involvement in groups and activities outside the classroom should be emphasized on your application. These beneficial educational experiences include membership in school clubs, volunteer work, or community service projects you've done as a student. You should provide details to the hiring agency about these activities and how they relate to your field of interest.

Writing About Your Work Experience

To develop an effective Federal Resume, you will need to keep the following points in mind:

- **Describe your professional experience in detail.** You will have to provide more details than you would for a typical private-sector job application. Even if the questions seem obvious or repetitive, complete them anyway.

- **Do more than re-describe your official job duties and job description.** Most competent employees do much more than their job descriptions indicate, and most official job descriptions don't adequately describe the complexity of a capable employee's work. Unfortunately, instead of writing about what they *really* do in their jobs, many people just repeat the language used for their official job descriptions.

- **Give yourself credit.** You've earned it with your good work in school or in the private sector. But you've got to let federal hiring managers know about your strengths and achievements. Federal screening panels are quite literal in the way they review and score your application, giving you points for what is relevant in your application. And remember, they *don't* give you any points for what is not included. So don't be bashful! You don't have to sound conceited, but you *do* have to point out your accomplishments.

- **Narrate your professional victories.** One good way to spotlight your accomplishments is to describe these professional "victories." Your narrative might relate how you've dealt effectively with problems, special projects, and/or troubleshooting assignments—times when you've really demonstrated your value to the organizations for which you've worked. Properly described, these stories are like money in the bank. Unlike the verbiage of official job descriptions, narratives have greater impact on the screening panel and make you and your abilities come alive.

- **Highlight your professional skills by using an "action/result" presentation.** Do your best to use concrete, action-oriented examples of how the skills you learned in school and on the job have benefited other employers. Try to demonstrate how these actions achieved positive results. If your work has generated effective bottom-line results for your employers, then say so. Did your innovative idea save them money? Did your initiative and persistence make them money? Say so—and how much. Describe what happened, and don't shortchange yourself. There's nothing more convincing to a skeptical screening panel than seeing a list of well-thought-out actions and successful outcomes throughout your application. It lets them know that *you* know where the bottom line is—and how to get there. *That's* what they are looking for in an employee.

- **Stop scaring yourself.** Writing an effective resume depends more on your attitude than your writing skills. Crafting a Federal Resume that meets all the specifications presented in the job announcement can be tedious, but don't let that discourage you. The task is certainly within your abilities. And remember, a Federal Resume is not a test. There are no right or wrong answers. There are only other competitors who find the process just as difficult as you do. If you compete with other applicants effectively, you stand a good chance of winning.

- **Write concisely and straightforwardly.** To make your Federal Resume highly readable, choose your words wisely. Excess "wordiness" should be eliminated, and sentences should be short and clear. Paragraphs should be no more than 5 to 10 lines long, and subheads may be used to highlight the main point of each paragraph.

- **Resist sending additional materials.** As tempting as it may be, resist the urge to send an additional package containing awards, letters of reference, certificates, writing samples, or any other materials to the hiring agency unless you are specifically asked to do so in the job vacancy announcement. Keep important additional materials in your application or resume folder and send them only if they are requested.

Remember: *Someone's* going to be selected for the position—it might as well be you.

Presenting Your Other Qualifications

In addition to your educational and work experience, a hiring agency will be interested in seeing what other qualifications you might have for a particular federal position, including the following:

- **Honors and awards.** Many are modest about honors and awards and fail to mention them, but these accolades may help distinguish you from other applicants and should be included. Be sure to cite scholarships, educational awards, community awards and nominations, and election to honorary societies and groups. You may also include brief excerpts from official or unofficial letters in which your work was praised. Recent awards are usually the most relevant, but if you've received only a few awards, list them all.

- **Special qualifications, experience, and skills.** You may possess special talents or abilities that can strengthen your candidacy for a particular job, even if these qualifications are not listed in the job announcement. For example, if you have competence with a foreign language, computer skills, typing skills, licenses and certificates you have earned, or experience with special equipment or machines, these abilities should be listed on your application because they may set you apart from other applicants. You should also mention any memberships in professional organizations, materials you have written (even if unpublished), public speaking engagements, and relevant hobbies.

- **Unpaid experience or volunteer work.** Hiring agencies may give credit for unpaid work you've performed that is similar to paid employment, so be sure to include descriptions of any volunteer experience along with your paid work history.

Online Resume Builders

Although many government agencies will still accept Federal Resumes created by individual applicants, the trend in recent years is for a more standardized resume format to streamline the application process across various government agencies. As a result, USAJOBS and certain federal agencies have developed online resume builders that allow job seekers to create one resume to apply for multiple federal job openings.

The USAJOBS Web site's Resume Builder can be used to help you put together one Federal Resume that may be used to apply for vacancies with many government agencies. You can create, save, edit, and print a Federal Resume that has already been formatted to most hiring agencies' specifications. Many federal vacancy announcements direct applicants to the USAJOBS Resume Builder as part of the online application process. Other federal agencies have their own online resume builders and submission systems or direct applicants to use Resumix™, a computer-scannable resume. (Several resume examples and a Resumix-formatted resume can be found in Part IV of this guide.) The Department of Defense, for example, uses online resume builders and submission systems for civilian job applications. Each military branch has a different application system. Let's take a look at Resumix and other electronic resume systems now.

The Computer-Scannable Resume, or Resumix

The computer-scannable resume and Resumix are one in the same. Resumix is simply the name of the company that invented this form. This is an application document used by several Department of Defense agencies, including the Army.

Unlike the OF-612 or the 1203-FX (which are reviewed by actual people), the computer-scannable resume is fed into the database of a mainframe computer system. An artificial intelligence program then scans your material, looking for certain keywords and phrases. Because of this fact, especially when writing this kind of resume, you need to mirror the language contained in the vacancy announcement to which you are responding. The database will keep a tally of certain relevant words and phrases to evaluate qualifications and rank candidates.

You also need to produce a document that will scan easily without errors. Forget the different fonts and stylistic creativity that might help your private-sector resume stand out from the crowd. Here are some simple tips for creating a scannable resume:

- Do not underline for emphasis.
- Do not use bold or italic type.
- Do not use forward or backward slashes (i.e., "supervised each employee in drawing up his/her professional goals").
- Do not use fancy or unusual fonts. Simple fonts, such as Courier, Arial, or Times New Roman, are recommended.
- No part of any letter must touch any part of any other letter.
- Do not use very small or very large type sizes. The standard size is 10 or 12 point.
- As with every document that will be scanned, do not bend, fold, staple, tape, or mutilate your resume in any way.

Hiring agencies that allow Resumix applications may ask that you cover only specific points, so your completed resume may end up being rather short. However, in those cases, the agency will also give you a *supplemental data sheet* with a list of questions to be submitted as a separate document. The supplemental data sheet solicits additional information, such as your lowest acceptable pay grade, willingness to accept temporary or part-time work, military experience, and so on.

Other Electronic Resumes

Army

Civilian vacancies with the U.S. Army are posted on both USAJOBS and the Army Employment Web site at http://acpol.army.mil/employment/apply_jobs.htm. If you are interested in applying for a civilian position in the U.S. Army, you will be asked to use the Army's *Resume Builder*. At the beginning of your job search, you can create and store a resume through the Army's Resume Builder. Your resume may be updated at any time and used to apply for future vacancies of interest. Although the U.S. Army prefers electronic application submissions, they will also accept Federal Resumes by e-mail or regular mail—the job vacancies will provide further details regarding how to send your resume and to whom. If you decide to apply with a traditional resume, however, you need to follow the instructions provided in the Army Job Application kit (found at http://cpol.army.mil/library/employment/jobkit/) such as formatting your resume to the exact specifications of the Army's Resume Builder.

Air Force

In September 2007, the U.S. Air Force completely revised its hiring process and began a new automated recruitment process. All Air Force jobs are now posted exclusively to the OPM's USAJOBS Web site at www.usajobs.gov. Applicants can both search for and apply to positions of interest through USAJOBS, and they may create and store up to five resumes, allowing for multiple submissions.

If you would like to apply for a U.S. Air Force vacancy listed on USAJOBS, simply click on the "Apply Online" button at the bottom of the page. You will be directed to a field that allows you to choose your preferred resume format to apply for a specific vacancy. Finally, the browser will take you to the Application Manager in order to complete further bibliographic information, answer the Online Questionnaire (assessment questions related to the job announcement), upload any other requested documents, and submit your application.

Although the U.S. Air Force encourages online submissions for vacant positions, they do offer another application method for those who, for some reason, cannot apply using the USAJOBS Web site. In this case, an applicant can fax his or her resume along with a copy of OPM Form 1203-FX (which replaces the Online Questionnaire) and any other supporting documents to 1-478-757-3144. Each job announcement with the U.S. Air Force will contain a "How to Apply" section, so be sure to review it carefully for any further application instructions.

Navy

The U.S. Department of Navy has its own application system called CHART, an acronym for Civilian Hiring And Recruitment Tool. CHART (https://chart.donhr.navy.mil/index.asp) offers those interested in a position with the Department of Navy a job search database and subscription service; *My Resume*, an online resume builder; and a record of applications submitted. You can also complete an Additional Data Sheet (ADS) through the CHART system.

Here's the procedure you should follow. First, conduct your job search through CHART, the Navy's automated online application tool. Read the vacancy announcement carefully, and then follow the instructions found on the announcement under the "Apply Now" link. Your resume and ADS will be sent from CHART to the Navy's resume database, and you will receive confirmation that your application materials were received. Once you have a resume and ADS stored in the CHART system, you can use these materials to apply for any job vacancy within the Department of Navy.

CREATING WINNING KSAs

Most federal agencies will require you to reflect on and write about how your background uniquely suits you for a government position. What knowledge, skills, and abilities have you acquired from your experience? These requests for KSAs will be found in job announcements or another specific list of questions, such as the U.S. Air Force's Online Questionnaire or the Department of Navy's Additional Data Sheet. To respond effectively, you'll need to think about how your education, experiences, and accomplishments distinguish you from other applicants and qualify you for a federal position. Below, you'll find some helpful tips for writing great KSAs to strengthen this vital part of your public service application.

The KSAs or Ranking Factors

Almost every federal vacancy lists criteria that the hiring agency feels are essential for strong job performance. These criteria are called various names by different federal agencies. Some agencies call these "ranking factors" while others label them "selection criteria" or "rating factors." Most agencies, however, refer to this list of criteria as "KSAs."

KSAs are the general qualifications an agency expects a successful candidate to possess to do the job. Examples of typical KSAs might include statements like "Ability to communicate orally and in writing," or "Knowledge of the federal budgeting system," or "Skill in negotiating contracts with vendors and suppliers." Usually there are four to six KSAs contained within each vacancy announcement.

When you are writing your KSAs, it is important to try and quantify the things you have done. For example, how much money did you save the company? How many convictions did you get? How many people did you supervise? How many new programs did you start?

Many KSAs repeat from one vacancy announcement to another. If you're applying for eight different positions as an Accounting Technician, for example, you'll probably find that all eight vacancy announcements are fairly similar—the KSAs you wrote for the first one can be used again almost verbatim for the others.

You must respond to each of these KSAs in order to be selected for an interview. As a general rule of thumb, if you are applying for a position at the GS-5 level or below, a half-page response to each KSA factor is usually sufficient. However, if you are applying at the GS-7 level or above, you should submit a full-page written response to each KSA factor, providing detailed examples of times when you used the types of knowledge, skills, or abilities referred to in the vacancy announcement.

Although responding to KSA factors may seem like it will take a great deal of time and effort, this section of your application can be of vital importance during the final selection process. Often, addressing KSAs effectively makes the difference between a decent application and a winning one. Sometimes an application is not required to include a description of the applicant's KSAs to be considered for a job—but it really should. If more than one applicant passes the initial screening, KSAs are used to rank these qualified applicants. An application with no or inadequate KSAs will drop to the bottom of the list.

Sponsored by the U.S. Department of Labor/Employment, and developed through a grant to the North Carolina Employment Security Commission, the O*NET database provides excellent examples of KSAs for nearly every imaginable position in both the public and private sectors. The O*NET database (http://online.onetcenter.org) program surveys a wide range of employees in hundreds of different occupations and presents descriptive information pertaining to each of these careers through its database. Included in each occupational description are sections listing knowledge, skills, and abilities needed to excel at each profession. Not only are these KSAs helpful for those exploring career possibilities, but they also provide valuable examples of what types of KSAs an applicant should possess for any given position.

Examples

Descriptions of Major Duties

Needs Improvement:

> Coordinated complex civil cases. Developed detailed reviews and analyses. Researched and prepared comprehensive legal memoranda.

Now see how much detail has been added to the following job-winning version.

Good:

> Coordinated complex civil cases with various departments or divisions within FDIC. Developed detailed reviews and analyses, in preparation for counseling client representatives to improve their request for legal services.

> Researched and prepared comprehensive legal memoranda for clients, drawing on my extensive knowledge and experience litigating various issues under the FDI Act, FIRREA, the FDIC Improvement Act, commercial law, real estate law, and the Bankruptcy Code.

Here is another example.

Needs Improvement:

> Served as a contracting officer and contract administrator. Performed pre-award, award, and contract administration duties. Headed evaluation teams reviewing potential contractors. Prepared lease agreements.

The added details in the following show how the applicant's duties were much more responsible and varied.

Good:

> Served as contracting officer and contract administrator for multimillion-dollar supplies and services, construction, and architectural and engineering contracts. Possessed a contracting officer's warrant. Performed pre-award, award, and contract administration duties. Prepared *Commerce Business Daily* synopses and advertisements, developed and reviewed technical specifications, and issued solicitations and Requests for Proposals (RFPs). Headed evaluation teams reviewing potential contractors' financial data. Prepared lease agreements for properties where contractors performed construction work.

Descriptions of Advanced Training

Needs Improvement:

> FBI/RTC Bank Failure School (December 7–10, 1993); Basic Examination School for Attorneys (January 1998).

Good:

> FBI/RTC Bank Failure School (December 7–10, 1993). This was a highly intensive course focusing on the aspects of fraud involving financial institutions, covering such topics as Fraud Detection and Investigation, Forensic Accounting Approach, Prosecution of Financial Institution Fraud Cases, and The Importance of CPAs to Bank Examiners and Criminal Investigations.

> Basic Examination School for Attorneys (January 1998). This was a week-long concentrated course focusing on fundamentals of bank supervision, basic report analysis, bank accrual accounting, loan classifications, and financial analysis.

Description for an Upper-Level Position

Needs Improvement:

Knowledge of materiel life-cycle management functions, programs, and systems used to provide logistical support:

> Gained valuable understanding of military facilities planning while serving as Acting Chief of the Facilities Management Office. Responsible for issuing policy pertaining to the total acquisition life-cycle baseline parameters. Strong working knowledge of PPBES. Broad experience writing, revising, and implementing policy.

Areas for Improvement:

For upper-level federal positions, applicants should include a full page for each KSA, explaining how and when their knowledge, skills, or abilities were demonstrated. The paragraph above, however, does provide a helpful outline for the following detailed, job-winning entry.

Good:

Knowledge of materiel life-cycle management functions, programs, and systems used to provide logistical support:

My current job includes substantial life-cycle management responsibility. For example, I currently run the policy operation of Acquisition Life Cycle management. In this capacity, the information related to guidance addresses the Army's Acquisition Program Baselines (APBs) for Army Acquisition Category (ACAT) I, II, and some representative III programs.

Examples of my strong working knowledge of this area include the following:

Analyze the content of the APBs and ensure that APBs adequately address program requirements.

Result:

I recently issued APB policy which now requires APBs to address "total life-cycle costs" which, by definition, includes operating and support (O&S) costs. Furthermore, I keep Army and OSD leadership informed regarding how the Army executes its cost, schedule, and performance parameters within their respective APBs.

Result:

Maintain close ties and frequent contacts with officials at all levels in the Army and DoD as well as the respective PEOs and PMs and Command Groups. Any known logistical support requirements would also be captured within the respective APBs.

I have gained substantial working knowledge and hands-on experience through interacting with officials in the Comptroller and Acquisition communities related to acquisition life-cycle subject matter contained within APBs, SARs, and DAES reports, as well as through managing these processes.

Result:

My effort to include O&S costs within APBs is unique. To this point, the other Military Services have not yet followed suit but will likely do so soon, because it is DoD policy to make Program Managers responsible for "total life-cycle management." If and when this happens, these Program Managers would have total "cradle-to-grave" program responsibility—as well as operational control of the budget dollars to make sure that this level of responsibility is discharged fully and effectively.

The previous example addresses just one factor. Now, let's take a look at a complete set of KSAs or ranking factors as they would appear as part of a completed job application. You can see the level of detail that is required to develop a winning set of KSAs.

XXXXXXX
XXXXX

EVALUATION FACTORS

1.   **ABILITY TO SELECT, DEVELOP, AND SUPERVISE A SUBORDINATE STAFF, WHICH INCLUDED THE ABILITY TO ACTIVELY PURSUE MANAGEMENT GOALS AND SUPPORT THE EQUAL OPPORTUNITY PROGRAM.**

I believe my ability to lead and facilitate the work of others has been demonstrably evident throughout my career. For example, on numerous occasions I have interacted with staffs that I have led by (1) providing a clear sense of direction and (2) setting my expected performance levels at a level that is commensurate with these organizations' objectives, thereby (3) motivating my staff toward a higher level of goal accomplishments.

In addition, I have promoted quality performance through effective use of the agency's performance management system and I have established performance standards, appraised subordinate staffs' accomplishments, and acted to reward or counsel them, as their performance indicated was appropriate. I also have made it my practice to assess my employees' developmental needs and provide opportunities to help maximize their skills, capabilities, and ongoing professional development.

I welcome and value cultural diversity and I use these and other differences as one more tool to foster an environment where people can work together cooperatively, while achieving organizational goals. In all of my leadership roles, I have worked to promote commitment, pride, trust and group identity, and I have sought to prevent situations that could have resulted in unpleasant confrontations.

Examples of my ability in this area include:

Recruited, supervised and led the activities of subordinate staff in five (5) separate assignments.

RESULT   • Managed planning efforts, devised organizational structures to support quality control, task management, technical and administrative functions.

• Established work schedules, assigned tasks, advised subordinates on proper techniques and procedures; prepared annual performance reviews.

Conducted local Title 10 training sessions to familiarize personnel with Army MDAPs and associated reporting requirements and to equip them to recognize potential threshold breaches when they occur.

RESULT   • Sponsored an Army developmental assignment program whereby individuals within Army competed to participate at HQ, DA. Candidates were screened from applications received from HQ, DA and PEO/PM offices. Those participating gained hands-on experience with the various Title 10 reporting requirements associated with the Army's Major Defense Acquisition Programs (MDAPs).

SEE NEXT PAGE

XXXXXXX

xxxxx

<u>EVALUATION FACTORS</u>

1.   **ABILITY TO SELECT, DEVELOP, AND SUPERVISE A
     SUBORDINATE STAFF, WHICH INCLUDED THE ABILITY
     TO ACTIVELY PURSUE MANAGEMENT GOALS AND SUPPORT
     THE EQUAL OPPORTUNITY PROGRAM.** (continued)

Served as Team Leader during major financial management exercises, making
determinations regarding proper and effective procedures.
<u>RESULT</u>   • Designed studies, coordinated planning, developed strategy, and identified
             potential sources for reliable and responsive information and assigned
             tasks. Teamwork included the compilation and review of budget data
             reflecting existing operations and data from feasibility studies on proposed
             programs.

Participated in the development and implementation of recruiting programs to meet
EEO requirements and Affirmative Action objectives.
<u>RESULT</u>   • Identified appropriate advertising vehicles for minority recruiting.
             • Provided assistance and input in matters involving career development,
               training, disciplinary actions, grievances, EEO complaints and separations.

Actively recruited, interviewed, and selected individuals from or for the following
positions: Computer Programmers, Budget Analyst, Program Analysts, Budget Clerks,
Facilities Managers, and Engineering Technicians.
<u>RESULT</u>   • I have maintained a better than 50% ratio of women/minority positions
             within the organizations affected.
             • Successfully achieved minority representation in key staff positions within
               both the Program Management Resource Divison and in the Directorate
               for Assessment and Evaluation.
             • All offices in which I have worked have met or exceeded workplace
               diversity goals during my tenure. I believe that having diversity tools
               available is crucial for managers to help ensure fair and equitable
               treatment of employees. Also, I believe if done right, culturally diverse
               offices can be rewarding and conducive to a high-performing, healthy
               work environment.

Actively recruited and mentored individuals to fill developmental assignments within
the division.
<u>RESULT</u>   • Managed the developmental program in such a way that their parent
             organizations continued to support our developmental program by staffing
             vacancies. I keep in touch with many of our former developmental
             employees and monitor their professional development and progress.

XXXXXXX
xxxxx

EVALUATION FACTORS

2. **KNOWLEDGE OF MATERIEL LIFE CYCLE MANAGEMENT FUNCTIONS, PROGRAMS AND SYSTEMS USED TO PROVIDE LOGISTICAL SUPPORT.**

My current job includes a very substantial degree of life-cycle management responsibility.

For example, I currently run the policy operation of Acquisition Life Cycle management. In this capacity, the information related to guidance addressing Army's Acquisition Program Baselines (APBs) for Army Acquisition Category (ACAT) I, II and some representative III programs.

Examples of my strong working knowledge in this area include the following:

Analyze the content of the APBs and ensure that APBs adequately address program requirements.

RESULT • I recently issued APB policy which now requires APBs to address "total life cycle costs" which by definition includes operating and support (O&S) costs.

Keep Army and OSD leadership informed regarding how the Army executes their cost, schedule and performance parameters within their respective APBs.

RESULT • Maintain close ties and frequent contacts with officials at all levels in the Army and DoD as well as the respective PEOs and PMs and Command Groups.
        • Any known logistical support requirements would also be captured within the respective APBs.

I have gained substantial working knowledge and hands-on experience through interacting with officials in the Comptroller and Acquisition communities related to acquisition life cycle subject matter contained within APBs, SARs and DAES reports, as well as through managing these processes.

RESULT • My effort to include O&S costs within APBs is unique. To this point, the other Military Services have not yet followed suit but will likely do so soon, since it is DoD policy to make Program Managers responsible for "total life cycle management".
        • If and when this happens, these Program Managers would have total "cradle-to-grave" program responsibility—as well as operational control of the budget dollars to make sure that this level of responsibility is discharged fully and effectively.

XXXXXXX
xxxxx

<u>EVALUATION FACTORS</u>

3. **KNOWLEDGE OF ADVANCED LIFE CYCLE MANAGEMENT PLANNING PRINCIPLES AND PRACTICES.**

My strong background in the Comptrollership and Acquisition areas has given me an unusually broad set of qualifications in this area.

Examples of my knowledge in this area include the following:

Gained valuable understanding of military facilities planning while serving as Acting Chief of the Facilities Management office.

<u>RESULT</u>
- This experience exposed me to requirements associated with our proposed military construction, Army (MCA) projects and the MCA processor.

Currently responsible for issuing policy at HQ, DA level, pertaining to the total acquisition life cycle baseline parameters (cost, schedule and performance) for the Armyís major programs.

<u>RESULT</u>
- In 1996, the Army adopted the idea to include operating and support cost estimates within Acquisition Program Baselines (APBs). I began enforcing the policy in earnest several months later .
- Soon, the Army will have "total life cycle" cost data captured routinely in the APBs. This is one example of the "high-level" Army policy areas for which I am responsible (APBs, CARS, DAES, UCRs and SECDEF program certification) and in which I am intimately involved.

Strong working knowledge of PPBES, the DoD planning, programming, budgeting and execution system.

<u>RESULT</u>
- Oversee the submission of three budget cycle positions each year (POM, BES and PB) as they relate to the Armyís ACAT I programs.
- Prepared substantial portions of the internal operating budget (IOB) at the installation level.

Broad experience writing, revising, and implementing policy at HQ, DA level, as it relates to legal reporting requirements associated with Title 10, United States Code.

<u>RESULT</u>
- Review, update and issue revised policy and guidance pertaining to the required content of Major Defense Acquisition Programs (MDAPs - Section 2430), Selected Acquisition Reports (SARs - Section 2432), Nunn-McCurdy Unit Cost Reporting (UCRs - Section 2433) and Acquisition Program Baselines (APBs-Section 2435). Since Title 10 is generally DoD-wide in scope, it must not conflict with DoD policy and guidance. I work closely with the other services and DoD to ensure communication is clear.

XXXXXXX
xxxxx

<u>EVALUATION FACTORS</u>

4.   ABILITY TO EFFECTIVELY COMMUNICATE BOTH ORALLY AND IN WRITING REGARDING THE DUTIES OF THIS POSITION.

I have had extensive experience communicating, both orally and in writing. For example, I have defended/advocated my organizations' programs to Congress, DoD, DA and industry. As a steward of government funds, I often have written to determine the disposition of un-liquidated obligations to ensure that the government's money was properly accounted for.

Examples of my ability in this critical skill area include the following:

Frequently prepare written correspondence for senior officials of the Army, DoD, and Congress.

<u>RESULT</u>
- Represent the Army in writing—and in person—in a variety of areas. Much of the interaction is in the form of Integrated Product Teams (IPTs) which often includes aspects of Title 10, DoD 5000 and AR 70-1, which requires substantial subject matter expertise which must be communicated either by written policy or correspondence or both. Some of these areas include:
  - Major Defense Acquisition Programs (MDAPs)- 10, USC, Section 2430.
  - Selected Acquisition Reports (SARs) - 10, USC, Section 2432.
  - Nunn-McCurdy Unit Cost Reporting (UCRs) - 10, USC, Section 2433
  - Acquisition Program Baselines (APBs) - 10, USC, Section 2435
  - Defense Acquisition Executive Summary (DAES - DoD 5000)

Extensive personal liaison with senior Army and other DoD officials.

<u>RESULT</u>
- Selected to brief the Secretary and Under Secretary of the Army regarding our Title 10, United States Code reporting requirements.

Issue written guidance and policy related to a broad area of responsibilities under my authority.

<u>RESULT</u>
- Recently issued new Title 10 policy to the Program Executive Offices (PEOs) and their Project Managers (PMs).
- Wrote Congressional Notification Letters to the House and Senate Leaders informing them of the NM unit cost breaches, for which we subsequently sent Congress reports.

Held managerial and staff leadership positions at installation and HQ, DA levels.

<u>RESULT</u>
- At the installation level, was intimately involved with frequent manpower surveys and writing justifications to defend our TDA.

SUMMING IT UP

- Your Social Security Number is requested under the authority of Public Law, a law specifying that anyone doing business with the federal government provide this information.

- Many government agencies will accept a Federal Resume.

- Unlike a private-sector resume, which often is no more than one or two pages, a Federal Resume can be as long or short as you want it to be.

- To make your Federal Resume highly readable, choose your words carefully. Excess wordiness should be eliminated, and sentences should be short and clear.

PART IV
PUTTING IT ALL TOGETHER

Applying for a Federal Job

chapter 7

OVERVIEW

- Writing an eye-catching cover letter
- Cover letter checklist
- Sample cover letters
- Assembling your resume and application
- A completed federal resume
- Submitting your application package
- Following up
- When you're called for an interview
- The job offer: negotiating your salary
- Summing it up

The federal job application process is the "make or break point" of aspiring federal employees. This is the place where dreams either *remain* dreams or become reality. You cannot approach the application process the same way as you would in the private sector. You cannot simply send the same resume and cover letter to multiple positions found on a Web site. Instead, to be successful, you must track down specific job openings, apply separately for each one, and tailor your application or resume to the listed requirements.

Above all, you must follow procedure—no matter how brilliant or qualified you may be. Even though you haven't yet been hired, it's time to start thinking like a bureaucrat. The better you are at following the rules, the more likely you'll be to succeed! This means you need to know how to "read" the federal job announcement—to pull out all of the information you'll need in order to craft the best application. Then, you must find and correctly complete the right application form. You must prepare the *entire* application, answer all the questions, and recognize that in this case, *more* information is *better* information. Your diligence can set you apart from other applicants!

WRITING AN EYE-CATCHING COVER LETTER

When a federal screening panel receives your application materials, the first document they will review is your cover letter. Because most federal vacancies attract numerous applicants, you will want to make sure that your cover letter is not only thoughtful and polished, but also sparks their interest. Ideally, your cover letter should help to set you apart from other applicants and persuade the hiring agency to look over the rest of your materials.

Although cover letters may not be mandatory for all federal job applications, they are highly recommended. Unless you are specifically instructed not to send a cover letter, it's a good idea to send one with your other application materials. Cover letters give you the chance to provide a personal introduction to the hiring panel and explain, in brief, your interest in the position. In a concise, one-page letter, you can capture the screening committee's attention by offering a succinct list of your most relevant qualifications and experience.

A well-written cover letter can complement your resume and pique the hiring manager's interest, so you'll want to make the most of this opportunity to create a positive first impression. The following tips should help you craft an engaging, effective letter:

- **Follow a standard business letter format.** Look carefully at how other business letters are typically formatted. Your cover letter should be no longer than one page and contain several paragraphs that are short and to-the-point. At the beginning of your letter, refer to the exact position for which you are applying, using the correct title as stated in the federal job announcement. You'll also want to be sure to include the announcement number at the top of your letter.

- **Address your letter to a specific person.** It's worth the extra effort to find the contact person's name (be sure it's spelled correctly) and title. Opening your letter with a salutation to the hiring manager is much more personal than a general greeting to an agency or department and shows you pay close attention to detail.

- **Express your interest in the position.** The opening paragraph of your letter should convey your purpose in writing and compel the hiring manager to read further. Explain why you are interested in that particular government agency or the type of work that agency does. If you would need to relocate for the position, you might also mention why the prospective geographic area appeals to you.

- **Highlight your qualifications.** In this middle section of your letter, you should point out your top two or three qualifications for the position and how the job would be a good match for your unique skills and experience. Using specific examples or achievements, briefly describe why you are a strong candidate for the position and why you would be an asset to the agency.

- **Repeat keywords.** Using keywords—words that are specific to your chosen industry or profession—will help showcase your knowledge of the government agency and the position. Keywords that appeared frequently in the job announcement (and also, ideally, in your other application materials) should be used in your cover letter as well.

- **Thank the employer and give contact information.** In the closing paragraph, remember to reiterate your interest in the position, provide your current contact information, and express your appreciation to the agency for reviewing your application materials.

- **Proofread your letter.** Your cover letter must be free of any spelling or grammatical errors, so be sure to review it several times. If possible, have another person double-check the letter for you.

COVER LETTER CHECKLIST

Overall

☐ No longer than one page

☐ Contains several paragraphs that are short and to-the-point

☐ At the beginning, refers to the exact position for which you are applying (uses the correct title as stated in the federal job announcement)

☐ Includes the announcement number

Address and Salutation

☐ Addressed to a specific person (name and title are spelled correctly)—hiring manager

Opening Paragraph

☐ Conveys your purpose in writing

☐ Explains why you are interested in that particular government agency or the type of work that agency does

☐ If you would need to relocate for the position, mention why the prospective geographic area appeals to you

Middle Paragraphs

☐ Point out your top two or three qualifications for the position

☐ Explain how the job would be a good match for your unique skills and experience

☐ Use specific examples or achievements

☐ Describe why you are a strong candidate for the position

☐ Describe why you would be an asset to the agency

☐ Use keywords that appeared frequently in the job announcement (and also, ideally, in your other application materials)

Closing Paragraph

☐ Reiterate your interest in the position

☐ Provide your current contact information

☐ Express your appreciation to the agency for reviewing your application materials

SAMPLE COVER LETTERS

Here are five examples of well-written cover letters.

SAMPLE COVER LETTER: CORRECTIONAL OFFICER

147 E. Ellsworth Street
Newton, MA 02474

September 30, 2009

Federal Bureau of Prisons
Consolidated Staffing Unit/BOP-HIRES
346 Marine Forces Drive
Grand Prairie, TX 75051

RE: Job Announcement Number BOP-N-0007-001

Dear Hiring Manager:

I am interested in applying for the position of Correctional Officer that has recently become available within your department.

I have a strong background in correctional facility work, having served as a correctional officer in the Massachusetts prison system for the past 10 years. I am planning a move to Texas this year for personal reasons and am seeking a position that allows me to continue to utilize my professional experience in my new locale.

As my resume shows, I have extensive experience with standard corrections facility practices and procedures, such as those I would be required to carry out in this position. I am skilled in disaster intervention and am proficient in the use of firearms and other weapons of self defense. My training includes a B.A. in Criminal Justice from Hope International University, and a DOC certification from the Philadelphia Training Institute in Philadelphia, Pa.

In my most recent position as a Correctional Officer with the Bay State Correctional Facility in Norfolk, Mass., I was awarded the Officer of the Year title in 2007. This award honors correctional officers for their ethical conduct on the job and for their ability to uphold facility security standards. If hired, I would bring the same level of competence and professionalism to my work at your facility.

I would welcome the opportunity for a personal interview, which would allow me to share with you in more depth the positive contributions I can bring to your organization's future success. I can be reached by phone at (617) 555-5155 or by e-mail at S.Hines@ressample.com. Thank you for your time and consideration; I look forward to hearing from you.

Sincerely,

Samantha Garcia-Hines

SAMPLE COVER LETTER: REGISTERED NURSE

2407 W. Chattanooga Drive
Milford, CA 96121

September 30, 2009

Regina Portchak, Hiring Manager
Department of Veterans Affairs
Janesville VA Medical Center
1 VA Center
Janesville, CA 96114

Dear Ms. Portchak:

I am writing to apply for the position of Registered Nurse in the Janesville VA Medical Center Nursing Home. Please accept these materials in application for the position advertised in job announcement number RN 12-64, printed in the *Milford Journal*.

As you can see from the attached resume, I have 12 years of experience working in the nursing field. Although my environment changed from the Surgical Unit to the Emergency Room over the course of this time, I have maintained a consistently high level of care in my work in both areas. I have proven leadership ability in a medical setting, and I bring the confidence of crisis management experience as a benefit in any emergency situation.

I wish to work at your medical center because of its excellent reputation for quality patient care. I have also performed volunteer work with nurses from your hospice who were very enthusiastic about the nursing home environment and career advancement opportunities.

I am available for interviews beginning October 15, 2009. Please let me know if it would be convenient for you to meet with me then. My phone number is (530) 555-1111, and I can be reached by e-mail as well at leslieshea@ressample.com. I appreciate your consideration of my application and look forward to discussing the position further with you.

Best regards,

Leslie Sheay, R.N.

Encl.

SAMPLE COVER LETTER: ELECTRONICS ENGINEER

7500 N. Princeton Place
New York, NY 10013

August 17, 2009

Buford Jones, Director of Personnel
New York Electric
314 Johnson Street
New York, NY 10013-2875

Dear Mr. Jones:

I am applying in response to job announcement # STU876YL712181X, for the position of Electronics Engineer with New York Electric.

I served in this capacity for Shipton Multimedia for nine years under the direction of the senior engineering staff. Some of my duties included conceptualizing and designing remote control units for DVD systems; preparing safety and test reporting; and conducting research on design and safety. I am proficient in working with PLC and PC control interfaces and have high-level skill in both AutoCAD and SolidWorks, as your job announcement mentions.

In addition, as the position requires, I have a four-year Bachelor of Science degree in Electronic Engineering from the University of Texas, and a consistent track record in helping my employers achieve their business goals. At Shipton, I consistently met or exceeded company production quotas, maintaining a rejection rate 200 percent below the acceptable company threshold. I was also directly responsible for introducing product innovations that saved the company $150,000 over a three-year period.

I am very interested in interviewing for this position and am available to begin work as soon as possible. Would it be convenient for you to meet in person to review my credentials and to speak with me about becoming part of your team at New York Electric?

I will follow up with you the week of August 23 to determine potential times for an interview. I may also be reached directly at (718) 234-1234 or by e-mail at markrshepherd@ressample.com. Thank you for considering my application for employment with your company. Enclosed is my resume for your review; I am happy to provide references at your request.

Sincerely,

Mark Shepherd

Encl.

SAMPLE COVER LETTER: ACCOUNTANT

123 Main Street
Atlanta, GA 30339

September 23, 2009

Jefferson Tyler, Hiring Manager
Environmental Protection Agency
Atlanta Federal Center
61 Forsyth Street, SW
Atlanta, GA 30303-3104

RE: Job Vacancy No. Reg 4-MP-2009-0780

Dear Mr. Tyler:

Please accept my resume in consideration for the Accountant position with the Region 4 office of the Environmental Protection Agency, recently advertised on the USAJobs Web site. With extensive Accounting experience and a strong track record of achieving business objectives, I am confident that my professional contributions will enhance your agency's success.

Over the past six years I have progressed from an internship with Ernst and Young to my current position with the City of Atlanta Office of the Controller. To illustrate my skills and abilities, I would like to mention a few notable accomplishments with my current employer:

Accounting Accuracy and Attention to Detail—By providing accurate and detailed accounting services, I am able to prepare multiple types of financial statements for the City of Atlanta departments. I also prepare the city's annual financial statements for public distribution.

Forecasting Utility—Part of my role is to provide city personnel with reconciled expenditure and revenue account reports, which allow staff members to effectively plan for the future year's budget. My strong knowledge of public agency budgeting practices and principles allows me to provide department staff members the most accurate depiction of their current financial status.

As my resume shows, I have demonstrated the ability to provide accounting services in a variety of professional environments. I am certain that I will contribute a strong level of performance to the Environmental Protection Agency as well. Thank you in advance for reviewing my materials. I would welcome the opportunity to meet with you and discuss my qualifications.

If you would like more information or to schedule an interview, I can be reached by phone at (555) 555-1235, and by e-mail at patred@ressample.com. I look forward to hearing from you.

Sincerely,

Patricia R. Edwards, CPA

SAMPLE COVER LETTER: HUMAN RESOURCES SPECIALIST

3155 E. 104th Street
Thornton, CO 80233

October 5, 2009

Office of Personnel Management
Center for Human Capital Management Services
1900 E Street NW, Room 1469
Washington, DC 20415

Dear Hiring Manager:

Please accept this letter and attached resume for your consideration. I am applying for the position of Human Resources Specialist with the OPM Center for Human Capital Management Services, job announcement number 09-567-AHAKJ-431. I am highly interested in this position, because I will be relocating to the DC area within the next month and would like to continue to contribute my skills to supporting an agency in the Human Resources field.

A combination of factors leads me to believe that I would be a prime candidate for the position described in your job announcement. First, I have had extensive experience in candidate screening and hiring, as the job announcement specifies. I have also had three years of hands-on training experience, similar to that which would be required in the position you advertise.

On a personal level, I am a conscientious employee, with strong communication skills, both verbally and in writing. In addition, I have a positive, team-oriented attitude, with a dedicated and responsible work ethic. I believe that my qualifications will help me achieve the professional goals expected of me, and I feel confident that I can be an asset to your organization.

Please feel free to contact me with any questions you may have, or to request references. I may be reached by phone at (303) 555-5445 or by e-mail at grsprague@ressample.com. Thank you for your time in considering my application. I am enthusiastic about the possibility of working with the OPM, and I look forward to hearing from you.

Sincerely,

Geraldine Sprague

Encl.

ASSEMBLING YOUR RESUME AND APPLICATION

The key to filling out an attention-grabbing federal job application is attitude. Just keep reminding yourself how capable you are and that what you're being asked to do is no different from what many other people have successfully done. Below is a checklist of items to be sure to cover when assembling your application package.

☐ **Make a first draft.** First, write up a rough draft of your federal resume or answers to KSA questions. Then go back and "write" these materials again, using the first drafts as an outline and expanding wherever possible. Rewrite these drafts as many times as needed to produce a complete, well-written account of your experience and expertise.

☐ **Be extremely thorough.** If you are required to complete a government form with your application, be sure to answer every question and include all the information requested in the job vacancy announcement. Even if you have nothing to enter on a particular line, don't leave the line blank. Fill in "N/A" or "not applicable" to show you're responding to it.

☐ **Provide a complete employment history.** Provide an in-depth listing of each job you've held and your major responsibilities and accomplishments. Be sure to label any attachments with your name, address, and the job announcement number. Be specific about what tasks you performed in each job. Do not summarize; explain fully.

☐ **Quantify where possible.** How much money did you save the company? How many people did you supervise? How many convictions were you responsible for? How many programs did you institute?

☐ **Provide a complete educational history.** Include the names of all schools you attended (back to high school), with their locations, the dates you attended, the subjects you studied, the number of classroom or credit hours you earned, the diplomas or degrees you received, and any other pertinent data. Also list in-service workshops, seminars, professional conferences, private study, correspondence courses, military training, leadership orientation, career specialty training, and the like. If you are filling out a government form, you may need to include separate sheets. Again, be sure to include your name, address, and the job announcement number on any additional pages.

☐ **List honors and awards.** Honors and awards should also be featured in your application. You may list scholarships, safety awards, community awards and nominations, and election to honorary societies and groups. Include brief excerpts from official or unofficial letters in which your work was praised. If you've received many awards, just list the most recent; otherwise, list them all.

☐ **List special qualifications, experience, and skills.** Any familiarity with a foreign language, computer skills, typing skills, licenses, and certificates should be mentioned in your application, along with any experience with equipment or machines, membership in professional organizations, material you have written even if unpublished, examples of public speaking, and relevant hobbies. Be sure to include unpaid experience or volunteer work because you may receive the same amount of credit for these as you would for paid work experience.

☐ **List available, professional references.** The people who ideally should be included on this list are those who know you and who know your work. Make sure they can easily be reached and include their phone numbers. Do not list people who are out of the country, have no phone, or whose whereabouts are unknown to you. Be sure you ask these people for permission to use them as references.

☐ **Be honest.** Don't embellish or falsify any information on the application. Your application will be closely checked. If you were ever fired, say so. It is better to state this openly than for the examiner to find out the truth from your former employer.

☐ **Aim for a clear, well-organized presentation.** Don't put employment history or other material into one long paragraph. Break up long descriptions into short sentences and paragraphs, and use headings. This is especially important if you are completing a government form and use more space (such as in an attachment) than is provided on the application.

☐ **Put the job announcement number on all application materials.** You will find this number on the front of the job announcement. You should also list your name, birth date, and the position on all materials in the event they become separated.

☐ **Sign and mail.** If you are mailing or faxing your application materials, be sure they are signed in colored ink, not black ink, and remember to mail or fax the original, not the copy.

Application Examples

Taking an exam for a civil service position is now much less common than submitting an application package for a job. For some positions, applicants are still required to take and pass an exam; however, most positions today do not require this. These jobs are obtained based on competitive evaluation of applicants' experience and education.

Following are examples of completed applications for three federal government positions. Each example contains an application form, cover letter, and resume tailored to the specific position.

Bank Examiner Trainee

Kathryn Johnson
123 Easy Street
Dallas, TX 53132
P: 555.222.1212

August 8, 2008

Human Resources Office
New York State Banking Department
One State Street
New York, NY 10004-1417

Re: Bank Examiner Trainee I (Exam 20-598); OC-APP-3 #20598 (4/07)

Dear Hiring Manager:

I am responding to your position listing for Bank Examiner Trainee I, dated August 8, 2008. The application, my resume, and three (3) letters of reference are attached. For the past year, I have provided consulting and training services but I am now eager to continue with a career in banking. I would be honored to make a strong contribution to your team's efforts in this position.

After having carefully reviewed the requirements of this position, I am confident that my skills, abilities, and experience effectively match your requirements for this position. I have over 15 years' experience in banking and the financial industry, both in the private sector and in the government arena.

Throughout my career in banking, I have derived great satisfaction from serving clients well. I enjoy working with dynamic teams. I also enjoy working with the public, demonstrating banking service. I believe I would contribute to your professional environment because I find the banking industry to be both challenging and rewarding.

May I arrange an interview to further discuss my qualifications? I am available to meet with you at a mutually convenient time. Thank you for your consideration of my application.

Sincerely,

Kathryn Johnson

Encl.

123 Easy St., Dallas, TX 53132 | P: 555.222.1212

Kathryn Johnson

Objective

To work in banking as a loan officer or a bank examiner

Experience

2006–2010   Progressive Bank   Dallas, TX
Bank Teller

- Served customers from diverse backgrounds in the Dallas metropolitan area
- Worked with bank officers to ensure efficient delivery of services
- Suggested new methods to increase retention of customers

2005–2006   Friendly Bank of Dallas   Dallas, TX
Bank Teller Assistant

- Helped assess the level of customer service and methods to increase delivery of great customer service
- Supervised interns in developing customer satisfaction surveys

2004–2005   Duffy Vineyards   Dallas, TX
Junior Sales Associate

- Worked with team to market local vineyard products

2003–2004   Lit Ware, Inc.   Dallas, TX
Sales Representative

- Worked in direct sales of plastic containers for home use
- Received company's highest sales award in 2004
- Helped develop training course in sales

Education

2002-2004   South Ridge State University   Dallas, TX

- Course of study: Finance and accounting

Interests

Running, gardening, nutrition, computers.

OC-APP-3 # 20598 (4/07)

APPLICATION FOR NYS EXAMINATIONS
OPEN TO THE PUBLIC

Send Completed Application To:

Human Resources Office
New York State Banking Department
One State Street
New York, NY 10004-1417

Read instructions on the exam announcement and Page 1 of SUPP #20598 first before completing.

Please Print Clearly

Exam No:	Titles:
20-598	Bank Examiner Trainee I

Last Name: JOHNSON   First Name: Kathryn   MI

Mailing Address: No., Street, or P.O. Box: 123 EASY STREET

Apt. No.

City or Post Office: DALLAS   State: TX   ZIP Code: 53132

Social Security Number: 123 | 456 | 7890

Home Phone: (555) 222 1212   Day Phone: (555) 222-1213

PERSONAL PRIVACY PROTECTION LAW NOTIFICATION

The information you provide on this form is being requested in accordance with Section 50(3) of the New York State Civil Service Law for the principal purpose of determining the eligibility to participate in the examination(s) for which you are applying, and to evaluate your merit and fitness for appointment. This information will be used in accordance with Section 96(1) of the Personal Privacy Protection Law, particularly subdivisions (b), (e), and (f). Failure to provide this information may result in disapproval of the application, and/or interfere with our ability to measure your merit and fitness. This information will be maintained by the Human Resources Office, New York State Banking Department, One State Street, New York, New York 10004-1417. For further information, relating only to the Personal Privacy Protection Law, call (518) 457-9375. (For examination information on this examination, call (212) 709-5448.)

CITIZENSHIP / ELIGIBILITY FOR EMPLOYMENT

Before you can be employed in any position in State Service, you will be required to produce documents which establish your identity and your eligibility to be employed in the United States.

STUDENT LOANS

YES ☐ NO ☐ Are you currently in default on any outstanding student loan(s) made or guaranteed by the New York State Higher Education Services Corporation?

ADDITIONAL QUESTIONS

YES ☐ NO ☑ Were you ever discharged from any employment except for lack of work or funds, disability or medical condition?

YES ☐ NO ☑ Did you ever resign from any employment rather than face discharge?

YES ☐ NO ☑ Did you ever receive a discharge from the Armed Forces of the United States which was other than "Honorable" or which was issued under other than honorable conditions?

YES ☐ NO ☑ Have you ever been convicted of any crime (felony or misdemeanor)?

YES ☐ NO ☑ Are you now under charges for any crime?

If you answered YES to any of these questions, provide details under REMARKS on Page 3 of the Supplement. Your failure to answer any of these questions or to provide details will significantly delay any determination concerning your qualifications and may deprive you of potential employment opportunities.

I affirm under penalties of perjury that all statements made on this application (including any attached papers) are true. I understand that all statements made by me in connection with this application are subject to investigation and verification and that a material misstatement or fraud may disqualify me from appointment and/or lead to revocation of my appointment.

X Kathryn Johnson   Aug. 8, 2008

Signature of Applicant   Date

Please print any other last name by which you are or have been known.

EXTRA CREDITS FOR WAR TIME VETERANS

DO NOT COMPLETE THIS SECTION UNLESS YOU:
1. Wish to claim War Time Veterans Credits, AND
2. Have NOT used veterans credits for appointment to a position in New York State or Local Government employment.

Answering these questions means that you are requesting the extra credits. Do not answer the questions if you are not a wartime active duty member of the armed forces or a war time veteran or if you do not want to request the extra credits.

If you are currently in the Armed Forces on full-time active duty (other than for training) or if you are a War Time Veteran or Disabled Veteran, you are eligible for extra credits added to your exam score if you pass. These extra credits can be used only once for any permanent government employment in New York State. If you want to have these extra credits added to your exam score, you must answer the questions now. You can waive the extra credits later if you wish. At the time of interview and appointment you will be required to produce the documentation, such as discharge papers, to prove that you are eligible for the extra credits.

YOUR ANSWERS MUST BE "YES" TO BE ELIGIBLE FOR ADDITIONAL CREDITS.

YES ☐ NO ☐ I received, or expect to receive, a discharge which was honorable or release under honorable circumstances from the Armed Forces of the United States. (The "Armed Forces of the United States" means the Army, Navy, Marine Corps, Air Force and Coast Guard, including all components thereof, and the National Guard when in the service of the United States pursuant to call as provided by law on a full-time active duty basis other than active duty for training purposes.)

YES ☐ NO ☐ I served, or am serving, on an active duty basis other than active duty for training purposes during one or more of the following Time of War periods.

In the Armed Forces:
- Aug. 2, 1990 to the date when the Persian Gulf hostilities ends;
- Feb. 28, 1961 to May 7, 1975;
- June 27, 1950 to Jan. 31, 1955;
- Dec. 7, 1941 to Dec. 31, 1946;

or earned the armed forces, navy, or marine corps expeditionary medal for service in:
- (Panama) Dec. 20, 1989 to Jan. 31, 1990;
- (Lebanon) June 1, 1983 to Dec. 1, 1987;
- (Grenada) Oct. 23, 1983 to Nov. 21, 1983;

or in the U.S. Public Health Service:
- June 26, 1950 to July 3, 1952;
- July 29, 1945 to Sept. 2, 1945.

YES ☐ NO ☐ I am a United States citizen or an alien lawfully admitted for permanent residence.

YES ☐ NO ☐ I am a New York State resident.

YES ☐ NO ☐ I am receiving payments from the U.S. Dept. of Veterans Affairs for a service connected disability rated at 10% or more incurred during a "Time of War" period listed above.

To claim additional credits as a Disabled Veteran, you must also answer YES to this question:

It is the policy of the New York State Department of Civil Service to provide for and promote equal opportunity in employment, compensation and other terms and conditions of employment without discrimination on the basis of age, race, creed, color, national origin, gender, sexual orientation, disability or marital status or genetic predisposition or carrier status.

It is the policy of the New York State Department of Civil Service to provide qualified persons with disabilities equal opportunity to participate in and receive the benefits, services, programs and activities of the Department, and to provide such persons reasonable accommodations and reasonable modifications as are necessary to enjoy such equal opportunity, including accommodations in the examination process. Further it is the policy of the Department to provide reasonable accommodations for religious observers.

SUPP #20598 (4/07)   **SUPPLEMENTAL QUESTIONNAIRE**
Page 1

| 1 | 2 | 3 | 4 | 5 | 6 | 7 | 8 | 9 |
SOCIAL SECURITY NUMBER

CONTINUOUS RECRUITMENT EXAMINATION NO. 20-598
FOR ENTRY LEVEL BANK EXAMINER TRAINEES
IN THE NEW YORK STATE BANKING DEPARTMENT

This is a training and experience examination. Your rating will be based on a review of your responses to this questionnaire. All information provided is subject to verification.

There is no application fee for this examination.

INSTRUCTIONS:

1. **Type or print legibly in ink.**

2. Answer all questions on this questionnaire and application form OC-APP 3 (attached) completely and accurately. **Incomplete information may result in a lower score.**

3. **Do not submit a resume with your application.**

4. Your degree and/or college credits must have been awarded by a regionally accredited college or university or one recognized by the New York State Education Department as following acceptable educational practices. If your degree and/or college credit was awarded by an educational institution outside the United States and its territories, you must provide independent verification of equivalency and a course by course evaluation. You can write to the address below for a list of acceptable companies who provide this service or this information can be found on the internet at: http://www.cs.state.ny.us/jobseeker/degrees.cfm. You must pay the required evaluation fee.

5. **Mail this APPLICATION FORM OC-APP-3 #20598 and SUPPLEMENTAL QUESTIONNAIRE SUPP #20598, and transcripts to:**

   Transcripts downloaded from college websites *will not* be accepted.

   **Human Resources Office
   NYS Banking Department
   One State Street
   New York, NY 10004-1417**

6. Retest Policy - You may reapply for this exam after one year.

7. Appropriate part-time and volunteer experience, which can be verified, will be accepted on a pro-rated basis.

I. ACADEMIC RECORD

A. Indicate any degrees received or expected to receive.

College, University, Professional or Technical School(s)	Semester Credits Received	Quarter Hours Received	Type of Degree Received	Major Subject or Type of Course	Did You Graduate	Degree Expected
Name SOUTH RIDGE STATE UNIVERSITY DALLAS, TEXAS	30			Account-ing	☐ Yes ☑ No	MO. YR. /
Name					☐ Yes ☐ No	MO. YR. /

SUPP #20598 (4/07)   **SUPPLEMENTAL QUESTIONNAIRE**
                                        Page 2

1	2	3	4	5	6	7	8	9

SOCIAL SECURITY NUMBER

CONTINUOUS RECRUITMENT EXAMINATION NO. 20-598
FOR ENTRY LEVEL BANK EXAMINER TRAINEES
IN THE NEW YORK STATE BANKING DEPARTMENT

I. ACADEMIC RECORD - continued

B. **Provide transcripts from all colleges attended. Only copies of transcripts with the registrar's seal or signature will be accepted. TRANSCRIPTS DOWNLOADED FROM COLLEGE WEBSITES WILL NOT BE ACCEPTED.**

C. Indicate Grade Point Average (G.P.A.) for all colleges you have attended through your last completed semester. Accurate information on your G.P.A. is vital to the selection process. Provide numerical G.P.A. only, based on a 4.0 grading system. **Incomplete information may result in a lower score.**

Undergraduate Course Work   Graduate Course Work

Overall G.P.A. __3.0__   Overall G.P.A. _____

Major G.P.A. __3.0__

II. ACCOUNTING, AUDITING, BANKING OR FINANCE PART-TIME WORK EXPERIENCE OR INTERNSHIP

Describe any accounting, auditing, banking or finance part-time work experience(s) or internship(s) while a student.

☑ Part-time Work Experience   ☐ Internship

DATES	FIRM NAME	ADDRESS	CITY AND STATE
FROM 06/2005 TO 06/2006	FRIENDLY BANK OF DALLAS	123 HOLLOW AVE.	DALLAS, TX
No. of hours worked per week: 20	DUTIES: Helped assess level of customer service and methods to increase delivery of customer service; supervised interns in developing customer service surveys.		
Name of Contact Person: JAMES REDFORD			
Telephone No. (555) 222-7890	YOUR TITLE: Bank Teller Assistant		

☐ Part-time Work Experience   ☐ Internship

DATES	FIRM NAME	ADDRESS	CITY AND STATE
FROM / TO /			
No. of hours worked per week	DUTIES:		
Name of Contact Person			
Telephone No. ( )	YOUR TITLE:		

III. CAMPUS/COMMUNITY/PROFESSIONAL ACTIVITIES

Describe your active involvement in campus, community groups or with professional organizations.

☑ Campus Activity   ☐ Community Group   ☐ Professional Activity

DATES	NAME OF ORGANIZATION	ADDRESS	CITY AND STATE
FROM 06/2002 TO 06/2003	FUTURE CPAs	SOUTH RIDGE STATE UNIV.	DALLAS, TX
No. of hours per week: 10	Goal of Organization: Teach accounting standards and ethics.		
	Position Held (if any): N/A		
Name of Contact Person: JOSEPH BROWN	Describe the nature and level of your involvement in this organization.		
Telephone No. (555) 222-4444	Prepared presentations to freshman-level students at university. Presentations demonstrated career opportunities in accounting		

SUPP #20598 (4/07)   **SUPPLEMENTAL QUESTIONNAIRE**
Page 3

/	2	3	4	5	6	7	8	9

SOCIAL SECURITY NUMBER

**CONTINUOUS RECRUITMENT EXAMINATION NO. 20-598
FOR ENTRY LEVEL BANK EXAMINER TRAINEES
IN THE NEW YORK STATE BANKING DEPARTMENT**

III.   CAMPUS/COMMUNITY/PROFESSIONAL ACTIVITIES - continued

☐ Campus Activity   ☐ Community Group   ☐ Professional Activity

DATES MO YR MO YR FROM / TO /	NAME OF ORGANIZATION	ADDRESS	CITY AND STATE
No. of hours per week	Goal of Organization:		
	Position Held (if any):		
Name of Contact Person	Describe the nature and level of your involvement in this organization.		
Telephone No. ( )			

IV. WORK EXPERIENCE

Describe any full-time work experience in the accounting, auditing, banking or finance field.

DATES MO YR MO YR FROM 06/2006 TO 08/2008	FIRM NAME Progressive Bank	ADDRESS 721 Oster Way	CITY AND STATE Dallas, TX
No. of hours per week 40	DUTIES: Served customers from diverse backgrounds and businesses in Dallas; worked with bank officers to ensure		
Contact Person Fred Jones	efficient delivery of services; suggested, after research, new ways to increased		
Telephone No. (555) 222.1717	YOUR TITLE: Bank Teller /customer satisfaction.		

DATES MO YR MO YR FROM / TO /	FIRM NAME	ADDRESS	CITY AND STATE
No. of hours per week	DUTIES:		
Contact Person			
Telephone No. ( )	YOUR TITLE:		

DATES MO YR MO YR FROM / TO /	FIRM NAME	ADDRESS	CITY AND STATE
No. of hours per week	DUTIES:		
Contact Person			
Telephone No. ( )	YOUR TITLE:		

Use additional sheets if necessary to complete information.

Remarks: (Use this space to provide any additional information as necessary. Attach additional
8 1/2" x 11" sheets if necessary.)

Use additional sheets if necessary to complete information.

Developmental Aide Trainee

Kathryn Johnson
123 Easy Street
Dallas, TX 53132
P: 555.222.1212

August 8, 2008

Human Resources Office
New York State
Department of Human Resources
One State Street
New York, NY 10004-1417

Re: Developmental Aide Trainee; OC-APP #4 10-010 / 10-011 (2-07L)

Dear Hiring Manager:

I am responding to your position listing for Developmental Aide Trainee, dated August 8, 2008. The application, my resume, and three letters of reference are attached. After having carefully reviewed the requirements of this position, I am confident that my skills, abilities, and experience will match your requirements for this position.

For the past year, I have served as a Developmental Aide with Kinder Kids as I pursue a degree in early childhood education. Prior to that, I worked as a Developmental Aide with the Institute for Childhood Development in Dallas. Both of these positions provided me with the opportunity to deepen my understanding of child development and teaching strategies.

I would be grateful for an opportunity to work for the State of New York as a Developmental Aide Trainee. Such an experience would be valuable to me as I pursue a career that utilizes my skills in a learning environment. I can assure you that I will devote my strong work ethic to serving your agency in this capacity.

May I arrange an interview to further discuss my qualifications? I am available for an interview at a mutually convenient time. Please feel free to contact me at the telephone number above.

Thank you for your time and consideration.

Sincerely,

Kathryn Johnson

Encl.

123 Easy St., Dallas, TX 53132 | P: 555.222.1212

Kathryn Johnson

Objective

To contribute to the understanding of early childhood development through study and application of innovative methods in education and testing

Experience

2007–Present   Kinder Kids   Dallas, TX
Developmental Aide

- Emphasized learning for children 4 to 6 years of age
- Worked with children to help them understand the role of preschool in preparing them for elementary school
- Suggested new methods to increase retention of new reading skills

2005–2007   The Institute for Childhood Development Dallas, TX
Developmental Aide

- Helped assess the level of preparedness of children 6 to 8 years old for foreign language education
- Supervised interns in early childhood development

2004–2005   Duffy Vineyards   Dallas, TX
Junior Sales Associate

- Worked with team to market local vineyard products

2003–2004   Lit Ware, Inc.   Dallas, TX
Sales Representative

- Worked in direct sales of plastic containers for home use
- Received company's highest sales award in 2004
- Helped develop training course in sales

Education

2002-2004   South Ridge State University   Dallas, TX

- Course of study: Early Childhood Development

Interests

Running, gardening, nutrition, computers.

APPLICATION FOR NEW YORK STATE EXAMINATIONS OPEN TO STATE EMPLOYEES

| PLEASE CHECK THE EXAM(S) YOU ARE APPLYING FOR: | ☐ 10-010 Developmental Aide Trainee
☐ 10-011 Developmental Aide Trainee (Spanish Language) | **Transition** | OC-APP #4 10-010 / 10-011 (2-07L) SIDE/PAGE 1 **XD-92B** |

Please read the announcement carefully before completing this application.

Send your completed and signed application to the Office of Mental Retardation and Developmental Disabilities facility where you would like to take the Developmental Aide Trainee *examination*.

PLEASE PRINT

Your Last Name	First Name	MI	Social Security Number
JOHNSON	KATHRYN		1 2 3 4 5 6 7 8 9

Street Number, Apt. or P.O. Box	Home Phone
123 EASY STREET	(555) 222 - 1212 Area Code

City or Post Office	State	ZIP Code	Business Phone
DALLAS	TX	53132	(555) 222 - 1213 Area Code

Please note: You may take these Developmental Aide Trainee exam(s) *only* <u>ONCE</u> every testform period. (See details on the announcement.)

REASONABLE ACCOMMODATIONS IN TESTING

☐ I require reasonable accommodations to take this test. (See the announcement for details.)

STUDENT LOANS

YES ☐ NO ☑ Are you currently in default on any outstanding student loan(s) made or guaranteed by the New York State Higher Education Services Corporation?

FOR TRANSITION EXAMS:

On or before the test date, you must have had full-time or part-time permanent or contingent permanent service in a qualifying title as specified on the examination announcement. Please provide the title, grade and dates of service for the title in which you gained qualifying experience as well as the other information requested below.

| Present Agency and Title:
(whether or not it is qualifying for the exam)

KINDER KIDS
DEVELOPMENTAL INTERN | Qualifying Permanent Title and Grade:
DEVELOPMENTAL AIDE
Dates of Qualifying Service:
From: (Mo./Yr.)   JUNE 2007   To: (Mo./Yr.)   AUGUST 2008 |

FOR ADDITIONAL LANGUAGE PARENTHETIC TITLES

In order to provide the best service to those individuals for whom English is not a primary language, additional language-specific positions may be created during the life of the list. If you are interested in a language-specific Developmental Aide Trainee position, indicate the language(s) in which you are fluent:

☐ French ☐ Creole ☐ Korean ☐ Russian ☐ Chinese ☐ American Sign Language ☐ Other (specify) _____

CITIZENSHIP / ELIGIBILITY FOR EMPLOYMENT

Before you can be employed in any position in State Service, you will be required to produce documents which establish your identity and your eligibility to be employed in the United States.

MEDICAL EXAMINATION, FINGER PRINTING AND BACKGROUND INVESTIGATION

A medical examination may be required for appointment.
Fingerprinting and a criminal background check will be conducted if you are selected for appointment.

NOTE: *Have you provided all requested information? An incomplete application may be disapproved.*

I affirm under penalties of perjury that all statements made on this application (including any attached papers) are true. I understand that all statements made by me in connection with this application are subject to investigation and verification and that a material misstatement or fraud may disqualify me from appointment and/or lead to revocation of my appointment.

X _Kathryn Johnson_   AUGUST 8, 2008
Signature of Applicant   Date   Please print any other last name by which you are or have been known.

Please continue application on Side/Page 2

APPLICATION FOR NEW YORK STATE EXAMINATIONS OPEN TO STATE EMPLOYEES

10-010 Developmental Aide Trainee **10-011** Developmental Aide Trainee (Spanish Language)	OC-APP #4 10-010 / 10-011 (2-07L) SIDE/PAGE 2 **XD-92B**

EXTRA CREDITS FOR WAR TIME VETERANS

Answering these questions means that you are requesting the extra credits. Do not answer the questions if you are not a wartime active duty member of the armed forces or a war time veteran or if you do not want to request the extra credits.

If you are currently in the Armed Forces on full-time active duty (other than for training) or if you are a War Time Veteran or Disabled Veteran, you are eligible for extra credits added to your exam score if you pass. These extra credits can be used only once for any permanent government employment in New York State. If you want to have these extra credits added to your exam score, you must answer the questions now. You can waive the extra credits later if you wish. At the time of interview and appointment you will be required to produce the documentation, such as discharge papers, to prove that you are eligible for the extra credits.

DO NOT COMPLETE THIS SECTION UNLESS YOU:	1. Wish to claim War Time Veterans Credits, AND 2. Have NOT used veterans credits for appointment to a position in New York State or Local Government employment.

YOUR ANSWERS MUST BE "YES" TO BE ELIGIBLE FOR ADDITIONAL CREDITS.

YES ☐ NO ☐ I expect to receive or have already received, a discharge which was honorable or release under honorable circumstances from the Armed Forces of the United States. The "Armed Forces of the United States" means the Army, Navy, Marine Corps, Air Force and Coast Guard, including all components thereof, and the National Guard when in the service of the United States pursuant to call as provided by Law, on a **full-time active duty basis other than active duty for training purposes.**

YES ☐ NO ☐ I am now serving, or have served, on an active duty basis other than active duty for training purposes during one or more of the following Time of War periods.

In the Armed Forces:	*or* **earned the armed forces, navy, or marine corps expeditionary medal for service in:**	*or* **in the U.S. Public Health Service:**
• Aug. 2, 1990 to the date when the **Persian Gulf hostilities** ends; • Feb. 28, 1961 to May 7, 1975; • June 27, 1950 to Jan. 31, 1955; • Dec. 7, 1941 to Dec. 31, 1946;	• **(Panama)** Dec. 20, 1989 to Jan. 31, 1990; • **(Lebanon)** June 1, 1983 to Dec. 1, 1987; • **(Grenada)** Oct. 23, 1983 to Nov. 21, 1983;	• June 26, 1950 to July 3, 1952; • July 29, 1945 to Sept. 2, 1945.

YES ☐ NO ☐ I am a United States citizen or an alien lawfully admitted for permanent residence.

YES ☐ NO ☐ I am a New York State resident.

To claim additional credits as a Disabled Veteran, you must also answer "YES" to this question:

YES ☐ NO ☐ I am receiving payments from the U.S. Dept. of Veterans Affairs for a service connected disability rated at 10% or more incurred during a "Time of War" period listed above.

REMARKS:

PERSONAL PRIVACY PROTECTION LAW NOTIFICATION

The information which you are providing on this application is being requested pursuant to Section 50(3) of the New York State Civil Service Law for the principal purpose of determining the eligibility of applicants to participate in the examination(s) for which they have applied. This information will be used in accordance with Section 96(1) of the Personal Privacy Protection law, particularly subdivisions (b), (e), and (f). Failure to provide this information may result in disapproval of the application. This information will be maintained by the Office of Mental Retardation and Developmental Disabilities. For further information, relating *only* to the Personal Privacy Protection Law, call (518) 457-9375. For exam information, call (518) 457-2487 (press 2, then press 3): or toll free at 1-877-697-5627 (press 2, then press 3).

It is the policy of the New York State Department of Civil Service to provide for and promote equal opportunity in employment, compensation and other terms and conditions of employment without discrimination on the basis of of age, race, creed, color, national origin, gender, sexual orientation, disability or marital status or genetic predisposition or carrier status.

It is the policy of the New York State Department of Civil Service to provide qualified persons with disabilities equal opportunity to participate in and receive the benefits, services, programs and activities of the Department, and to provide such persons reasonable accommodations and reasonable modifications as are necessary to enjoy such equal opportunity, including accommodations in the examination process. Further it is the policy of the Department to provide reasonable accommodations for religious observers.

Food Service Worker

> Kathryn Johnson
> 123 Easy Street
> Dallas, TX 53132
> P: 555.222.1212

August 8, 2008

Personnel Office
New York State
Department of Human Resources
One State Street
New York, NY 10004-1417

Re: Food Service Worker I; OMRDD, DOH, OC-APP #4 20-484 (12/04L)

Dear Hiring Manager:

I am responding to your position listing for Food Service Worker I, dated August 8, 2008. The application and my resume are attached. I am happy to provide letters of references upon request. After having carefully reviewed the requirements of this position, I am confident that my skills, abilities, and experience qualify me to serve as a Food Service Worker I for your organization.

For the past year, I have worked as a Food Service Technician in the cafeteria at a local hospital in Dallas, Texas. I am pursuing a degree in physical therapy, but I am also interested in the way that nutrition affects a person's physical well being. I would appreciate the chance to increase my knowledge and skills through hands-on experience working for the State of New York. I am a dedicated, reliable employee, and I bring enthusiasm to a team environment.

May I arrange an interview to further discuss my qualifications? I am available for an interview at a mutually convenient time. Please feel free to contact me at the telephone number above.

Thank you for your consideration of my application. I look forward to hearing from you.

Sincerely,

Kathryn Johnson

123 Easy St., Dallas, TX 53132   P: 555.222.1212

Kathryn Johnson

| **Objective** | To work as a food service worker in a progressive hospital |

Experience

2007–Present   Arbor Hospital   Dallas, TX
Food Service Technician

- Emphasized efficient, safe delivery of food to patients
- Learned to keep food and food delivery costs to a minimum without sacrificing quality
- Suggested new food products that increased efficiency and nutrition

2005–2007   Broadmoor Physical Therapy Institute   Dallas, TX
Food Service Technician

- Served staff and clients during breakfast and lunch
- Supervised interns learning food service trade

2004–2005   Duffy Vineyards   Dallas, TX
Junior Sales Associate

- Worked with team to market local vineyard products

2003–2004   Lit Ware, Inc.   Dallas, TX
Sales Representative

- Worked in direct sales of plastic containers for home use
- Received company's highest sales award in 2004
- Helped develop training course in sales

Education

2002-2004   South Ridge State University   Dallas, TX

- Course of study: Physical Therapy.

Interests

Running, gardening, nutrition, computers.

APPLICATION FOR NEW YORK STATE EXAMINATIONS OPEN TO THE PUBLIC

☒ 20-484 **Food Service Worker 1**
OMRDD, DOH,
agencies other than OMH
Please read the announcement carefully
before completing this application.

OC-APP #4 20-484 (12/04L)
SIDE/PAGE 1
XD-72

Send your completed and signed application to:
the facility Personnel Office where you
would like to take the
Food Service Worker 1 examination.

Your Last Name	First Name	MI	Social Security Number
JOHNSON	KATHRYN		1 2 3 4 5 6 7 8 9
Street Number, Apt. or P.O. Box			Home Phone
123 EASY STREET			(555) 222 - 1212 Area Code
City or Post Office	State	ZIP Code	Business Phone
DALLAS	TX	53132	(555) 222 - 1213 Area Code

(PLEASE PRINT)

Please note: 1 - An examination for Food Service Worker 1 is also offered for the Office of Mental Health. For information on these positions, refer to the announcement for Exam No. 20-483 Food Service Worker 1 - Office of Mental Health.

2 - The same Food Service Worker 1 written test is used for both exam numbers 20-483 and 20-484. You may take the FOOD SERVICE WORKER 1 written test only ONCE every testform period. (See details on the announcement.)

SPECIAL ACCOMMODATIONS IN TESTING

☐ I require special accommodations to take this test. (See the announcement.)

STUDENT LOANS

YES ☐ NO ☒ Are you currently in default on any outstanding student loan(s) made or guaranteed by the New York State Higher Education Services Corporation?

ADDITIONAL QUESTIONS

YES ☐ NO ☒ Were you ever discharged from any employment except for lack of work or funds, disability or medical condition?
YES ☐ NO ☒ Did you ever resign from any employment rather than face discharge?
YES ☐ NO ☒ Did you ever receive a discharge from the Armed Forces of the United States which was other than "Honorable" or which was issued under other than honorable conditions?
YES ☐ NO ☒ Have you ever been convicted of any crime (felony or misdemeanor)?
YES ☐ NO ☒ Are you now under charges for any crime?

If you answered YES to any of these questions, provide details under REMARKS on Page 2. Your failure to answer any of these questions or to provide details will significantly delay any determination concerning your qualifications and may deprive you of potential employment opportunities.

CITIZENSHIP / ELIGIBILITY FOR EMPLOYMENT

Before you can be employed in any position in State Service, you will be required to produce documents which establish your identity and your eligibility to be employed in the United States.

MEDICAL EXAMINATION, FINGER PRINTING AND BACKGROUND INVESTIGATION

A medical examination will be required for appointment.
Fingerprinting and a criminal background check will be conducted if you are selected for appointment.

NOTE: *Have you provided all requested information? An incomplete application may be disapproved.*

I affirm under penalties of perjury that all statements made on this application (including any attached papers) are true. I understand that all statements made by me in connection with this application are subject to investigation and verification and that a material misstatement or fraud may disqualify me from appointment and/or lead to revocation of my appointment.

X *Kathryn Johnson* AUGUST 8, 2008
Signature of Applicant   Date   Please print any other last name by which you are or have been known.

Please continue application on Side/Page 2

APPLICATION FOR NEW YORK STATE EXAMINATIONS OPEN TO THE PUBLIC

20-484 Food Service Worker 1

OMRDD, DOH, agencies other than OMH

OC-APP #4 20-484 (12/04L)

SIDE/PAGE 2

XD-72

EXTRA CREDITS FOR WAR TIME VETERANS

Answering these questions means that you are requesting the extra credits. Do not answer the questions if you are not a wartime active duty member of the armed forces or a war time veteran or if you do not want to request the extra credits.

If you are currently in the Armed Forces on full-time active duty (other than for training) or if you are a War Time Veteran or Disabled Veteran, you are eligible for extra credits added to your exam score if you pass. These extra credits can be used only once for any permanent government employment in New York State. If you want to have these extra credits added to your exam score, you must answer the questions now. You can waive the extra credits later if you wish. At the time of interview and appointment you will be required to produce the documentation, such as discharge papers, to prove that you are eligible for the extra credits.

| DO NOT COMPLETE THIS SECTION UNLESS YOU: | 1. Wish to claim War Time Veterans Credits, AND |
| | 2. Have NOT used veterans credits for appointment to a position in New York State or Local Government employment. |

YOUR ANSWERS MUST BE "YES" TO BE ELIGIBLE FOR ADDITIONAL CREDITS.

YES ☐ NO ☑ I expect to receive or have already received, a discharge which was honorable or release under honorable circumstances from the Armed Forces of the United States. The "Armed Forces of the United States" means the Army, Navy, Marine Corps, Air Force and Coast Guard, including all components thereof, and the National Guard when in the service of the United States pursuant to call as provided by Law, on a **full-time active duty basis other than active duty for training purposes.**

YES ☐ NO ☑ I am now serving, or have served, on an active duty basis other than active duty for training purposes during one or more of the following Time of War periods.

In the Armed Forces:	*or earned the armed forces, navy, or marine corps expeditionary medal for service in:*	*or in the U.S. Public Health Service:*
• Aug. 2, 1990 to the date when the **Persian Gulf hostilities** ends; • Dec. 22, 1961 to May 7, 1975; • June 27, 1950 to Jan. 31, 1955; • Dec. 7, 1941 to Dec. 31, 1946;	• **(Panama)** Dec. 20, 1989 to Jan. 31, 1990; • **(Lebanon)** June 1, 1983 to Dec. 1, 1987; • **(Grenada)** Oct. 23, 1983 to Nov. 21, 1983;	• June 26, 1950 to July 3, 1952; • July 29, 1945 to Sept. 2, 1945.

YES ☐ NO ☐ I am a United States citizen or an alien lawfully admitted for permanent residence.

YES ☐ NO ☐ I am a New York State resident.

To claim additional credits as a Disabled Veteran, you must also answer "YES" to this question:

YES ☐ NO ☐ I am receiving payments from the U.S. Dept. of Veterans Affairs for a service connected disability rated at 10% or more incurred during a "Time of War" period listed above.

REMARKS:

ADDITIONAL EXAMINATION CREDITS PURSUANT TO CIVIL SERVICE LAW SECTION 85-a

If you are a child of a police officer or firefighter who was killed in the line of duty in the service of New York State, you may be entitled to additional examination credits pursuant to Civil Service Law Section 85-a. For further information, please contact the Department of Civil Service at (518) 457-5507.

PERSONAL PRIVACY PROTECTION LAW NOTIFICATION

The information which you are providing on this application is being requested pursuant to Section 50(3) of the New York State Civil Service Law for the principal purpose of determining the eligibility of applicants to participate in the examination(s) for which they have applied. This information will be used in accordance with Section 96(1) of the Personal Privacy Protection law, particularly subdivisions (b), (e), and (f). Failure to provide this information may result in disapproval of the application. This information will be maintained by the Personnel Office of the facility where you applied to take this examination. For further information, relating *only* to the Personal Privacy Protection Law, call (518) 457-9375. For information on other Civil Service exams, call (518) 457-6216.

It is the policy of the New York State Department of Civil Service to provide for and promote equal opportunity in employment, compensation and other terms and conditions of employment without discrimination because of age, race, creed, color, national origin, gender, sexual orientation, disability or marital status or genetic predisposition or carrier status.

It is the policy of the New York State Department of Civil Service to provide qualified persons with disabilities equal opportunity to participate in and receive the benefits, services, programs and activities of the Department, and to provide such persons reasonable accommodations and reasonable modifications as are necessary to enjoy such equal opportunity, including accommodations in the examination process. Further it is the policy of the Department to provide reasonable accommodations for religious observers.

A COMPLETED FEDERAL RESUME

XXXX XXXXXXX
Announcement number:

XXXXX XXXXXXXX

000000 Alex Guerrero Circle
El Paso, Texas 79936

Home / Fax: (915) 000-0000
Email: xxxxxx@xxx.com
Office: xxxxxxxxxx
Email: xxxxx@xxx.org
U.S. citizen
Highest security clearance held: TOP SECRET (1985-90)
Highest Federal civilian grade: GG-1102-12
Date of last promotion : December, 1996

GOAL   Announcement Number:
Position title:

PROFILE   **Current responsibility:**
Contracting Officer
Border Environment Cooperation Commission
Assigned to facility in Juarez, Mexico

Proven experience managing budgets for contracts ranging in value up to $200 million. Experience supervising up to 5 employees.

Primary focal point for the award of several multi-million-dollar construction, architectural and engineering, and management services contracts.

Strategic liaison responsibility. Frequently interact with high-ranking city, county, and state officials, as well as consultants and the general public to provide funding and construction of border projects in Mexico and the United States.

Served as Equal Employment Opportunity Counselor. Also served on Qualification Review Boards to rank applicants for Federal positions.

Designed and implemented operating policies and procedures. Automated library operations and recorded retrieval procedures. Participated in establishment of computerized accounting program for non-appropriated funds.

Accomplished communicator. Principal point-of-contact and lead negotiator during contract deliberations.

Strong written communication skills. Developed and wrote Agency-wide operating standards.

XXXX XXXXXXX
Announcement number:

CURRENT TITLE: CONTRACTING OFFICER
Border Environment Cooperation Commission (BECC)   Juarez, Mexico 32470
GRADE: N/A   **SALARY:** $57,000   **HOURS:** 40/week
DATE: January 1998-present   **SUPERVISOR:** XXXXXX

Direct, monitor, and personally oversee the award of architectural and engineering and other management services contracts for the BECC, a quasi-government agency.

RESULT   Responsible for the development of water/waste water and sanitation master plans, cost and price analysis, development of pre-negotiation memorandums and projects' negotiations, and assembling documentation required to certify projects for construction funds. Selected to fill in for the incumbent Technical Assistance Program Manager during her travel or absence.

Serve as lead negotiator and facilitator for the evaluation team. Responsible for coordinating all business development and contract administration activities for the organization. Direct proposal efforts, lead negotiation teams and chair status meetings with all disciplines involved in complex, high-dollar development projects.

RESULT   Expertly guiding principals through the contracting process, successfully directed contracting efforts (cradle to grave) for multi-year, multi-million-dollar projects.

Supervise and coordinate the work of subordinate staff of U.S. and Mexican nationals, managing planning efforts, devising organizational structures to support quality control, task management, technical operations and administrative functions.

RESULT   Establish work schedules, assign tasks, advise subordinates on proper techniques and procedures and prepare annual performance reviews.

Review Mexico's contracting law and procedures and the United Nations Model Law on Procurement in order to develop Agency specific procurement standards. Because the BECC was created under a North American Free Trade Agreement (NAFTA) side-agreement and is a bi-national agency, funded by both the United States and Mexican governments and the U.S. Environmental Protection Agency (USEPA), the BECC is not required to conform to Federal Acquisition Regulations (FAR). As a result, no such procurement regulations were in place.

RESULT   Developed procurement standards and procedures for this relatively new Agency.

IMPACT   These procedures are written in a clear, concise and detailed manner and contain information that is vital to the efficient and effective administration of the procurement program. These procedures were instrumental in securing new contracts with the corporate community and launched the procurement program.

Prepare reviews for the agency's Legal Counsel on contract clauses and other legal issues. Review financial feasibility of projects. Examine environmental and sustainability aspects, as well as criteria required to qualify for construction funding. Where possible, work is coordinated with graduate studies in the MPA program at the University of Texas at El Paso (UTEP).

RESULT   Successfully handled two protests for disqualification of proposals during the evaluation stage.

IMPACT   This early resolution of the problem prevented a more serious challenge.

Point-of-Contact for management study and internal needs assessment.

RESULT   Coordinate project tracking systems, electronic and hard copy record keeping, general operating procedures, manual writing, and accounting/budgeting processes.

IMPACT   Until my intervention there were few standards or operational practices in place. Recipient, "Excellent" job performance rating.

XXXX XXXXXXX
Announcement number:

TITLE: **Contract Specialist** (NOTE: hired as GS-1102-7 Intern; promoted to GS-9/11/12)
U.S. Section, International Boundary and Water Commission   El Paso, TX 79902-1441
GRADE: GG-1102-12   **SALARY:** $45,000   **HOURS:** 40/week
DATE: 12/90-1/98   **SUPERVISOR:** XXXXXX

Served as contracting officer and contract administrator for multi-million-dollar supplies and services, construction, and architectural and engineering contracts. Possessed a contracting officer's warrant. Performed pre-award, award, and contract administration duties.

RESULT   Prepared *Commerce Business Daily* synopses and advertisements, developed and reviewed technical specifications, and issued solicitations and Requests For Proposals (RFPs). Headed evaluation teams reviewing potential contractors' financial data. Prepared lease agreements for properties where contractors performed construction work.

Performed price and costs analyses, conducted contract negotiations, monitored expenditures, and developed legal interpretations. Presided over bid openings and site visits.

Set priorities and demonstrated effective leadership. Since contracting does not leave much room for variance, it was my responsibility to ensure that rules were strictly adhered to.

RESULT   Established good working relationships with diverse groups of individuals in order to effectively solicit compliance with regulatory requirements.

IMPACT   Anticipated questions and provided necessary information and guidance.

Instituted policy and procedures for Acquisition Division in areas of Ethics, Imprest Funds, and Memorandums of Understanding for grants and cooperative agreements with Federal agencies.

RESULT   Developed technical expertise in all phases of the contracting cycle from per-award through negotiations and contract administration.

IMPACT   Led staff members through the process of changing and updating old habits and implementing required procedures.

Coordinated with technical and engineering staff, end users, and senior executives within the client organizations and Federal contract managers to ensure timely compliance with all terms of the contracts and the Federal Acquisition Regulations (FAR).

RESULT   Worked with diverse individuals to create cohesive plans and strategies, incorporating the often-divergent objectives of many disciplines. Oversaw several projects of national interest.

IMPACT   In the operation and maintenance of the Nogales International Wastewater Treatment Plant, made the determination that it would be more cost effective to contract the work out to a private firm than to have the government continue its operation of the plant. As a result of contracting out, the government was able to realize a cost savings over a five-year period.

Main point-of-contact, internally and externally, ensuring that client organizations were satisfied and that contractors delivered goods/services in accordance with Statements-of-Work documents.

Served as Equal Employment Opportunity (EEO) Counselor. Provided supervisors and managers with detailed explanations of applicable EEO laws and regulations prohibiting discrimination. Participated in EEO workshops.

RESULT   Often called upon to provide assistance in matters involving disciplinary actions, grievances, EEO complaints and illegal separations.

IMPACT   Used tact to provide practical advisory services in potentially volatile situations.

XXXX XXXXXXX
Announcement number:

Facilitated affirmative action hiring, providing advice and support for manager involved. explaining Federal regulations to assist them in devising effective job search strategies.

RESULT   Gained the support of management and employees throughout the organization.

IMPACT   As a result, was able to resolve all issues presented to me at the local level without the need for expensive and disruptive litigation.

Recipient of several "Excellent" job performance ratings during this period.

TITLE: Records Officer (Mail and File Assistant)
U.S. Section, International Boundary and Water Commission   El Paso, TX 79902-1441
GRADE: GG-307-07   **SALARY:** $25,000   **HOURS:** 40/week
DATE: 6/85-6/90   **SUPERVISOR:** XXXXXX
Chief, Headquarters Communications and Records Branch with TOP SECRET security clearance and purview over 12 field offices throughout the U.S. and Mexico border region.

RESULT   Exercised primary responsibility for the Agency's records management, mail management, correspondence management, library (legal and technical) operations, Freedom of Information and Privacy Act programs, and public relations program.

Conducted assistance visits to field offices to conduct operational audits in records management. Wrote reports of my findings and made recommendations. Taught classes in records management, records disposition, correspondence management, mail management, micrographics management, directives management, copier use and ADP management.

RESULT   Wrote the Agency's Freedom of Information Act regulations, and rewrote the records disposition and correspondence manuals.

Initiated a records control program for Privacy Act records.

RESULT   Established a directives system, and initiated a micrographics program. Computerized the library's operations as well as its records retrieval procedures.

IMPACT   My ideas were adopted, implemented, and maintained. When completed, these new or revised documents and procedures went a long way in reducing turnaround time, enabling our staff members to make renewed progress toward mission goals.

Supervised and directed the activities of subordinate staff.

RESULT   Managed planning and designed organizational structures capable of supporting strong quality control, task management, technical and administrative functions.

IMPACT   Established work schedules, assigned tasks, advised subordinates on proper techniques and procedures and prepared annual performance reviews.

Recipient, several "Excellent" job performance ratings during this period.

TITLE: Administrative Clerk
Loan Servicing Department, Small Business Administration   El Paso, TX 79935
GRADE: GS-301-4   **SALARY:** $16,800   **HOURS:** 40/week
DATE: 5/84-6/85   **SUPERVISOR:** XXXXXXX
Planned, organized, and coordinated administrative activities of the office.

RESULT   Completed special projects that involved contact with administrative and management staff at all levels within the Agency.

IMPACT   Given greater responsibilities than the job called for while in this position.

NOTE: *Accepted this position in order to return to Federal service.*

TITLE: Homemaker
xxxxxx Alex Guerrero Circle   xxxxx, Texas 00000
GRADE: N/A   **SALARY:** N/A   **HOURS:** N/A
DATE: 5/83-5/84   **SUPERVISOR:** N/A

Stayed home to care for newborn child. Responsible for child care, home operations, budgeting and family support.

TITLE: Administrative Officer
Administration Division, Department of the Army   WSMR, NM 88022
GRADE: GS-341-9   **SALARY:** $21,000   **HOURS:** 40/week
DATE: 9/81-5/83   **SUPERVISOR:** XXXXXX

Administrative management for Morale Support Activities Division's budget, procurement of supplies, publicity, personnel and manpower, and property and facilities management. **Monitored expenditures and developed annual budget forecasts.** Established five-year budget plans. Funding was provided through either non-appropriated (self earning) or appropriated means. Served as principal conduit for all information flow to the Director.
  RESULT   Applied accounting techniques which determined if activities were profitable, identified ways of improving activities' income, and determined the need for supplemental funding through appropriated means.
  IMPACT   Computerized accounting program for non-appropriated funds resulted in savings to the government.
            Recipient, Letter of Appreciation (1982).
Main point-of-contact for all budget issues for the Division, providing interpretation of accounting statements to supervisor, activity managers, and the Colonel. Worked with both appropriated and non-appropriated funds. Performed audits of private organizations at the Missile Range to assure their financial soundness and their compliance with regulatory requirements.
  RESULT   Implemented mandated financial data format changes for private organizations.
  IMPACT   Earned the trust and cooperation of all private organizations serviced and brought them into compliance with regulatory requirements.
            Recipient, Special Act Award for working with private organization (1982).
Supervised and directed the work of five staff members (3 civilians and 2 military). Managed planning efforts, devised organizational structures to support quality control, task management, technical operations and administrative functions.
  RESULT   Established work schedules, assigned tasks, advised subordinates on proper techniques and procedures and prepared annual performance reviews.

TITLE: Management Assistant
Administration Division, Department of the Army   WSMR, NM 88002
GRADE: GS-344-7   **SALARY:** $16,000   **HOURS:** 40/week
DATE: 8/79-9/81   **SUPERVISOR:** XXXXXX

Assisted in the analysis and assessment of management issues for the Administrative Management Branch.

RESULT   Suggested solutions to administrative and management problems. Collected data, reviewed and analyzed information. Interviewed managers and employees while observing their operations, taking into account the nature of the organization, the relationship it had with other organizations, its internal organization and culture.

IMPACT   Reported findings and recommendations to client organization, often in writing. In addition, made oral recommendations. Assisted in implementation of suggestions.

Taught classes in records management, records disposition, correspondence management, mail management, micrographics and directives management, copier use and ADP management.

RESULT   Recipient, Letter of Appreciation for instructing military personnel in records management (1980).

Conducted audits, and wrote reports of findings with recommendations. Allocated timeframes to offices to correct deficiencies and did follow-up visits where appropriate. Held secret security clearance. Acted in behalf of supervisor during her absence.

RESULT   Led individuals to change what they were doing incorrectly in order to conform to regulatory requirements.

IMPACT   Facility was upgraded to exceed all records management requirements.

EDUCATION
Bachelor of Business Administration (B.B.A.)
University of Texas at El Paso, 1993

Masters of Public Administration candidate (M.P.A. degree due: May 1999)
University of Texas at El Paso

PROFESSIONAL ORGANIZATIONS
National Institute of Government Purchasing (NIGP)
National and Local Chapters

RELATED SKILLS
Computer literate in Windows, WordPerfect, MS Word and Works, Lotus (Quattro Pro), and database management software, the Internet, intranets, and on-line services.

LANGUAGE SKILLS
Fluent in spoken and written Spanish

XXXXXXXXX
SSN 000-00-0000

XXXXXX XXXXX
SSN 000-00-0000
0000 Spain Drive
Stafford, Virginia 00000
Home: (540) 000-0000
Work: (703) 000-0000
DSN: 000-0000
E-mail: xxxx@xxx.xxx

SUMMARY OF SKILLS
Military Satellite Communications
Manager, Defense Satellite Communications System (DSCS)
Proven Staff Leadership
Task Manager
Lead Evaluator
Contractor Supervision
Liaison and representation
Technical Troubleshooting
Spacecraft Reconfiguration
Data Integration
Operating Parameters
Control and Coordination
Operational Assessments
Contingency Planning
Specialized Engineering
Contingency Communications
Earth Terminals Optimization
System Reliability
Maintainability Standards
Control Concepts
System Capabilities
Interface Requirements
Requirements Analysis
Project Coordination
High-level Briefings
Frequency Modulation
Digital Baseband Equipment
Common-user Communications
Modeling and Simulation
Network Management
Information Security
Communications Link Configurations
System Optimization
Detection of Degradations

EXPERIENCE:
January 1991 to present. 40-50 hours/week.
Telecommunications Manager.
TOP SECRET / SCI security clearance
Defense Information Systems Agency (DISA)
Supervisor: XXXXXXX
Pay-grade: GS-391-14
Functional leader within DOD for the DSCS Operational Control System. Integrate complex data and conclusions from various functional areas to formulate policy and develop procedures for operating DSCS to serve DOD and other Federal agencies. Recruited by DSCS Operations Branch (DOT) at DCA/DISA. Promoted to GS-0391-14 as of 10-19-92 due to "accretion of duties" and assigned as Deputy/Assistant to the Senior Satellite Communications System Manager; served as primary in his absence. Assumed all management duties effective October 1998 during his transition to retirement. Acting in that capacity to date. Supervise management of DSCS and technical direction of DSCS Operations Control Centers. Manage satellite communication payloads and network coordination. Establish parameters of satellite service. Exercise managerial authority regarding access to DSCS. Prepare and issue Telecommunications Service Requests (TSR). Develop implementation directives for the O&M commands. Coordinate execution of these directives. Develop objectives, policies and procedures for the Joint Staff concerning current and projected DSCS operations. Provide liaison and representation regarding operational requirements in the planning, development, programming, budgeting, acquisition and deployment of DSCS space and ground equipment and related operational control systems. Extensive use of DCAD 800-70-1 and 310-65-1 for TSR services, as governed by MOP 37. Evaluate all requests for DSCS access; prepare DISA's recommendations to the Joint Staff for its approval/disapproval and subsequent entry into the Integrated Consolidated SATCOM Data Base (ICDB). Serve as DNSO representative on ICDB-related matters. Extensive interaction with, and instruction of, DISA and other Defense and Intelligence Community managers, frequently including decision-makers with limited knowledge of satellite technology. Provide recommendations for communications link configurations that optimize the use of DSCS satellite resources. Plan satellite cut-overs and frequency plans to optimize loading of operational satellites.
RESULTS PRODUCED: Key player in ensuring highly efficient utilization of assets. Instrumental in developing and implementing a reconstitution effort during unexpected transponder failures. Planned and implemented error-free satellite Telecommunications Service Requests. Develop and maintain policies, procedures, concepts of operation, parameters and standards for DSCS, including ECCM and the use of partial satellites. Develop, produce, and publish operational and control concepts for DSCS in DISAC 800-70-1. Develop new and modified concepts and configurations in support of ongoing missions. Extensive troubleshooting in the following areas: limited bandwidth, restricted available power from satellite transponders, antenna patterns and earth terminal characteristics, shortage of specific filters or multiplexers, front-line coordination with field sites, creating cut-over plans. Provide inputs for updated edition of DCAC 800-70-1. Initiated change of ENR codes for all strategic satellite terminals in use worldwide.

XXXXXXXX
SSN 000-00-0000

1989 to 1991. 40-50 hours/week. **MilNet Manager.**
Defense Data Network, Operations
Supervisor: XXXXXXXX
Assigned to DDN Operations as DDN MilNetManger. Operational manager of the DOD
global MilNet. Provided direction in network design and implementation from user level to
nodal points, including fielding of NACs and CISCO routers.

1987 to 1989. 40 hours/week. **Integrated Test Facility Manager.**
Defense Data Network
Supervisor: LTC XXXX
Managed the Defense Data Network (DDN) Integrated Test Facility (ITF) in Reston, VA.
Responsible for baseline development of BLACKER encryption device. Was detailed into
position as Branch Chief upon transfer of LTC XXXX.

1985 to 1987. 50-60 hours/week. **Head, Communications Department.**
NAVELEXDETPAX, Patuxent River, MD.
Supervisor: XXXXXXX
Managed four (4) Telecommuncation Facilities (2 Strategic Genser, 1 Tactical, 1
SCIF) providing Air, Land and Sea Test & Evaluation Platforms. Conducted
performance evaluations at all participating test facilities.

SECURITY CLEARANCE:
TOP SECRET / SCI

EDUCATION
Graduate, Southwest XXXX XXXXX Public High School, April 1961

ADVANCED PROFESSIONAL TRAINING
Customer Service Orientation (40-hour course), 1995
DSCS DOSS/DASA Course (80-hour course), 1991
DSCS Network Engineering Course (40-hour course), 1991
Orientation to Contracting (16-hour course), 1987
COTR Training (40-hour course), 1985
Leadership Management Education and Training, 1981
Satellite Controller Course (three-month course), 1978
Radioman "B" School, (six-month course),1971
Teletype Maintenance and Operation, 1966
Radioman "A" School (seven-month course), 1962

AWARDS AND HONORS
Joint Service Commendation Medal
Vietnam Service Medal, with two Bronze Stars
Recipient of continuous "Outstanding" performance appraisals throughout my tenure at DISA.

XXXXXXX
xxxxx

EVALUATION FACTORS

1.   **ABILITY TO SELECT, DEVELOP, AND SUPERVISE A
      SUBORDINATE STAFF, WHICH INCLUDED THE ABILITY
      TO ACTIVELY PURSUE MANAGEMENT GOALS AND SUPPORT
      THE EQUAL OPPORTUNITY PROGRAM.**

I believe my ability to lead and facilitate the work of others has been demonstrably evident throughout my career. For example, on numerous occasions I have interacted with staffs that I have led by (1) providing a clear sense of direction and (2) setting my expected performance levels at a level that is commensurate with these organizations' objectives, thereby (3) motivating my staff toward a higher level of goal accomplishments.

In addition, I have promoted quality performance through effective use of the agency's performance management system and I have established performance standards, appraised subordinate staffs' accomplishments, and acted to reward or counsel them, as their performance indicated was appropriate. I also have made it my practice to assess my employees' developmental needs and provide opportunities to help maximize their skills, capabilities, and ongoing professional development.

I welcome and value cultural diversity and I use these and other differences as one more tool to foster an environment where people can work together cooperatively, while achieving organizational goals. In all of my leadership roles, I have worked to promote commitment, pride, trust and group identity, and I have sought to prevent situations that could have resulted in unpleasant confrontations.

Examples of my ability in this area include:

Recruited, supervised and led the activities of subordinate staff in five (5) separate assignments.

RESULT
- Managed planning efforts, devised organizational structures to support quality control, task management, technical and administrative functions.
- Established work schedules, assigned tasks, advised subordinates on proper techniques and procedures; prepared annual performance reviews.

Conducted local Title 10 training sessions to familiarize personnel with Army MDAPs and associated reporting requirements and to equip them to recognize potential threshold breaches when they occur.

RESULT
- Sponsored an Army developmental assignment program whereby individuals within Army competed to participate at HQ, DA. Candidates were screened from applications received from HQ, DA and PEO/PM offices. Those participating gained hands-on experience with the various Title 10 reporting requirements associated with the Armyís Major Defense Acquisition Programs (MDAPs).

SEE NEXT PAGE

XXXXXXX

xxxxx

EVALUATION FACTORS

1. ABILITY TO SELECT, DEVELOP, AND SUPERVISE A SUBORDINATE STAFF, WHICH INCLUDED THE ABILITY TO ACTIVELY PURSUE MANAGEMENT GOALS AND SUPPORT THE EQUAL OPPORTUNITY PROGRAM. (continued)

Served as Team Leader during major financial management exercises, making determinations regarding proper and effective procedures.

RESULT
- Designed studies, coordinated planning, developed strategy, and identified potential sources for reliable and responsive information and assigned tasks. Teamwork included the compilation and review of budget data reflecting existing operations and data from feasibility studies on proposed programs.

Participated in the development and implementation of recruiting programs to meet EEO requirements and Affirmative Action objectives.

RESULT
- Identified appropriate advertising vehicles for minority recruiting.
- Provided assistance and input in matters involving career development, training, disciplinary actions, grievances, EEO complaints and separations.

Actively recruited, interviewed, and selected individuals from or for the following positions: Computer Programmers, Budget Analyst, Program Analysts, Budget Clerks, Facilities Managers, and Engineering Technicians.

RESULT
- I have maintained a better than 50% ratio of women/minority positions within the organizations affected.
- Successfully achieved minority representation in key staff positions within both the Program Management Resource Divison and in the Directorate for Assessment and Evaluation.
- All offices in which I have worked have met or exceeded workplace diversity goals during my tenure. I believe that having diversity tools available is crucial for managers to help ensure fair and equitable treatment of employees. Also, I believe if done right, culturally diverse offices can be rewarding and conducive to a high-performing, healthy work environment.

Actively recruited and mentored individuals to fill developmental assignments within the division.

RESULT
- Managed the developmental program in such a way that their parent organizations continued to support our developmental program by staffing vacancies. I keep in touch with many of our former developmental employees and monitor their professional development and progress.

XXXXXXX
xxxxx

<u>EVALUATION FACTORS</u>

2.   **KNOWLEDGE OF MATERIEL LIFE CYCLE MANAGEMENT FUNCTIONS, PROGRAMS AND SYSTEMS USED TO PROVIDE LOGISTICAL SUPPORT.**

My current job includes a very substantial degree of life cycle management responsibility.

For example, I currently run the policy operation of Acquisition Life Cycle management. In this capacity, the information related to guidance addressing Army's Acquisition Program Baselines (APBs) for Army Acquisition Category (ACAT) I, II and some representative III programs.

Examples of my strong working knowledge in this area include the following:

Analyze the content of the APBs and ensure that APBs adequately address program requirements.

<u>RESULT</u>   • I recently issued APB policy which now requires APBs to address "total life cycle costs" which by definition includes operating and support (O&S) costs.

Keep Army and OSD leadership informed regarding how the Army executes their cost, schedule and performance parameters within their respective APBs.

<u>RESULT</u>   • Maintain close ties and frequent contacts with officials at all levels in the Army and DoD as well as the respective PEOs and PMs and Command Groups.
   • Any known logistical support requirements would also be captured within the respective APBs.

I have gained substantial working knowledge and hands-on experience through interacting with officials in the Comptroller and Acquisition communities related to acquisition life cycle subject matter contained within APBs, SARs and DAES reports, as well as through managing these processes.

<u>RESULT</u>   • My effort to include O&S costs within APBs is unique. To this point, the other Military Services have not yet followed suit but will likely do so soon, since it is DoD policy to make Program Managers responsible for "total life cycle management".
   • If and when this happens, these Program Managers would have total "cradle-to-grave" program responsibility—as well as operational control of the budget dollars to make sure that this level of responsibility is discharged fully and effectively.

XXXXXXX
xxxxx

EVALUATION FACTORS

3. KNOWLEDGE OF ADVANCED LIFE CYCLE MANAGEMENT PLANNING PRINCIPLES AND PRACTICES.

My strong background in the Comptrollership and Acquisition areas has given me an unusually broad set of qualifications in this area.

Examples of my knowledge in this area include the following:

Gained valuable understanding of military facilities planning while serving as Acting Chief of the Facilities Management office.

RESULT • This experience exposed me to requirements associated with our proposed military construction, Army (MCA) projects and the MCA processor.

Currently responsible for issuing policy at HQ, DA level, pertaining to the total acquisition life cycle baseline parameters (cost, schedule and performance) for the Army's major programs.

RESULT • In 1996, the Army adopted the idea to include operating and support cost estimates within Acquisition Program Baselines (APBs). I began enforcing the policy in earnest several months later.

• Soon, the Army will have "total life cycle" cost data captured routinely in the APBs. This is one example of the "high-level" Army policy areas for which I am responsible (APBs, CARS, DAES, UCRs and SECDEF program certification) and in which I am intimately involved.

Strong working knowledge of PPBES, the DoD planning, programming, budgeting and execution system.

RESULT • Oversee the submission of three budget cycle positions each year (POM, BES and PB) as they relate to the Army's ACAT I programs.

• Prepared substantial portions of the internal operating budget (IOB) at the installation level.

Broad experience writing, revising, and implementing policy at HQ, DA level, as it relates to legal reporting requirements associated with Title 10, United States Code.

RESULT • Review, update and issue revised policy and guidance pertaining to the required content of Major Defense Acquisition Programs (MDAPs - Section 2430), Selected Acquisition Reports (SARs - Section 2432), Nunn-McCurdy Unit Cost Reporting (UCRs - Section 2433) and Acquisition Program Baselines (APBs-Section 2435). Since Title 10 is generally DoD-wide in scope, it must not conflict with DoD policy and guidance. I work closely with the other services and DoD to ensure communication is clear.

XXXXXXX
xxxxx

EVALUATION FACTORS

4.   ABILITY TO EFFECTIVELY COMMUNICATE BOTH ORALLY AND IN WRITING REGARDING THE DUTIES OF THIS POSITION.

I have had extensive experience communicating, both orally and in writing. For example, I have defended/advocated my organizations' programs to Congress, DoD, DA and industry. As a steward of government funds, I often have written to determine the disposition of un-liquidated obligations to ensure that the government's money was properly accounted for.

Examples of my ability in this critical skill area include the following:

Frequently prepare written correspondence for senior officials of the Army, DoD, and Congress.

RESULT   • Represent the Army in writing—and in person—in a variety of areas. Much of the interaction is in the form of Integrated Product Teams (IPTs) which often includes aspects of Title 10, DoD 5000 and AR 70-1, which requires substantial subject matter expertise which must be communicated either by written policy or correspondence or both. Some of these areas include:
   • Major Defense Acquisition Programs (MDAPs)- 10, USC, Section 2430.
   • Selected Acquisition Reports (SARs) - 10, USC, Section 2432.
   • Nunn-McCurdy Unit Cost Reporting (UCRs) - 10, USC, Section 2433
   • Acquisition Program Baselines (APBs) - 10, USC, Section 2435
   • Defense Acquisition Executive Summary (DAES - DoD 5000)

Extensive personal liaison with senior Army and other DoD officials.

RESULT   • Selected to brief the Secretary and Under Secretary of the Army regarding our Title 10, United States Code reporting requirements.

Issue written guidance and policy related to a broad area of responsibilities under my authority.

RESULT   • Recently issued new Title 10 policy to the Program Executive Offices (PEOs) and their Project Managers (PMs).
   • Wrote Congressional Notification Letters to the House and Senate Leaders informing them of the NM unit cost breaches, for which we subsequently sent Congress reports.

Held managerial and staff leadership positions at installation and HQ, DA levels.

RESULT   • At the installation level, was intimately involved with frequent manpower surveys and writing justifications to defend our TDA.

SUBMITTING YOUR APPLICATION PACKAGE

Before your federal application is complete, you need to submit an application package. Most job announcements provide a link to the *Application Manager*, an online program that makes applying for federal positions quicker and more convenient. Using the Application Manager not only makes it easier to send all your application materials, but also allows you to track the progress of your application package through checklist and status displays.

Once you are directed to the Application Manager at https://applicationmanager.gov/, you'll be asked for your User ID and password; if you have not yet established an account, you'll need to follow the link to "Register Now." The program will provide instructions for uploading your resume and other supporting documents to complete your application package. Depending on the agency and position, you may be asked to submit a federal resume, answers to an assessment questionnaire, responses to KSAs, government forms, and/or other specific documents. If you've created a federal resume through the USAJOBS Resume Builder, the Application Manager will provide instructions for attaching this resume to your application package.

Although most federal agencies prefer that you submit your application package through the online Application Manager, it is also possible to apply by fax. In this case, you will need to read the job vacancy announcement carefully for a list of required documents. These documents might include specific government forms, your federal resume, a list of KSAs, and/or an assessment questionnaire. Your federal application package may then be faxed to 1-478-757-3144.

Even though most government agencies will still accept faxed application materials, the OPM does not recommend this option because the time agencies take to scan documents may vary. It may take 24 hours or longer for your application package to be processed; therefore, your materials may be received after the position's closing date. Faxing your application has another disadvantage—the agency is not able to track the status of your submission. If at all possible, it will be more efficient and you will enjoy greater peace of mind if you are able to apply online through the Application Manager.

FOLLOWING UP

The federal hiring process is notoriously slow, and waiting to hear back from an agency after you've applied for a position can seem like an eternity. According to the USAJOBS Web site, agencies generally take between 15 and 30 days following the position's closing date to contact applicants. Other federal sources place the time frame for hiring at 45 days, and for some positions requiring security clearance, up to several months. During this time, there is often little or no direct communication from the agency, aside from an e-mail confirmation of application materials following online submissions.

What can you do to ease the frustration involved with a long wait and remind the hiring manager of your continuing interest in the position? If you haven't heard anything from the agency one month after the position's closing date, it is perfectly fine to call and check on the status of your application. You can find the agency contact information listed on the job announcement, either in the lower right-hand corner of the announcement or under the "How to Apply" tab.

When you speak to the contact person, politely ask about the status of your application and whether candidates for the position have been chosen. You might also inquire whether the hiring manager has any questions or would like any further materials from you in order to evaluate your qualifications. Thank the contact person for taking your call and providing information, and then resign yourself to waiting patiently for the outcome. With a little luck and perseverance, your next communication with the hiring agency may be for that coveted job interview.

WHEN YOU'RE CALLED FOR AN INTERVIEW

You've searched for a federal position, submitted your application materials, waited patiently, and at long last, landed a federal job interview! Once you've been offered the chance to interview for the position, you'll probably feel both elated and apprehensive. Try not to worry too much—the federal interview process is not that much different from what you'd find in the private sector. Although a federal interview has some important differences from private sector interviews, in both cases, prospective employers use the interview process to determine the most qualified applicant who will be the best match for the company or agency.

A federal interview gives you the opportunity to impress the hiring agency by promoting your skills, achievements, education, and experience. Remember that the interview is also an opportunity for you to ask questions and display your interest in both the agency and the position. Whether this is your first professional interview or your first interview in a long while, now is the time to brush up on your interviewing skills. The following are some suggestions to help you prepare for a successful federal interview:

- **Do your homework.** Perhaps the best way to get ready for your interview is by thoroughly researching the agency beforehand, including its mission, key personnel, and current issues and concerns. In addition to spending time looking over the agency's Web site, you should conduct a general search online for recent news items relating to that agency. Not only will this knowledge help you answer the interviewer's questions intelligently, but also demonstrate your enthusiasm for the agency and the position.

- **Practice in advance.** Interviewing well is a skill that may be perfected through practice and repetition. Using the job announcement as a guide, try to anticipate some of the questions you'll be asked and develop thoughtful responses that include specific examples and details. There are sure to be questions pertaining to your skills, achievements, and experience and how these relate to the position for which you've applied. It can be very helpful to rehearse your answers to typical interview questions with a friend or family member beforehand.

- **Arrive early.** Over the past few years, government agencies have tightened their security measures significantly. Don't be surprised if you're asked to sign in with security, obtain a visitor's pass, walk through a metal detector, and/or be escorted to the interview by security personnel. Try to find out about these procedures in advance by asking the human resources representative who contacts you for the interview. At some agencies, you may need to arrive up to 45 minutes early.

- **Set a positive tone.** As soon as you arrive at the agency, your interview begins. Be sure to behave professionally and politely to everyone you meet, and remember to use a firm handshake, make eye contact, and smile. At the beginning of the interview, you'll probably be asked to introduce yourself, so be prepared to offer a brief summary of your career goals, skills, and interests.

- **Respond knowledgeably to questions.** Try to answer each of the interviewer's questions as clearly and concisely as possible with specific examples, data, evidence, or anecdotes. The hiring panel may ask about your motivation to perform public service because government jobs sometimes pay less than their private-sector counterparts, so be ready to explain your incentive for seeking civil service employment.

- **Ask insightful questions.** Here is your chance to discuss the job in more detail and display your knowledge of the hiring agency. Asking perceptive questions will not only impress the hiring committee, but also help you decide if the position is a good match for your talents and skills.

- **Close on a positive note.** It's perfectly fine to ask what you might expect next in the hiring process. For lower-level positions, one interview may suffice, but higher-level jobs may require multiple interviews, writing tests, and more extensive questionnaires. Remember to thank everyone who interviewed you and to express your continuing interest in the position. Sending a thank-you note to those with whom you interviewed is always appropriate and displays thoughtfulness and good manners.

THE JOB OFFER: NEGOTIATING YOUR SALARY

If you are offered a position with the federal government, congratulations—you've earned it! All your hard work and perseverance have paid off, and now you're faced with an important decision. Whether you are entering the workforce for the first time or contemplating a position or career change, deciding to accept (or decline) a job offer requires careful deliberation. Sometimes your decision will be based on your own personal preferences; other times, it will depend on more practical matters like location, working conditions, benefits, and perhaps most important, salary.

Most federal positions fall within a salary range, or pay grade, established by the OPM's General Schedule Pay Scale. Within each pay grade, there exists a series of steps. If you are offered a position at the GS-9 level, for example, you may be placed at the first of 10 steps that make up that pay grade. With the assistance of the agency's human resources personnel, the hiring manager determines the grade and step you'll be offered based on your educational attainments, work experience, skill set, and the agency's budget.

If you are interested in accepting a federal job offer but feel that the salary is too low, you may be able to negotiate a higher salary by requesting a step increase within the established pay grade for the position. You'll need to provide a solid rationale to the hiring manager that might be based on one of the following points:

- **Salaries for comparable work:** Before beginning any salary negotiation, make sure you are well informed about current salaries in your field for those with equivalent skills, experience, or degrees. You can research salaries by looking at Internet job sites (many feature online salary calculators) to determine what is fair compensation.

- **Specialized experience or critical skills:** If you have several years of related experience that will enable you to be highly productive from your first day forward, you may be able to justify starting at a higher step within your pay grade. Similarly, if you posses certain critical skills that are in high demand at a particular agency, you may have extra leverage for negotiating a higher wage.

- **Higher cost of living or relocation expenses:** You may be able to make the case for a better starting salary if accepting the position would entail substantial travel and moving costs, or if the new job is located in a more expensive area. If accepting the position will require a larger income to support yourself or your family, the agency may be willing to pay you a higher salary.

Before you decide to accept or decline a federal job offer based on salary alone, be sure to think about other factors that may enhance the starting salary, including tuition reimbursement and student loan repayment programs. You might also consider the federal government's excellent benefits package and prospects for career advancement, along with the personal growth and satisfaction possible from a career in public service.

SUMMING IT UP

- When a federal screening panel receives your application materials, the first document they will review is your cover letter.

- Although cover letters are not mandatory for all federal job applications, they are highly recommended. Cover letters give you the chance to provide a personal introduction to the hiring panel and explain, in brief, your interest in the position.

- The opening paragraph of your letter should convey your purpose in writing and compel the hiring manager to read further.

- Taking an exam for a civil service position is now much less common than submitting an application package for a job.

PART V

APPENDIXES

Sample Resumes

SAMPLE RESUME: CORRECTIONAL OFFICER

SAMANTHA GARCIA-HINES   CONTACT:
147 E. Ellsworth Street   Tel: (617) 555-5155
Newton, MA 02474   E-mail: S.Hines@ressample.com

CAREER OBJECTIVE

To obtain a position as Correctional Officer within the Department of
Corrections that utilizes my experience in correctional therapy with
inmates.

SUMMARY OF QUALIFICATIONS

- ➤ Excellent organizational skills.

- ➤ Excellent oral and written communication skills.

- ➤ Excellent problem-solving and decision-making skills.

- ➤ Facility with preparing and maintaining routine records and
  logs.

- ➤ Comprehensive knowledge of laws and ordinances regarding
  the confinement of inmates in the state of Massachusetts.

- ➤ Extensive familiarity with standard corrections facility
  practices and procedures.

- ➤ Demonstrated effectiveness in using interpersonal skills to
  interact with inmate population, prison staff, and community at
  large.

EMPLOYMENT EXPERIENCE

Correctional Officer, 2003–Present
Bay State Correctional Center (Norfolk, MA)

Responsibilities include:

- Oversee daily activities of inmates.

- Register new and transferred inmates; process intake paperwork.

- Communicate facility policies to inmates and enforce facility rules and regulations.

- Maintain security in prison system and assist in preventing disturbances, assaults, and escapes.

- Control disruptive behavior by giving verbal orders and using force as necessary.

- Supervise inmate recreational activity as well as personal visits.

- Prepare confidential reports describing prison incidents, disciplinary action, and special observations.

- Provide counseling to inmates as necessary.

Correctional Officer, 1999–2003
Philadelphia Industrial Correctional Center (Philadelphia, PA)

Responsibilities included:

- Oversaw inmate activity within assigned area of the jail.

- Kept records on inmate population and cell assignments.

- Completed activity logs and reports.

- Reviewed logs and report from previous shift.

- Monitored correctional facility area on an ongoing basis to maintain security.

- Oversaw work of prison trustees in kitchen.

- Collected outgoing mail from prisoners and distributed incoming mail.

EDUCATIONAL BACKGROUND

Teaching English as a Foreign Language (TEFL) Certificate, 2003
The Boston Language Institute (Boston, MA)

DOC Certification, 1999
Philadelphia Training Institute (Philadelphia, PA)

BA in Criminal Justice, 1998
Hope International University (Fullerton, CA)

<u>JOB-RELATED SKILLS</u>

➢ Proficient in the use of firearms and weapons of self-defense

➢ Demonstrated ability to solicit cooperation within correctional facility environment

➢ Skilled in disaster intervention with DOC employees and family members

➢ Bilingual and bicultural (Spanish and English); native Spanish speaker

References provided upon request.

SAMPLE RESUME: REGISTERED NURSE

Leslie Sheay, R.N.
2407 W. Chattanooga Drive
Milford, CA 96121
(530) 555-1111 | leslieshea@ressample.com

PROFESSIONAL
OBJECTIVE

Seeking a rewarding position as a registered nurse.

CAREER PROFILE

- Registered nurse with 12 years' professional experience

- Strong interpersonal communication skills; relate well with patients, family members, and medical staff

- In-depth knowledge of clinical medicine principles as applied to patient care

- Proven leadership ability in medical setting

- Crisis management experience as a trauma nurse in an emergency room setting

EMPLOYMENT
EXPERIENCE

Emergency Room Nurse, Lassen Community Hospital, 2004-2009 (Susanville, CA)

- Provide specialized care for emergency patients.
- Coordinate and delegate duties involved in patient care.
- Assess incoming patients and provide triage for case management.
- Deliver patient-focused care in collaboration with emergency health care team.
- Provide continuity of care, including discharge planning.
- Assist in communicating with patients' families and notifying family members regarding treatment progress.
- Maintain patient charts and files.

Surgical Nurse, Mattel Children's Hospital, 1997-2003
UCLA (Los Angeles, CA)

- Provided nursing care for surgery patients at UCLA Children's Hospital.
- Conducted medical assessments for new patients.
- Performed treatments as authorized by attending physicians.
- Maintained written documentation on treatment protocols and results.

Student Nurse, Mattel Children's Hospital, 1995-1996
UCLA (Los Angeles, CA)

- Under RN supervision, provided treatment and clinical documentation for pediatric surgery patients.
- Administered medications and provided general nursing care.
- Maintained patient charts and documented treatment protocols.

EDUCATION

Bachelor of Science in Nursing, 1996
UCLA (Los Angeles, CA)
Dean's List—GPA: 3.6

Master of Science in Nursing, 1999
UCLA (Los Angeles, CA)
Dean's List—GPA: 3.9

LICENSES &
CERTIFICATIONS

Registered Nurse, State of California
Registered Nurse, American Medical Association

PROFESSIONAL
AFFILIATIONS

Volunteer, Milford Hospice, 2008-Present
Member, California Nurses Association, 2006-Present
Member, Association of Perioperative Registered Nurses, 2005-Present

SAMPLE RESUME: ELECTRONICS ENGINEER

MARK SHEPHERD

7500 N. Princeton Place
New York, NY 10013
(718) 234-1234
markrshepherd@ressample.com

Objective: Seeking a position as electronics engineer.

Professional Summary: Efficient designer with 17 years of professional experience. Organized team player with excellent interpersonal communication skills. Expertise in product development, testing, and safety oversight. Strong record of on-time delivery to meet customer expectations.

Employment Experience: **Electronics Engineer**, 2000-Present
Shipton Multimedia, New York, NY

- Conceptualize and design remote control units for DVD systems.
- Conduct research on innovative design and product safety.
- Develop design plans and implement processes to improve product efficiency.
- Prepare safety and testing reports; modify product design based on testing results.

Results:
- ✓ Assisted company in obtaining 75% reduction in product returns due to design improvements over a 5-year period.
- ✓ Directly responsible for product innovations that resulted in $150,000 per year personnel savings (averaged over 3 years) due to reduced customer service inquiries.
- ✓ Consistently met or exceeded company production quotas.
- ✓ Maintained rejection rate 200% below acceptable company threshold.

Electronics Engineer, 1994-2000
Farrier Auto, Topeka, KS

- Developed preliminary designs for engineers in product laboratory.
- Tested features of new equipment and modify design as required.
- Oversaw operations of testing equipment for plant-wide applications.
- Trained technicians on efficient product use.

Engineering Intern, Product Development, 1993
Western Electronics, Midfield, TX

- Assisted in the design of testing equipment for new machinery.

Engineering Intern, Product Design, 1992
Western Electronics, Midfield, TX

- Assisted engineers with product design for heavy machinery.
- Assembled design models and performed product quality checks.
- Received employee-of-the-month award—first ever awarded to an intern.

Education: **AutoCAD Certification**, 2000
Manhattan Community College, New York, NY

Bachelor of Science Degree, Electronic Engineering, 1993
University of Houston, Houston, TX

Related Skills:
- Familiarity with PLC and PC control interfaces for industrial electronic equipment
- Proficiency with basic hand tools, soldering tools, and electronic assembly tools
- High-level skills in AutoCAD and SolidWorks

SAMPLE RESUME: ACCOUNTANT

PATRICIA R. EDWARDS, CPA
123 Main Street • Atlanta, Georgia • 30339
Home: (555) 555-1234 • Cell: (555) 555-1235
patred@ressample.com

Objective: Seek the position of Accountant

Summary:

- More than six years of professional accounting experience
- Auditor internship with Ernst and Young, Chicago, IL
- In-depth knowledge of municipal accounting practices and procedures
- Expertise includes preparing year-end audit reports, financial analysis reports, and annual and mid-year budgets

Summary of Qualifications

- Solid knowledge of fund and governmental accounting practices and principles.
- Strong knowledge of auditing practices and principles.
- Strong knowledge of public agency budgeting practices and principles.
- Sound knowledge of computer applications related to accounting work.
- Exceptional ability to reconcile accounts, records, reports, and journals.
- Strong ability to make accurate mathematical calculations and to identify and correct math errors made by others.
- Works efficiently with keen attention to detail.

Professional Experience

Office of the Controller, City of Atlanta, Atlanta, GA
2006–Present

Accountant II

- Prepare, audit, and analyze a variety of financial statements, including distributing monthly revenue and expenditure reports to departments.
- Prepare journal entries and reconcile general ledger and subsidiary accounts.

- Analyze and reconcile expenditure and revenue accounts.

- Calculate and prepare reimbursement billings and track receivables; reconcile monthly accounts receivable.

- Prepare and file annual financial statements for the City.

- Assist with the preparation of the annual and mid-year budgets.

Leon Gunther Builders, Inc., Athens, GA
2003–2006

Accountant

- Handled accounts payable and accounts receivable for construction company.

- Administered payroll twice monthly for 145 company employees.

- Managed benefits plan reporting on a timely basis for all company employees.

- Created mid-year, end-of-year, and project-specific budgets.

- Prepared company financial statements and tax returns.

- Prepared business financial records for audit.

Ernst and Young, Chicago, IL
2002

Accountant

- Assisted in yearly and quarterly audits of major clients.

- Developed final certification report for one annual audit.

- Developed Excel macros to assist in identifying accounting errors.

Education

Bachelor of Science Degree in Accounting
University of San Diego (1999)

Graduated *magna cum laude*
3.8 GPA

Professional Associations

Georgia Society of Certified Public Accountants
Member (2003–Present)

American Accounting Association
Member (2006–Present)

Licenses

Certified Public Accounting
Georgia, #11111

SAMPLE RESUME: HUMAN RESOURCES SPECIA

GERALDINE SPRAGUE
3155 E. 104th Street
Thornton, CO 80233
(303) 555-5445   grsprague@ressample.com

OBJECTIVE:
Seeking a position as Director of Human Resources in the health care industry.

PROFESSIONAL EXPERIENCE:

Human Resources Administrator, Bryant Health–Denver, CO (2000–Present)

- Responsible for hiring and new employee training for health care consulting firm
- Determine staffing requirements in consultation with executive management team
- Create and post job vacancy notices; collect and screen candidate applications
- Contact potential applicants to arrange in-person interviews
- Participate in new candidate selection process
- Serve as resource to executive management team regarding personnel policies and procedures
- Conduct negotiations with potential hires regarding job-offer packages
- Provide orientation to new employees
- Administer company benefits program

Human Resources Trainer, Hammond Consulting–Seattle, WA (1996–1999)

- Conducted new employee orientations
- Trained company employees on improved customer service techniques
- Assisted with continuing education and certification of company personnel
- Provided regular training updates to keep consultants current on changing health care industry regulations

Human Resources Intern, Hammond Consulting–Seattle, WA (1995)

- Assisted a 14-member consulting team in conducting candidate screenings for new personnel
- Provided research support for special HR projects

- Distributed payroll checks to company employees on a monthly basis
- Attended training on EEOC Compliance
- Managed HR filing system

ADDITIONAL EXPERIENCE:

Customer Service Assistant Manager, Finley's Department Store–Seattle, WA (1990–1994)

- Trained 7-person sales staff in customer service skills
- Implemented customer service improvements that resulted in 34% reduction in customer complaints over 2-year period
- Responsible for responding to customer inquiries and resolving customer service issues in a timely manner

EDUCATION:

Bachelor of Science in Human Resources; 1994
Seattle State University, Seattle, WA
Overall GPA: 3.3/4.0; Major GPA: 3.7/4.0

Master of Science in Human Resource Management; 1996
Seattle State University, Seattle, WA
Overall GPA: 3.5/4.0

AFFILIATIONS, HONORS, and SKILLS:

- Member, National Human Resources Association 2003–Present

- Member, Colorado Human Resource Association 1999–Present

- Member, Society for Human Resource Management 1995–Present

- Seattle State University Dean's List: 6 Semesters
-
- Recipient of Frank Hutchinson Scholarship, 1994–1996

- Advanced Microsoft Office Skills: Word, Excel, PowerPoint, Access, and Publisher

SAMPLE RESUME: PATENT EXAMINER

CHAD LOUIS ARTHUR
225 Worthington Court
Alexandria, VA 22313
(703) 555-1212
clarthur@ressample.com

Objective: Seek the position of Patent Examiner

Summary of Qualifications

- Five years' experience as assistant patent examiner

- Chemical engineer with three years of hands-on experience in wastewater treatment

- Strong technical research skills, with keen understanding of advanced chemistry principles

Professional Experience

Assistant Patent Examiner, Department of Commerce (August 2004–Present)
U.S. Patent and Trademark Office, Alexandria, VA

- Review applications to assess whether submissions meet established patent requirements

- Research applications to understand the scope and extent of the invention under review

- Research existing technology to verify authenticity and originality of claimant's invention

Chemical Engineer, Wastewater Treatment (July 2001–July 2004)
Woodcliff Treatment Plant, North Bergen, NJ

- Prepared water treatment plans for systems under facility oversight

- Assisted in developing design plans for new projects under construction

Education

Master's of Science in Chemical Engineering, 2004
Columbia University School of Engineering, New York, NY

Bachelor's of Science in Chemical Engineering, 2001
Columbia University School of Engineering, New York, NY

SAMPLE RESUME: LOGISTICS MANAGER

LORRAINE C. PRICE
146 Templeton Way, #203
Albuquerque, NM 87101
505-555-1234
lcprice@ressample.com

OBJECTIVE
Position of Logistics Manager in transportation industry

PROFILE
- Skilled manager with strong problem-solving and interpersonal skills
- Five years' experience in transportation industry working for major private shipper
- Familiarity with transportation management concerns for both shippers and carriers

PROFESSIONAL EXPERIENCE

Logistics Manager, 2004–2009
Newberg Shipping, Santa Fe, NM

- Coordinate inbound and outbound trucking operations between U.S. and Canada
- Manage truck fleet transporting biohazardous materials
- Oversee management of warehouse storing hazardous materials for transportation

Accomplishments:
- Increased company profitability by 8% annually through cost-reduction measures designed to lower direct shipping expenditures
- Implemented inventory control system that reduced overhead costs by $35,000 in two months
- Shortened transport time by 20% on key routes between U.S. and Canada

Distribution Manager, 2002–2004
Bristol Warehousing, Albuquerque, NM

- Oversaw distribution logistics for warehousing facility
- Managed operating budget for distribution center
- Coordinated implementation of new warehouse management software to automate receiving system

EDUCATION AND AFFILIATIONS

Bachelor of Science in Business Management, 2002
University of New Mexico, Albuquerque

Supply Chain Management Certification, 2003
Association for Operations Management

Council of Logistics Management
Member since 2003

SAMPLE RESUME: AIR TRAFFIC CONTROLLER

Trevor Bourne
922 Stratford Court
Oak Park, IL 16801
708-555-1234
t_bourne@ressample.com

OBJECTIVE

To obtain an air traffic controller position that enables me to utilize my expertise to help maintain a safe and efficient flow of air traffic within local airspace.

PROFILE

- Licensed air traffic controller
- Over six years of experience in air traffic management
- Certifications as private and commercial pilot
- Experienced non-destructive inspections technician

PROFESSIONAL EXPERIENCE

AIR TRAFFIC CONTROL TECIINICIAN
Chicago Executive Airport, Wheeling, IL (2005-Present)

- Work with control team to coordinate aircraft movement to ensure safety and expedient traffic flow
- Facilitate aircraft movement within vicinity by maintaining radio and telephone contact with nearby control centers
- Organize flight plans for planes entering assigned airspace
- Compile information about flights from flight plans, pilot reports, radar, and observations

ASSISTANT AIR TRAFFIC CONTROLLER
Lansing Municipal Airport, Lansing, IL (2003-2005)

- Assisted in ensuring spacing, separation, and sequencing of aircraft at city airport
- Coordinated with neighboring airports for safe air traffic flow
- Assisted in operations of airport radar and communications equipment

NON-DESTRUCTIVE INSPECTION TECHNICIAN
AAR CORP, Wood Dale, IL (2000-2002)

- Performed non-destructive inspections on aircraft to ensure airworthiness
- Inspection methods used: optical, penetrant, eddy current, radiographic, magnetic particle, X-ray, and ultrasonic
- Completed inspections in compliance with customer work instructions, and AAR procedures and policies
- Recorded inspection data and completed applicable paperwork to meet customer and AAR guidelines

EDUCATION, PROFESSIONAL TRAINING, AND CERTIFICATIONS

Undergraduate Education

- B.S. in Air Traffic Management, Arizona State University (2000)

Professional Training Courses

- Technical Training Instruction
- Non-Destructive Inspection Techniques
- Air Traffic Control Operation

Certifications

- Certified Professional Air Traffic Controller
- All-Star Safety Certification
- Licensed Commercial Pilot
- Licensed Private Pilot

SAMPLE RESUME: INFORMATION TECHNOLOGY SPECIALIST

THOMAS NOVAK
1475 E. OKLAHOMA AVENUE
WICHITA, KS 67202
(316) 555-1211
thomas_novak@ressample.com

Objective

To obtain a management-level Information Technology Specialist position.

Summary of Qualifications

- *Networking Experience:* Microsoft Exchange, IIS, SQL, VPN, Internet/Intranet, and Citrix server connections and applications

- *Hardware Expertise:* Citrix Server/Windows 2000/NT Server 4.0

- *Software Expertise:* Windows XP, NT, 2000, 9X, 3.1; Microsoft Office Suite, including Access, Word, Excel, PowerPoint, and Outlook

- Excellent written and verbal communication skills

- More than 10 years of supervisory leadership experience

Professional Experience

Senior Network Administrator, Public Works Department (1999–Present)
City of Wichita, Wichita, KS

- Supervise network programming staff
- Complete budgets for major programming projects and network enhancements
- Administer Citrix/2003 server AD and XP connections to the network LAN/WAN
- Resolve LAN, workstation, and application-related problems for department staff

Information Technology Specialist II, Department of Human Resources
(1995–1999)
City of Wichita, Wichita, KS

- Provided desktop support and technical assistance for user workstations
- Set up permissions and telecommunication error reporting
- Provided support for department systems main applications and hardware connectivity

Education

Computer Technology and Networking Administration
Wichita Technical Institute   Wichita, KS   1995

Bachelor of Science in Electrical Engineering
University of Kansas   Lawrence, KS   1992

Associate of Science in Information Technology
Brown Mackie College   Salina, KS   1990

Certifications

- Networking and Computer Security, 2001
- Unix and HTML/Java, 1998
- Novell Certification, 1995

SAMPLE RESUME: SUPERVISORY PROGRAM ANALYST

JAMES BEARDSON
2951 Beaufort Lane
Dallas, TX 75201
(972) 555-1111
jbeard@ressample.com

OBJECTIVE: Seeking Supervisory Program Analyst position with U.S. government agency in Dallas/Fort Worth area.

PROFILE: Experienced Supervisory Program Analyst with six years of professional experience. Specialization in audit management; three years of supervisor experience overseeing unit of 12 Program Analysts.

WORK EXPERIENCE: SUPERVISORY PROGRAM ANALYST, 2006–Present
U.S. Department of Labor
Office of the Inspector General (San Francisco, CA)

- Responsible for overseeing audit management
- Supervise 12 Program Analysts employed in unit
- Plan scope of major program audits, in collaboration with audit team
- Create audit guides and update/maintain as necessary to remain current with departmental policies
- Verify that audit reports comply with reporting standards; approve final reports

Accomplishments:
✓ Investigated errors in audit reports resulting in recovery of $50,000 of agency funds during 2007 review
✓ Successfully reduced staff attrition rate from 40% to 15% in a three-year period

PROGRAM ANALYST, 2003–2006
Sacramento County Office of Education
(Sacramento, CA)

- Developed budget estimates and operating plans
- Implemented and administered agency budget to ensure strategic goals were met

Accomplishments:
- ✓ Recognized for recommending budget cuts that saved over $150,000 in annual outlays while maintaining program operations at quality levels
- ✓ Received Departmental Excellence award for high productivity two consecutive months during 2006 budget review

PROPOSAL MANAGER, 1999–2003
Horchow Associates (Rancho Cordova, CA)

- Responsible for development of bids and RFPs for 6-person consulting firm
- Successfully proposed $2 million worth of contract projects during employment tenure
- Assisted senior management in improving proposal development process to more effectively respond to state and federal government Requests for Bid

EDUCATION:

Bachelor of Science in Business Administration, 2001
Sacramento State University (Sacramento, CA)
GPA: 3.6—Graduated Cum Laude

Associate's Degree in Business, 1997
Sacramento City College (Sacramento, CA)

AFFILIATIONS:

American Society for Public Administration
Member, 2001–Present

Important Contacts and Web Sites

MAJOR FEDERAL AGENCIES

Central Intelligence Agency (CIA)
Office of Public Affairs
Washington, D.C. 20505
301-504-7925
www.cia.gov

Consumer Product Safety Commission
4330 East-West Highway
Bethesda, MD 20814
301-504-7925
www.cpsc.gov

Environmental Protection Agency (EPA)
Ariel Rios Building
1200 Pennsylvania Avenue, NW
Washington, D.C. 20460
202-272-0167
www.epa.gov

Federal Bureau of Investigation (FBI)
935 Pennsylvania Avenue, NW
Washington, D.C. 20535
202-324-3000
www.fbi.gov

Federal Communications Commission (FCC)
445 12th Street, SW
Washington, D.C. 20554
202-418-0101
www.fcc.gov

Federal Deposit Insurance Corporation (FDIC)
500 C Street, SW
Washington, D.C. 20472
877-ASKFDIC
www.fdic.gov

Federal Highway Administration
1200 New Jersey Avenue, SE
Washington, D.C. 20590
202-366-0530
www.fhwa.dot.gov

Federal Trade Commission (FTC)
600 Pennsylvania Avenue, NW
Washington, D.C. 20580
202-326-2021
www.ftc.go

Food & Drug Administration (FDA)
10903 New Hampshire Avenue
Silver Spring, MD 20993-0002
888-463-6332
www.fda.gov

General Services Administration (GSA)
18th Street & F Street, NW
Washington, D.C. 20405
202-501-1805
www.gsa.gov

Library of Congress
1st Street and Independence, SE
Washington, D.C. 20540
202-707-5000
www.lcweb.loc.gov

National Aeronautics & Space Administration (NASA)
300 E. Street, SW
Washington, D.C. 20546
202-358-0000
www.nasa.gov

National Science Foundation
4201 Wilson Boulevard
Arlington, VA 22230
703-292-5111
www.nsf.gov

Securities and Exchange Commission (SEC)
450 5th Street, NW
Washington, D.C. 20549
202-942-8088
www.sec.gov

Social Security Administration
6401 Security Boulevard
Baltimore, MD 21235
800-772-1213
www.ssa.gov

U.S. Department of Homeland Security
245 Murray Lane, SW
Washington, D.C. 20528
www.dhs.gov

The Homeland Security Act of 2002 mobilized and organized our nation to protect the country from terrorist attacks. To this end, one primary reason for the establishment of the Department of Homeland Security (DHS) was to provide the unifying core for the vast national network of organizations and institutions involved in efforts to secure our nation. The agencies designated as part of the Department of Homeland Security are housed in one of four major directorates: Border and Transportation Security, Emergency Preparedness and Response, Science and Technology, and Information Analysis and Infrastructure Protection. The Secret Service and the Coast Guard are also located within the Department of Homeland Security.

U.S. Coast Guard
2100 Second Street, SW
Washington, D.C. 20593
877-NOW-USCG
http://www.uscg.mil/default.asp

U.S. Secret Service
Personnel Division
245 Murray Drive
Building 410
Washington, D.C. 20223
202-406-5800
www.secretservice.gov

Border and Transportation Safety

Animal and Plant Health Inspection Service
Office of the Director
Washington, D.C. 20535
202-720-2511
www.aphis.usda.gov

Customs and Border Protection
1300 Pennsylvania Avenue, NW
Washington, D.C. 20229
202-344-1250
www.customs.gov

Federal Law Enforcement Training Center
FLETC Washington Office
555 Eleventh Street, NW
Suite 400
Washington, D.C. 20004
912-267-2289
www.fletc.gov

Federal Protective Service
500 12th Street, SW
Washington, D.C. 20536
202-690-9632
www.ice.gov

Immigration and Naturalization Service
Washington District Office
111 Massachusetts Avenue, N.W.
Washington, D.C. 20529-2260
202-307-1557
http://uscis.gov

Office for Domestic Preparedness
810 Seventh Street, NW
Washington, D.C. 20531
800-368-6498
www.ojp.usdoj.gov/odp

Transportation Security Administration
601 South 12th Street
Arlington, VA 22202-4220
800-887-1895
www.tsa.gov

Emergency Preparedness and Response

Domestic Emergency Support Teams
www.dhs.gov

Federal Emergency Management Agency (FEMA)
500 C Street, SW
Washington, D.C. 20472
202-566-1600
www.fema.gov

Health Resources & Services Administration
5600 Fishers Lane
Rockville, MD 20857
301-443-3376
www.hrsa.gov

National Domestic Preparedness Office
810 Seventh Street, NW
Washington, D.C. 20531
800-368-6498
www.ojp.usdoj.gov/odp

Nuclear Incident Response Team
www.dhs.gov

Science and Technology

CBRN Countermeasures Programs
www.dhs.gov

Environmental Measurements Laboratory (EML)
www.dhs.gov

National BW Defense Analysis Center
www.dhs.gov

Plum Island Animal Disease Center
Jamie L. Whitten Building
1400 Independence Avenue, SW
Washington D.C., 20250
301-504-1638
www.ars.usda.gov/plum

Information Analysis and Infrastructure Protection

Energy Security and Assurance Program
U.S. Department of Energy
1000 Independence Avenue, SW
Washington, D.C. 20585
202-287-1808
www.ea.doe.gov

Federal Computer Incident Response Center
245 Murray Lane, SW, Bldg. 410
Washington, D.C. 20598
www.us-cert.gov/federal

National Communications System
703-607-6211
www.ncs.gov

National Infrastructure Protection Center
Information Analysis Infrastructure Protection
10302 Eaton Place, Suite 100
Fairfax, VA 22030-2215
800-368-3757
www.calea.org

FEDERAL EMPLOYMENT WEB SITES FOR JOB LISTINGS

- Career City (www.careercity.com): A guide to federal and local government employment.

- Federal Job Search (www.federaljobsearch.com): Listings for 40,000 federal jobs in the United States.

- FedWorld (www.fedworld.gov): Provides searchable abstracts of federal government jobs.

- HRS Federal Job Search (www.hrsjobs.com): A subscription job search and e-mail delivery service.

- The Internet Job Source (www.statejobs.com): The federal jobs section of this site links users to job listings at a variety of federal agencies and also to online newspapers listing federal job opportunities.

- Public Services Employees Network (www.pse-net.com): A guide to government employment, including job listings.

- U.S. Postal Service (www.usps.gov/employment): Listing of all available positions with the U.S. Postal Service.

- USAJOBS (www.usajobs.opm.gov): The official site for federal employment listings from the U.S. Office of Personnel Management.

Federal Job Applications and Other Forms

- Electronic forms (www.opm.gov/forms): All applications and forms relating to federal employment from the Office of Personnel Management.

- Frequently requested forms (www.usajobs.gov/forms.asp): Provides links to PDF files of frequently requested forms and forms found on the Office of Personnel Management Web site.

Tips for Taking Exams and the Jobs That Require Them

EXAMINATIONS FOR FEDERAL CIVIL SERVICE JOBS

You made it through filling out the application, the first step of the screening process, and the second step. Is it time to polish your shoes for the interview? Not yet. Many of the positions also require the results of competitive testing. The test must be passed, and test grades also become part of the factors that determine how you compare to other competitors.

There are generally two types of competitive tests: *assembled exams* and *unassembled exams*. An assembled exam means that all the applicants assemble at the same time to take the test—whether it's a written test or a physical test of performance. An unassembled exam actually means there's no exam at all. The applicant is judged on the education and experience presented in the application; proof of achievement is usually required (diplomas, training certificates, etc.).

A written test is usually a paper-and-pen, multiple-choice format. The format of the performance test depends on the physical tasks that need to be measured. You'll receive a notice in the mail telling you of the test date and where it is to be held. If the test or the test location presents a problem to applicants with disabilities, they should call personnel at once to make other arrangements. The section titled "Federal Occupations That Require Examinations" in this appendix contains a listing of more than 220 exam-dependent occupations and their grades and the type of exam required for each position. The results of the test also come in the mail, giving you your test score (70 is passing) and your place on the list of eligibles when ranked with the other applicants.

Remember that not every federal job applicant has to take a competitive exam. Some positions are by appointment rather than testing. And some groups of people *may* be eligible for appointment; in other words, they *may* be exempted from the requirement. These groups include the following:

- **Disabled veterans** who are 30 percent or more disabled
- **Persons with severe disabilities** who have either physical or mental impairments
- **Peace Corps or VISTA volunteers** who have left the service within the past year
- **Foreign Service employee*** who has been, whether presently or formerly, appointed under the Foreign Service Act of 1946
- **Overseas Federal employees or family member*** who seek appointments within three years of their return to the United States

appendix c

- **National Guard technician*** who has been involuntarily separated from service within the last year

*There may be restrictions on certain members of Foreign Service employees, overseas federal employees or family members, or National Guard technicians. See the hiring agency for details.

Preparing for an Exam

Many factors enter into a civil service test score. The most important factor should be the ability to answer the questions, which in turn indicates the ability to learn and perform the duties of the job. Assuming that you have this ability, knowing what to expect on the exam and familiarity with techniques of effective test taking should give you the confidence you need to do your best on the civil service exam.

There is no quick substitute for long-term study and development of your skills and abilities to prepare you for doing well on tests. However, there are some steps you can take to help you do the very best that you are prepared to do. Some of these steps are done before the test, and some are followed when you are taking the test. Knowing these steps is often called being "test wise." Following these steps may help you feel more confident as you take the actual test.

"Test wiseness" is a general term that simply means being familiar with some good procedures to follow when getting ready for and taking a test. The procedures fall into four major areas:

1. being informed
2. avoiding careless errors
3. managing your time
4. educated guessing

Be Informed

Do not make the civil service exam harder than it has to be by not preparing yourself. You are taking a very important step in preparation by reading this book and taking the sample tests that are included. This will help you to become familiar with the tests and the kinds of questions you will have to answer.

As you use this book, read the sample questions and directions for taking the test carefully. Then, when you take the sample tests, time yourself because you will be timed for the real exam.

As you are working on the sample questions, do not look at the correct answers before you try to answer them on your own. This can fool you into thinking you understand a question when you really do not. Try it on your own first, and then compare your answer with the one given. Remember, in a sample test, you are your own grader; you gain nothing by pretending to understand something you really don't.

On the examination day assigned to you, allow the civil service test itself to be the main attraction of the day. Do not squeeze it in between other activities. Be sure to bring your admission card, identification, and pencils, as instructed. Prepare these the night before to avoid being flustered by a last-minute search. Arrive rested, relaxed, and on time. In fact, plan to arrive a little bit early. Allow plenty of time for traffic tie-ups or other complications that might upset you and interfere with your test performance.

In the test room, the examiner will distribute forms for you to fill out. The examiner will give you the test instructions and tell you how to fill in the grids on the forms. Time limits and timing signals will be explained. If you do not understand any of the examiner's instructions, ASK QUESTIONS. It would be ridiculous to score less than your best because of poor communication and a misunderstanding.

At the examination, you must follow instructions exactly. Fill in the grids on the forms carefully and accurately. Mis-gridding may lead to loss of veteran's credits to which you may be entitled or misaddressing of your test results. Do not begin until you are told to begin. Stop as soon as the examiner tells you to stop. Do not turn pages until you are told to do so. Do not go back to parts you have already completed. Any infraction of the rules is considered cheating. If you cheat, your civil service test will not be scored, and you will not be eligible for appointment.

The answer sheet for most multiple-choice exams is machine scored. You cannot give any explanations to the machine, so you must fill out the answer sheet clearly and correctly.

How to Mark Your Answer Sheet

1. Blacken your answer space firmly and completely. ⬤ is the only correct way to mark the answer sheet. ◑, ✖, ◑, and ◿ are all unacceptable. The machine might not read them at all.

2. Mark only one answer for each question; otherwise, the answer is considered wrong.

3. If you change your mind, you must erase your mark. Attempting to cross out an incorrect answer like this ✖ will not work. You must erase any incorrect answer completely. An incomplete erasure might be read as a second answer.

4. All of your answering should be in the form of blackened spaces. The machine cannot read English. Do not write any notes in the margins. MOST IMPORTANT: Answer each question in the right place. Question 1 must be answered in space 1; question 2 in space 2. If you should skip an answer space and mark a series of answers in the wrong places, you must erase all those answers and do the questions over, marking your answers in the proper places. You cannot afford to use the limited time in this way. Therefore, as you answer each question, look at its number and check that you are marking your answer in the space with the same number.

5. For the typing tests, type steadily and carefully. Do not rush because that is when errors occur. Keep in mind that each error subtracts 1 wpm from your final score.

Avoid Careless Errors

Don't reduce your score by making careless mistakes. Always read the instructions for each test section carefully, even when you think you already know what the directions are. It is why we stress throughout this book that it is important to understand the directions for these different question types before you go into the actual exam. It will not only reduce errors, but will also save you time—time you will need for the questions.

What if you don't understand the directions? You risk getting the answers wrong for a whole test section. As an example, vocabulary questions can sometimes test synonyms (words that have similar meanings) and sometimes test antonyms (words with opposite meanings). You can easily see how a mistake in understanding in this case could make a whole set of answers incorrect.

If you have time, reread any complicated instructions after you do the first few questions to check that you really do understand them. Of course, if you are allowed, ask the examiner to clarify anything you find confusing.

Other careless mistakes affect only the response to particular questions. This often happens with arithmetic questions, but can happen with other questions as well. This type of error, called a "response error," usually stems from a momentary lapse of concentration.

Example

The question states, "The capital of Massachusetts is …." The answer is (D) Boston, and you mark (B) because "B" is the first letter of the word "Boston."

Example

The question states, "8 − 5 = …." The answer is (A) 3, but you mark (C) thinking "third letter."

A common error in reading comprehension questions is bringing your own information into the subject. For example, you may encounter a passage that discusses a subject you know something about. While this can make the passage easier to read, it can also tempt you to rely on your own knowledge about the subject. You must rely on information within the passage for your answers—in fact, sometimes the "wrong answer" for the questions is based on true information about the subject not given in the passage. Since the test-makers are testing your reading ability, rather than your general knowledge of the subject, an answer based on information not contained in the passage is considered incorrect.

Manage Your Time

Before you begin, take a moment to plan your progress through the test. Although you are usually not expected to finish all of the questions given on a test, you should at least get an idea of how much time you should spend on each question in order to answer them all. For example, if there are 60 questions to answer and you have 30 minutes, you will have about one-half minute to spend on each question.

Keep track of the time on your watch or the room clock, but do not fixate on the time remaining. Your task is to answer questions. Do not spend too much time on any one question. If you find yourself stuck, do not take the puzzler as a personal challenge. Guess and mark the question in the question booklet, or skip the question entirely. If you skip a question, make sure you mark the item as a skip and skip the answer space on the answer sheet. If there is time at the end of the exam or section, you can return to questions you have skipped and attempt to answer them.

Multiple-Choice Questions

Almost all of the tests given on civil service exams are multiple-choice format. This means that you normally have four or five answer choices. However, the questions should not be overwhelming. There is a basic technique to answering this type of question. Once you have understood this technique, it will make your test taking far less stressful.

First, there should only be one correct answer. Since these tests have been given repeatedly, and the test-developers have a sense of which questions work and which questions do not work, it will be rare that your choices will be ambiguous. They may be complex and somewhat confusing, but there will still be only one right answer.

The first step is to look at the question, without looking at the answer choices. Now select the correct answer. That may sound somewhat simplistic, but it is usually the case that your first choice is the correct one. If you go back and change it, or redo it repeatedly, you are more likely to end up with the wrong answer. Thus, follow your instinct. Once you have come up with the answer, look at the answer choices. If your answer is one of the choices, you are probably correct. The method is not perfect, but you have a strong possibility of selecting the correct answer.

With math questions, you should first solve the problem. If your answer is among the choices, you are probably correct. Do not ignore details like the proper function signs (adding, subtracting, multiplying, and dividing), negative and positive numbers, and so on.

What if you don't know the correct answer? You should use the "process of elimination." The process of elimination is a time-honored technique for test-takers. First, take a second to eliminate those answers that are obviously wrong, then quickly consider and guess from the remaining choices. A smaller number of possibilities increases your odds of making an accurate guess. Once you have decided to make a guess, be it an educated guess or a wild stab, do it right away and move on; do not keep thinking about it and wasting time. You should always mark the test questions at which you guess so that you can return later.

Educated Guessing

You may be wondering whether it is wise to guess when you are not sure of an answer (even if you have reduced the odds to 50 percent) or whether it is better to skip the question when you are uncertain. The wisdom of guessing depends on the scoring method for the particular examination. If the scoring is *rights only*, that is, one point for each correct answer and no subtraction for wrong answers, then you should guess. Read the question and all of the answer choices carefully. Eliminate those answer choices that you are certain are wrong. Then guess from among the remaining choices. You cannot gain a point if you leave the answer space blank; however, you may gain a point with an educated guess or even with a lucky guess. In fact, it is foolish to leave any spaces blank on a test that counts "rights only." If it appears that you are about to run out of time before completing such an exam, mark all the remaining blanks with the same letter. According to the law of averages, you should get some portion of those questions right.

If the scoring method is **rights minus wrongs**, such as the address checking test found on Postal Clerk Exam 470, DO NOT GUESS. A wrong answer counts heavily against you. On this type of test, do not rush to fill answer spaces randomly at the end. Work as quickly as possible while concentrating on accuracy. Keep working carefully until time expires. Then stop and leave the remaining answer spaces blank.

For those questions that are scored by *subtracting a fraction of a point for each wrong answer*, the decision as to whether or not to guess is really up to you. A correct answer gives you one point. A skipped space gives you nothing at all, but it costs you nothing except the chance of getting the answer right. A wrong answer costs you 1/4 point. If you are uncomfortable with guessing, you may skip a question, but you must then remember to skip its answer space as well. The risk of losing your place if you skip questions is so great that we advise you to guess even if you are not sure of the answer. Our suggestion is that you answer every question in order, even if you have to guess. It is better to lose a few 1/4 points for wrong guesses than to lose valuable seconds figuring where you started marking answers in the wrong place, erasing, and re-marking answers. On the other hand, do not mark random answers at the end. Work steadily until time is up.

One of the questions you should ask in the testing room is what scoring method will be used on your particular exam. You can then guide your guessing procedure accordingly.

HOW CIVIL SERVICE EXAMS ARE SCORED

If your exam is a short-answer exam, such as those often used by companies in the private sector, your answers will be scored by a personnel officer trained in grading test questions. If you blackened spaces on the separate answer sheet accompanying a multiple-choice exam, your answer sheet will be machine scanned or will be hand scored using a punched card stencil. Then a raw score will be calculated using the scoring formula that applies to that test or test portion—rights only, rights minus wrongs, or rights minus a fraction of wrongs. Raw scores on test parts are then added together for a total raw score.

A raw score is neither a final score nor the score that finds its way onto an eligibility list. The civil service testing authority, Postal Service, or other testing body converts raw scores to a scaled score according to an unpublicized formula of its own. The scaling formula allows for slight differences in difficulty of questions from one form of the exam to another and allows for equating the scores of all candidates. The entire process of conversion from raw to scaled score is confidential. The score you receive is not your number correct, raw score, or a percentage, despite being on a scale of 1 to 100. It is a scaled score. If you are entitled to veterans' service points, these are added to your passing scaled score to boost your rank on the eligibility list. Veterans' points are added only to passing scores. A failing score cannot be brought to passing level by adding veterans' points. The score earned, plus any veterans' service points, is the score that will be on the eligibility list rankings. Highest scores go to the top of the list.

TEST-TAKING TIPS

1. **Get to the test center early.** Make sure you give yourself plenty of extra time to get there, park your car, if necessary, and even grab a cup of coffee before the test.

2. **Listen to the test monitors** and follow their instructions carefully.

3. **Read every word of the instructions.** Read every word of every question.

4. **Mark your answers by completely darkening the answer space** of your choice. Do not use the test paper to work out your answers.

5. **Mark only ONE answer for each question,** even if you think that more than one answer is correct. You must choose only one. If you mark more than one answer, the scoring machine will consider you wrong.

6. **If you change your mind, erase completely.** Leave no doubt as to which answer you mean.

7. **Do not forget to mark the answer on the answer sheet** if you are using scratch paper or the margins of your test booklet. Only the answer sheet is scored.

8. **Check often to be sure that the question number matches the answer space,** that you have not skipped a space by mistake.

9. **Take educated guesses only.**

10. **Stay alert.** Be careful not to mark a wrong answer just because you were not concentrating.

11. **Do not panic.** If you cannot finish any part before time is up, do not worry. If you are accurate, you can do well even without finishing. It is even possible to earn a scaled score of 100 without entirely finishing an exam part if you are very accurate. At any rate, do not let your performance on any one part affect your performance on any other part.

12. **Check and recheck, time permitting.** If you finish any part before time is up, use the remaining time to check that each question is answered in the right space and that there is only one answer for each question. Return to the difficult questions and rethink them.

FEDERAL OCCUPATIONS THAT REQUIRE EXAMINATIONS

Although the great percentage of federal civil service jobs no longer require testing to qualify, some specialized occupations still require an exam or assessment. These tests usually help to determine a candidate's physical and mental abilities and his or her skills required for the position. Qualifying tests are still required for jobs in law enforcement, air traffic control, the Foreign Service, the U.S. Post Office, and other government areas.

The following table shows occupational series for which the OPM currently requires written and/or performance tests. This list is updated periodically to reflect changes in test coverages, so be sure to check the OPM Web site for the most current list. Test requirements are for competitive appointments only, unless otherwise specified.

Note that references to the ACWA, the Administrative Careers With America program, pertain only to positions that meet the ACWA criteria. In 2009, the OPM streamlined the assessments under the ACWA Program, which offers entry-level opportunities at the GS-5 and 7 levels, so that job applicants can complete a self-assessment in 10–15 minutes that can be used to apply for many other jobs.

FEDERAL OCCUPATIONS/POSITIONS FOR WHICH WRITTEN AND/OR PERFORMANCE TESTS ARE REQUIRED

Series, Title/Position(s)	Grade(s)	Requirement
011 Bond Sales Promotion	5/7	ACWA
018 Safety & Occupational Health Management	5/7	ACWA
020 Community Planning	5/7	ACWA
023 Outdoor Recreation Planning	5/7	ACWA
025 Park Ranger	5/7	ACWA
028 Environmental Protection Specialist	5/7	ACWA
029 Environmental Protection Assistant	2/3/4	written test
072 Fingerprint Identification	2/3/4	written test
080 Security Administration	5/7	ACWA
082 United States Marshal	5/7	written test
083 Police	2	written test
083 Park Police	5	written test
083a Police (Secret Service)	4/5	written test
085 Security Guard	2	written test
086 Security Clerical & Assistance	2/3/4	written test
101 Social Science	5/7	ACWA
105 Social Insurance Administration	5/7	ACWA
106 Unemployment Insurance	5/7	ACWA
107 Health Insurance Administration	5/7	ACWA
110 Economist	5/7	ACWA
130 Foreign Affairs	5/7	ACWA

131 International Relations	5/7	ACWA
132 Intelligence	5/7	ACWA
134 Intelligence Aide & Clerk	2/3/4	written test
140 Workforce Research and Analysis	5/7	ACWA
142 Workforce Development	5/7	ACWA
150 Geography	5/7	ACWA
170 History	5/7	ACWA
180 Psychology	5/7	ACWA
184 Sociology	5/7	ACWA
186 Social Services Aide & Assistant	2/3	written test
187 Social Services	5/7	ACWA
190 General Anthropology	5/7	ACWA
193 Archeology	5/7	ACWA
201 Human Resources Management	5/7	ACWA
244 Labor Manaagement Relations Examining	5/7	ACWA
301 Misc Administration & Program	5/7	ACWA
302 Messenger	2/3/4	written test
303 Misc Clerk & Assistant	2/3/4	written test
304 Information Receptionist	2/3/4	written test
305 Mail & File	2/3/4	written test
309 Correspondence Clerk	2/3/4	written test
312 Clerk-Stenographer	3/4/5	written and performance tests
312 Reporting Stenographer	5/6	performance test only; mandatory for competitive appointment and in-service placement
312 Shorthand Reporter	6/7/8/9	performance test only; mandatory for competitive appt. and in-service placement
318 Secretary	3/4	written test
319 Closed Microphone Reporting	6/7/8/9	performance test only; mandatory for competitive appointment and in-service placement

322 Clerk-Typist	2/3/4	written and perfor-mance tests
326 Office Automation Clerical & Assistance	2/3/4	written and perfor-mance tests
332 Computer Operation	2/3/4	written test
334 Computer Specialist	5/7	ACWA for Alternative B only
335 Computer Clerk & Assistant	2/3/4	written test
341 Administrative Officer	5/7	ACWA
343 Management and Program Analysis	5/7	ACWA
344 Management and Program Clerical & Assistance	2/3/4	written test
346 Logistics Management	5/7	ACWA
350 Equipment Operator	2/3/4	written test
351 Printing Clerical	2/3/4	written test
356 Data Transcriber	2/3/4	written and perfor-mance tests
357 Coding	2/3/4	written test
359 Electric Accounting Machine Operation	2/3/4	written test
382 Telephone Operating	2/3/4	written test
390 Telecommunications Processing	2/3/4	written test
391 Telecommunications	5/7	ACWA
392 General Telecommunications	2/3/4	written test
394 Communications Clerical	2/3/4	written test
421 Plant Protection Technician	2/3	written test
455 Range Technician	2/3	written test
458 Soil Conservation Technician	2/3	written test
459 Irrigation System Operation	2/3	written test
462 Forestry Technician	2/3	written test
501 Financial Administration & Program	5/7	ACWA
503 Financial Clerical & Assistance	2/3/4	written test
525 Accounting Technician	2/3/4	written test
526 Tax Specialist	5/7	ACWA
530 Cash Processing	2/3/4	written test
540 Voucher Examining	2/3/4	written test
544 Civilian Pay	2/3/4	written test
545 Military Pay	2/3/4	written test
560 Budget Analysis	5/7	ACWA
561 Budget Clerical & Assistance	2/3/4	written test
570 Financial Institution Examining	5/7	ACWA, except for FDIC positions

592 Tax Examining	2/3/4	written test
593 Insurance Accounts	2/3/4	written test
636 Rehabilitation Therapy Assistant	2/3	written test
640 Health Aide & Technician	2/3	written test
642 Nuclear Medicine Technician	2/3	written test
645 Medical Technician	2/3	written test
646 Pathology Technician	2/3	written test
647 Diagnostic Radiologic Technologist	2/3	written test
648 Therapeutic Radiologic Technologist	2/3	written test
649 Medical Instrument Technician	2/3	written test
651 Respiratory Therapist	2/3	written test
661 Pharmacy Technician	2/3	written test
667 Orthotist & Prosthetist	3	written test
673 Hospital Housekeeping Management	5/7	ACWA
675 Medical Records Technician	2/3/4	written test
679 Medical Clerk	2/3/4	written test
683 Dental Lab Aide & Technician	2/3	written test
685 Public Health Program Specialist	5/7	ACWA
704 Animal Health Technician	2/3	written test
802 Engineering Technician	2/3	written test
809 Construction Control	2/3	written test
817 Surveying Technician	2/3	written test
856 Electronics Technician	2/3	written test
895 Industrial Engineering Technician	2/3	written test
901 General Legal and Kindred Administration	5/7	ACWA
950 Paralegal Specialist	5/7	ACWA
958 Pension Law Specialist	5/7	ACWA
962 Contact Representative	3/4	written test
963 Legal Instruments Examining	2/3/4	written test
965 Land Law Examining	5/7	ACWA
967 Passport & Visa Examining	5/7	ACWA
986 Legal Clerk & Technician	2/3/4	written test
987 Tax Law Specialist	5/7	ACWA
990 General Claims Examining (One-grade interval)	4	written test
991 Workers' Comp Claims Examining	5/7	ACWA
993 Railroad Retirement Claims Examining	5/7	ACWA
994 Unemployment Comp Claims Examining	5/7	ACWA
996 Veterans Claims Examining	5/7	ACWA

998 Claims Clerical	2/3/4	written test
1001 General Arts and Information	5/7	ACWA
1015 Museum Curator	5/7	ACWA
1016 Museum Specialist & Technician	2/3	written test
1035 Public Affairs	5/7	ACWA
1046 Language Clerical	2/3/4	written test
1082 Writing & Editing	5/7	ACWA
1083 Technical Writing & Editing	5/7	ACWA
1087 Editorial Assistance	2/3/4	written test
1101 General Business and Industry	5/7	ACWA
1102 Contracting	5/7	ACWA
1103 Industrial Property Management	5/7	ACWA
1104 Property Disposal	5/7	ACWA
1105 Purchasing	2/3/4	written test
1106 Procurement Clerical & Technician	2/3/4	written test
1107 Property Disposal Clerical & Technician	2/3/4	written test
1130 Public Utilities Specialist	5/7	ACWA
1140 Trade Specialist	5/7	ACWA
1140 International Trade Specialist	5/7	written test
1145 Agricultural Program Specialist	5/7	ACWA
1146 Agricultural Marketing	5/7	ACWA
1146 Grain Marketing Specialist	5/7	ACWA
1147 Agricultural Market Reporting	5/7	ACWA
1150 Industrial Specialist	5/7	ACWA
1152 Production Control	2/3/4	written test
1160 Financial Analysis	5/7	ACWA
1163 Insurance Examining	5/7	ACWA
1165 Loan Specialist	5/7	ACWA
1169 Internal Revenue Officer	5/7	ACWA
1170 Realty	5/7	ACWA
1171 Appraising & Assessing	5/7	ACWA
1173 Housing Management	5/7	ACWA
1176 Building Management	5/7	ACWA
1316 Hydrologic Technician	2/3	written test
1341 Meteorological Technician	2/3	written test
1371 Cartographic Technician	2/3	written test
1374 Geodetic Technician	2/3	written test
1411 Library Technician	2/3/4	written test
1412 Technical Information Services	5/7	ACWA
1420 Archivist	5/7	ACWA

1421 Archives Specialist	5/7	ACWA (Two-grade interval only)
1521 Mathematics Technician	2/3	written test
1531 Statistical Assistant	2/3/4	written test
1654 Printing Management Specialist	5/7	ACWA
1701 General Education & Training	5/7	ACWA
1702 Education & Training Technician	2/3	written test
1715 Vocational Rehabilitation	5/7	ACWA
1720 Education Program	5/7	ACWA
1801 Civil Aviation Security Specialist	5/7	ACWA
1801 Center Adjudications Officer	5/7	ACWA
1801 District Adjudications Officer	5/7	ACWA
1810 General Investigation	5/7	ACWA
1811 Criminal Investigation	5/7	ACWA
1811 Criminal Investigator—Treasury Enforcement Agent	5/7	ACWA
1849 Wage & Hour Investigation (formerly 249 Wage & Hour Compliance)	5/7	ACWA
1863 Food Inspection	5/7	biographical data assessment
1889 Import Specialist	5/7	ACWA
1895 Customs & Border Protection Officer	5/7	written test
1896 Border Patrol Agent	5/7	written test & language proficiency
1910 Quality Assurance	5/7	ACWA
2001 General Supply	5/7	ACWA
2003 Supply Program Management	5/7	ACWA
2005 Supply Clerical & Technician	2/3/4	written test
2010 Inventory Management	5/7	ACWA
2030 Distribution Facilities & Storage Management	5/7	ACWA
2032 Packaging	5/7	ACWA
2050 Supply Cataloging	5/7	ACWA
2091 Sales Store Clerical	2/3/4	written test
2101 Transportation Specialist	5/7	ACWA
2101 Airway Transportation System Specialist Department of Transportation, FAA	5/7	written test
2102 Transportation Clerk & Assistant	2/3/4	written test
2110 Transportation Industry Analysis	5/7	ACWA
2125 Highway Safety	5/7	ACWA
2130 Traffic Management	5/7	ACWA

2131 Freight Rate	2/3/4	written test
2135 Transportation Loss & Damage Claims Examining	2/3/4	written test
2150 Transportation Operations	5/7	ACWA
2151 Dispatching	2/3/4	written test
2152 Air Traffic Control	5/7	written test for 5/7—mandatory for competitive appointment and in-service placement; optional above 7
2210 Information Technology Management (Alternative B only)	5/7	ACWA

Selected Federal Civil Service Jobs

Here you'll find descriptions of different kinds of jobs available in the federal government, with typical duties, salary levels, and requirements of those positions. Use this information to discover the range of available positions and determine those in which you might be interested.

In addition to the requirements described below, additional testing or continuing education may be mandatory for those who serve in high-security facilities such as penal institutions. Many federal jobs have been affected by the Department of Homeland Security's rules and regulations concerning detection and prevention of terrorist activity.

CLERICAL POSITIONS

Nearly one-half of the jobs in the federal civil service are clerical, and the government's demand for clerical workers often exceeds the supply. Agencies have not been able to fill all the positions for competent stenographers, typists, office machine operators, and file clerks.

In government, the title "clerk" describes more positions than it does in private industry. For instance, an editor or a writer may be called an editorial clerk, a purchasing agent with fairly important responsibilities may be called a purchasing clerk, or an accountant may be called a cost accounting clerk.

Other government clerical jobs include:

- correspondence clerk
- shorthand reporter
- mail clerk
- file clerk
- record clerk

Clerical salaries have risen sharply in recent years, probably exceeding average salaries for similar jobs in private industry. There are usually good opportunities for advancement, and clerical jobs can be the start of a real career in the government.

LABOR AND MECHANICAL POSITIONS

Most people do not realize that the U.S. government is the largest employer of mechanical, manual, and laboring workers in the country. The government is more than offices. It is also factories, shipyards, shops, docks, and power plants.

The government makes battleships, runs irrigation systems, and operates a printing office in Washington. There are more than one million mechanical and manual workers in the federal government.

Apprentices

The government hires fully qualified mechanics, artisans, and laborers, but several agencies conduct their own apprenticeship training programs for young people who want to learn a trade. Apprentices are employed in Navy yards, arsenals, other Department of Defense (DOD) establishments, and the Government Printing Office. There are apprenticeship training programs in many occupations, among them carpenter, coppersmith, electrician, electronics mechanic, glass apparatus maker, instrument maker, machinist, painter, plumber, refrigeration and air-conditioning mechanic, sheet-metal worker, toolmaker, and welder. Apprenticeships usually last four years, or eight 6-month periods, made up of approximately 1,025 shop and school hours. There are no educational requirements, but the applicant must take a written test. The minimum age for apprentices is usually 18. There is no maximum age limit.

When an apprentice has finished the prescribed period of training, he or she is promoted to the status of artisan, regardless of age. Advancement comes regularly to the apprentice who completes service satisfactorily. There is no hard and fast pay scale for all apprentices. The apprentice pay rate is usually set in ratio to the journeyman pay in the trade.

SKILLED AND SEMI-SKILLED POSITIONS

The full list of skilled and semi-skilled jobs in the government probably includes every kind of job in this class. The following is just a selection of positions in federal establishments: woodworker, aircraft mechanic, metalsmith, radio mechanic, mason, toolmaker, machinist, radio and electronics mechanic, radar mechanic, water plant operator, automotive mechanic, locksmith, cook, gardener, butcher, blacksmith, munitions handler, freight handler, and laundry helper.

The government usually follows the custom of the trade. Most, but not all, positions are paid at hourly rates, and often skill sets the rate of pay. In some cases, the government pays on a piecework basis. Overtime is on a time-and-a-half basis, rather than at straight time, as in jobs of other types.

Skilled and semi-skilled craft positions are also open on a full-time, annual-salary basis. Some typical positions of this kind include the following: electrician, plumber, carpenter, painter, operating engineer, office appliance technician, and photographer.

UNSKILLED POSITIONS

Thousands of positions in the government service are open to those with no skills or with only a small amount of training. The following are just a few:

- custodial laborers
- elevator operators
- general laborers
- housekeeping aides (restricted to veterans)
- janitors
- kitchen helpers
- laundry workers
- mess attendants (restricted to veterams)
- messengers (restricted to veterans)
- storekeeping clerks

PROFESSIONAL AND ADMINISTRATIVE POSITIONS

Many professional and administrative positions are available in government agencies, including the following: personnel management, computer science, general administration, economics, Social Security administration, management analysis, tax collection, electronic data processing, budget management, park ranger activities, statistics, investigation, procurement and supply, housing management, archival science, adjudication and other quasi-legal work, and food and drug inspection. Passing a civil service exam is required for many of these positions. The exam generally measures a candidate's aptitude for the position and ability to be trained, rather than prior knowledge of the position's duties.

LEGAL POSITIONS

Legal positions range from higher-grade positions that require full professional legal training to those in the lower grades, requiring legal training but little or no experience. They include attorneys and clerkships.

Attorneys

Attorney positions are filled on a more subjective basis than most civil service jobs and are based mainly on the attorney's achievements in law school, the scored resume, interviews, and recommendations from politicians, college professors, and other influential people. Attorneys should apply directly to the particular government agency where they want to work. The OPM ordinarily does not maintain lists of federal agencies that may want to employ attorneys. Each federal agency is responsible for determining the qualifications of attorneys who apply, as well as for making the appointments in accordance with appropriate standards. Congressional committees also use lawyers to investigate, question witnesses, gather evidence, and write reports. The lawyer who wants that kind of job should make the acquaintance of political leaders and cultivate the party leaders in a position to hand out such posts. Keeping posted on Congressional events and following up on the creation of special committees is also important.

Federal Clerks

Federal clerkships are perhaps the most eagerly sought short-term legal positions. All federal judges are provided at least two law clerks. A clerkship runs from one to two years, during which the clerk does legal research, writes briefs, and assists at various tasks in the office of the judge. A clerkship is excellent legal training and offers the clerk an opportunity to make lifelong contacts in both the legal and political worlds. Various factors enter into winning a federal clerkship: the prestige of the law school; law school grades; publications; honors; the desire of the judge for "balance" among the clerks in terms of gender, race, and geography; the interview; and the enthusiasm and standing of those who recommend the applicant.

INVESTIGATIVE AND LAW ENFORCEMENT POSITIONS

The highly publicized FBI is only one federal agency that enforces the law. A dozen agencies employ law enforcement officers for jobs that range from guarding property and patrolling borders to the most highly technical intelligence operations, including the following:

- Department of Homeland Security
- Department of Justice
- Department of State
- Department of the Treasury
- U.S. Postal Service
- U.S. Army
- U.S. Navy
- the NRC
- the FDA
- the SEC
- U.S. Customs and Border Protection

The work of law enforcement officers and investigators is dramatic, but it is often arduous and dangerous as well. Federal law enforcement frequently requires long absences from home and operating under trying physical conditions. In some of the security positions, the training is as tough as that given to commando units in the armed forces. Most of the posts naturally have stiff physical requirements, calling for well-proportioned, healthy, agile persons. Eyesight and hearing requirements are more stringent than for most other federal jobs, and candidates must have full use of their arms and legs.

FBI Special Agent

As the primary investigative arm of the federal government, the FBI is responsible for protecting the United States by preventing future terrorist attacks, conducting sensitive national security investigations, and enforcing over 300 federal statutes. The FBI's ten top investigative priorities are to:

- protect the United States from terrorist attack
- protect the United States against foreign intelligence operations and espionage
- protect the United States against cyber-based attacks and high-technology crimes
- combat public corruption at all levels
- protect civil rights
- combat transnational and national criminal organizations and enterprises
- combat major white-collar crime
- combat significant violent crime
- support federal, state, county, municipal, and international partners
- upgrade technology to successfully perform the FBI's mission

Although the FBI remains committed to other important national security and law enforcement responsibilities, the prevention of terrorism takes precedence in investigations.

The FBI has been given the authority to hire its own personnel. In addition to its agents, it hires clerical and specialized personnel. Applications may be filed at any time and may be obtained from the Director, FBI, Washington, DC, or from any of the bureau's offices, located in most larger cities.

The special agent enforces federal law, investigates its violations, gathers evidence for prosecution, checks the background of individuals, and traces criminals. The work extends from enforcing antitrust laws to tracing bribes to uncovering evidence of espionage and terrorism. There are five entrance programs for FBI Special Agents under which applicants can qualify:

1. Law
2. Accounting
3. Foreign Language
4. Science
5. Modified

Applicants must be citizens between 23 and 37 years old and must meet high educational requirements. They also must qualify on batteries of written and oral exams that measure emotional stability, resourcefulness, interpersonal and communication skills, and the ability to apply analytical methods to work assignments. Since special agents must be able to use firearms and defensive tactics, each applicant must pass a rigid physical examination, be capable of strenuous physical exertion, and have excellent hearing and eyesight. Before hiring, the FBI conducts an extensive background and character investigation.

Securities Investigator

Securities investigators examine the financial statements of national securities exchanges, brokers, and investment advisers to determine their financial condition and compliance with the regulations of the SEC. They also conduct investigations of fraud. Securities investigator positions require, at minimum, three years' general accounting experience and two to three years' specialized auditing, investigative, or administrative experience in the securities field—which is generally known in the trade as "back office" experience. Required undergraduate education includes major study in business, economics, or another field that was supplemented by at least 24 semester hours in business or economic subjects and that included 6 semester hours in accounting/auditing. Required graduate education includes major study in a field such as business administration, finance, or accounting. Applicants do not have to take a written test but are rated primarily on the quality, scope, and responsibility of their experience. Salaries start at grades GS-9 to GS-11.

In lieu of the education requirements listed above, the following experience may be substituted for Securities Investigator positions. For GS-5 positions, general experience should provide knowledge and skills pertaining to the business practices and management structure of organizations. Positions above the GS-5 level require specialized experience, including an extensive background in accounting, auditing, examining, or investigating practices related to the securities industry.

Treasury Enforcement Agent

Treasury enforcement agents enforce laws under the jurisdiction of the Treasury Department. Positions are located in the following enforcement arms of the Treasury:

- Bureau of Alcohol, Tobacco, and Firearms (ATF)
- Bureau of Engraving and Printing
- Customs Service
- IRS Criminal Investigation Division and Internal Security Division
- Secret Service

Duties range from surveillance and undercover work to presenting evidence to government prosecutors and testifying in court. Experience in dealing with groups and in criminal investigation, four years of college study, membership in the Bar, or a CPA certificate may be required. Applicants have to take the Treasury enforcement agent examination. Starting salaries range from grades GS-5 to GS-7.

For GS-5 positions, general experience includes a background in the criminal investigative or law enforcement fields. For positions above the GS-5 level, specialized experience should include an extensive background in the investigation of criminal violations. Examples of qualifying specialized experience include membership on a military intelligence team; experience investigating complex fraud claims; and law enforcement work requiring extensive surveillance.

IRS Agent and IRS Special Agent

The IRS agents examine and audit the accounting books and records of individuals, partnerships, fiduciaries, and corporations to determine their correct federal tax liabilities. These positions require an undergraduate and graduate education in a major field of study with concentration in accounting, three years of comparable experience, or a Certified Public Accountant (CPA) certificate. Applicants without a CPA certificate or accounting degree must take a written test on accounting principles. Starting salaries range from grades GS-5 to GS-7.

Special agents in the IRS investigate criminal violations of federal tax laws, make recommendations with respect to criminal prosecution, prepare technical reports, and assist the U.S. Attorney in preparing cases for trial. Major study fields must have been supplemented by 15 semester hours in accounting and 9 semester hours in another finance-related field. Applicants must also take the Treasury enforcement agent examination. Starting salaries range from GS-5 to GS-7.

In lieu of the required education, IRS special agents must demonstrate general experience utilizing accepted accounting, auditing, and business practices. Specialized experience required for IRS Special Agent positions is essentially the same as that described for Treasury enforcement agents above. This experience, however, must have been acquired in investigative work related to the finance or business practices of subjects investigated.

Corrections Officer

Corrections officers supervise, safeguard, and train inmates in federal prisons. Those who start out as corrections officers often advance to supervisory and administrative positions in such fields as custody, education, vocational training, skilled trades, social services, parole, recreation, culinary service, accounting, and farm activities. Applicants must be U.S. citizens, have comparable experience or education, have excellent character backgrounds, remain cool in emergencies, and have good morals, patience, and a capacity for leadership. There are strict vision, hearing, physical, and age requirements. Salaries start at grade GS-6.

The position of corrections officer involves the correctional treatment, custody, and supervision of criminal offenders in correctional institutions or community-based correctional treatment or rehabilitation facilities. Positions in this series have as their paramount requirement the knowledge and application of correctional skills and techniques.

The staff of correctional officers comprises the largest single group of employees in the correctional system. They have the primary responsibility for meeting the first objective of keeping the inmates safely in custody. They also play a very important role in the treatment and rehabilitative process as well.

Protective Officer

Protective officers patrol premises to prevent trespassing, fire, theft, damage, espionage, terrorism, or vandalism. They also protect the occupants of buildings from outside disturbances and interferences, control traffic, prevent unauthorized activities, search premises in the event of a bomb scare, stand guard during secret and hazardous experiments, and perform other duties. All applicants must pass a written test to qualify.

INSPECTOR POSITIONS

Inspection work is related to investigation. Inspectors see that building construction, elevators, fire escapes, plumbing, and other projects comply with regulations. They test weights and measures and act to enforce sanitary, food and drug, and public health laws. A government inspector may also check public works, playgrounds, street lighting and overhead lines, transportation, or public-safety devices.

Safety Inspector

The safety inspector enforces the Interstate Commerce Commission's motor carrier safety regulations. Safety inspectors advise transportation companies in the development of safety activities, accident prevention plans and driver education, inspect motor vehicles, investigate accidents, and work with state agencies. Two years' experience investigating highway accidents, inspecting motor vehicles, conducting hearings on traffic violations, maintaining motor carrier fleets, or important work on highway safety programs is required. Work as a traffic officer, motor vehicle dispatcher, or insurance claims adjuster does not qualify. Applicants are rated entirely on the basis of a written test. Salary is grade GS-5 at entrance.

Patent Examiner

The patent examiner performs professional scientific and technical work in examining applications for U.S. patents. The examiner evaluates an invention, determines if it will perform as claimed, uncovers any previous knowledge comparable to the invention, and determines whether the application and its claimed invention meets all legal requirements. All applicants must have a bachelor's degree or higher degree in professional engineering or science and are rated on the extent and quality of their relevant experience and training. Certain type of training or other experience may be substituted for specialized experience in patent work. A test is not required. Starting salaries range from grades GS-5 to GS-13.

MEDICAL POSITIONS

With the growth of social services in the past 50 years, the government has developed a need for physicians, medical researchers, nurses, dentists, and similar workers. The growth of psychiatric concepts, the development of occupational therapy, and the public demand that veterans who need medical care should have it all demand a force of medical practitioners working for the government.

Medical researchers study bacteriological warfare, hunt for protection against the effects of radioactivity, and prepare new vaccines, serums, and other biological products. Other medical jobs involve:

- administrating hospitals
- caring for Native Americans on reservations
- examining those entering the public service

- inspecting laboratories
- performing straight medical work
- running public relations campaigns
- testing pharmaceuticals

The VA employs the most medical workers in peacetime. The Army and Navy have medical and dental corps, which, of course, grow enormously during war. Other agencies that need medical workers are the Public Health Service, the FDA, the Children's Bureau of the Department of Health, and the Bureau of Indian Affairs (BIA) of the Interior Department. American physicians also accompany our missions in the Foreign Service. Many federal agencies employ nurses in the in-house medical facilities that they maintain for their employees. Nurses also serve in U.S. hospitals and serve as consultants to state health departments on programs to control tuberculosis and venereal disease.

Medical Officer

Medical officers occupy positions in the Public Health Service, FDA, the Children's Bureau of the Department of Health, the BIA, the VA, and many other federal agencies. Medical officers determine whether medicines are labeled properly. They conduct extensive research in maternal and child health and in services to physically and/or mentally challenged children. They serve in Native American hospitals and as district physicians in small government dispensaries. They have the opportunity of working in teaching hospitals in the federal service that are approved by the American Medical Association (AMA). There they obtain a wide variety of medical experience, particularly in the field of tropical diseases. They also inspect vessels and airplanes entering ports, harbors, and airfields and examine foreigners entering the United States.

Medical officers also work closely with all local, state, and national governmental agencies that support the Department of Homeland Security. They help to identify any threat to the United States, such as potential terrorism or biological agents.

Professional Nurse

Professional nurses serve in hospitals on Native American reservations, Army hospitals, and Navy hospitals. Most available positions are in Public Health Service hospitals located in major port cities and at the Clinical Center at the National Institutes of Health (NIH). Public health nursing consultants are employed in the Children's Bureau, where they work with state agencies. Positions range from staff nurse through nurse consultant and division chief.

Applicants for all professional nurse positions must have completed a full nursing course. Basic requirements in education include a degree or diploma from a professional nursing program. At the GS-4 level, one year of nursing experience as a military corpsman may be accepted in lieu of education. Applicants must also be currently registered as professional nurses in the United States. For positions in grades GS-6 and higher, they must have had specialized professional experience appropriate to the position. The entrance salary for a staff nurse is GS-5 to GS-7 and for a head nurse is GS-7 to GS-9. The pay of public-health nurse positions is from GS-7 to GS-9 at entrance. Nurse consultant positions pay GS-11 to GS-13.

Dental Assistant

Dental assistants perform a variety of supportive duties that facilitate the work of the dentist. Dental assistants may work in general dentistry or in a specialty field of dentistry such as periodontics or prosthodontics. They provide chairside assistance during treatment and perform clinic maintenance and radiographic duties. They also keep records of appointments, examinations, treatments, and supplies.

Applicants must have had two years of dental assistant experience, including one year of specialization in restoration, dental X-raying, or dental prosthetics. Dental assistant courses may be substituted for experience. No written test is required. Salaries start at grade GS-4.

Dental Hygienist

Dental hygienists give oral prophylaxis to patients in hospitals and clinics. They conduct oral hygiene educational programs and instruct hospital and clinic personnel in the oral hygiene maintenance techniques. Applicants for all grades must be currently licensed to practice as dental hygienists in the United States. Applicants for GS-4 and higher positions must have successfully completed a full course of dental hygiene and/or have comparable experience. No written test is required. Applicants are judged on the extent and quality of their educational experience and on personal qualities.

Other Medical and Nursing Positions

Other government positions in the medical and nursing fields include medical technician, laboratory helper, X-ray technician, occupational therapist, orthopedic technician, dental technician, and veterinarian. Entrance salaries for these positions range from grades GS-3 to GS-14.

ECONOMICS AND STATISTICS POSITIONS

The complexities of modern government require the services of people who "understand figures." Hardly an activity exists in any department that does not demand the work of an accountant, statistician, economist, or mathematician. Every citizen knows of the work done by the IRS. Statisticians in the U.S. Census Bureau prepare data for businesses and keep facts on the ups and downs of business. Other statisticians work with scientists, collecting and analyzing statistical reports that are frequently the basis of long-range national policy. They work on problems dealing with production, marketing, distribution, taxation, and other economic questions. Accountants and budget examiners go over the dollars and cents spent by various departments, submit estimates, and sometimes cut spending programs. They also:

- make up payrolls
- work on retirement mathematics
- examine the books of stock exchange firms
- study the background of bankruptcies
- audit the books of public utility companies
- check into the financial conditions of banks

In another sphere, they may analyze the fiscal policy of the United States and determine methods of adapting that policy to the economic needs of the country. They make up the nation's budget and suggest appropriations for all government activities.

Mathematicians work with scientists in all of their activities, from plotting the course of planets to devising formulas in atomic physics. They work with engineers building bridges, solve equations about heat conduction or electrical circuits, make computations to predict weather, and determine the path of missiles and the intensity of earthquakes.

The "figures" people are so important that it is not an overstatement to say that modern government could not function without them. The Department of Agriculture, Tennessee Valley Authority, Department of Labor, National Labor Relations Board, Census Bureau, Treasury Department, and SEC are only some of the agencies that need workers with mathematics or economics backgrounds. As the government grows more complex, the need for qualified people will increase.

Accounting Assistant

The duties of this position vary, depending on the agency. For GS-5 positions, applicants must meet one of the following requirements: study in accounting above the high school level, progressive experience, a combination of both, or a CPA certificate. For GS-7 positions, applicants must meet the requirements for GS-5 plus additional graduate study or experience in professional accounting. Applicants qualifying based on education or a CPA certificate do not take an exam. Salaries start in the GS-5 to GS-7 range.

Accountant and Auditor

Accountants and auditors collect and evaluate data, maintain and examine records, plan new accounting systems and revise old ones, prepare statements, examine transactions to determine accuracy and legality, and analyze financial reports. These positions require a high degree of professional accounting experience and/or education. Salaries range from the GS-9 grade through the GS-15 grade at entrance.

Basic requirements include a degree in accounting or a related field, such as business administration. Applicants may substitute four years of accounting experience for the required education.

Revenue Officer

Revenue officers collect delinquent taxes and secure delinquent tax returns. They investigate and analyze business situations, negotiate agreements to satisfy tax obligations, enforce tax law, and perform related work. Preferably, applicants should have taken college courses in subjects such as accounting, business administration, business economics, finance, and law. Starting salaries range from the GS-5 to GS-7 levels.

Tax Technician

Tax technicians represent the IRS in consulting with taxpayers to identify and explain tax issues and to determine the correct tax liability. An exam may be used to fill tax technician positions. Preferably, applicants should have studied accounting, business administration, business economics, finance, or law in college. General experience for the GS-5 level is that which provided a general knowledge of business practices. Specialized experience (for positions above GS-5) includes a substantive knowledge of business practices, basic accounting principles, and Federal tax laws and regulations. Starting salaries range from the GS-5 to GS-7 levels.

Statistician

The job duties of the statistician involve professional work regarding statistical processes. Statisticians provide professional consultation requiring the application of statistical theory and techniques in a variety of fields, including social, natural, and physical sciences and administration. Applicants must have a bachelor's degree in mathematics and statistics. They must also have had from two to three years' professional experience. No written test is given. Salaries range from grades GS-9 through GS-15.

Economist

Economists research economic phenomena, interpret economic data, prepare reports on economic facts and activities, investigate and evaluate reports for their economic implications, and consult with government policymakers. Applicants are rated on the amount and quality of their experience, education, and training. Salaries start at grade GS-9 and range from GS-11 through GS-15.

Management Analyst

The management analyst's work includes evaluating administrative systems and facilities for the management and control of government operations and developing new or improved procedures, systems, and organization structures. Management analysts help managers to evaluate the effectiveness of government programs and agencies. The work requires skill in application of fact-finding and investigative techniques; oral and written communications; and development of presentations and reports. Applicants must have had several years of experience or graduate study (depending on the grade applied for) in such fields as tabulation and machine accounting, forms control, records management, or budgetary preparation and presentation. They must also pass a written exam. Salaries start at grades GS-9 to GS-12.

Budget Examiner

Budget examiners survey government programs, review budgets, and present budgets to the proper authorities. They are often responsible for the development and operation of systems for reporting work performed and funds expended. Requirements and salary levels for this position are similar to those for the management analyst.

TEACHING AND LIBRARY POSITIONS

Although teaching is primarily a function of state and local government, the federal government employs teachers and educators for a number of services. With the new emphasis on vocational guidance, opportunities for qualified teachers in the federal service have increased. Pay rates compare favorably with those of larger cities.

Among the agencies that employ teachers and educators are the BIA, the VA, the Department of Agriculture, and Department of Education. In the VA, there is informal class teaching and individual instruction, and teachers assist in arranging correspondence courses. A number of teaching positions are also available abroad. The Department of Health uses highly trained education experts to work with colleges, universities, and state educational systems in setting up educational programs. Among the other teaching jobs in the federal service are educational research, in-service training work in all agencies, and playground and recreation directing.

Almost every federal agency has a librarian who takes care of the agency's reading and reference materials. Agencies that service the public with such information, such as the Departments of Agriculture and Commerce, use many libraries. In Washington, librarians assist federal employees by giving them reference materials and by doing research for them. Branches of the VA have libraries that offer limited opportunities for trained librarians.

The largest number of librarians is employed in the Library of Congress. The jobs there are diverse and complex—locating books and documents, looking for facts for Congress members, working on major research projects, and writing reports that sometimes influence national policies. Employees of the Library of Congress are not under the civil service. Applicants should write directly to the Director of the Library in Washington, DC. The following are some of the teaching and library posts available in the federal service.

Bureau of Indian Affairs

The BIA is responsible for the education of Native American children who are not educated by public schools in states where they live and for a program of adult education that can bridge the gap between life on the reservation and mainstream, contemporary America. The bureau operates more than 200 schools, serving nearly 50,000 students. Adult education aids more than 31,000 Native Americans and Alaska Natives in twenty-three states on sixty-three reservations. Arizona, New Mexico, Alaska, North Dakota, and South Dakota have the largest concentration of Native American schools, although some educators are needed each year in California, Oklahoma, Oregon, Utah, Kansas, Florida, Mississippi, Montana, North Carolina, and Louisiana. Classroom teachers and guidance counselors are especially needed. Most BIA schools are located in isolated, rural places more than 30 miles from the nearest city. The work involved in combating physical isolation, as well as physical and emotional poverty, demands dedication, imagination, and strength—but it can be very rewarding.

Agency for International Development

The Agency for International Development (AID) administers America's foreign aid program in the developing countries of Asia, Africa, and Latin America. Since the progress of a developing country hinges on the ability of its people to learn the skills by which they can support and govern themselves, education plays an important part in that program. AID educators work with local officials on projects ranging from selecting textbooks to setting up educational television. They also help plan educational programs that meet the needs for particular areas and train people of that area to run the programs themselves.

AID hires advisers in the fields of elementary education, higher education, human resources development, teacher education, trade-industrial education, and vocational education. Classroom teaching alone does not provide the experience needed, and positions usually require advanced degrees and several years of administrative and program responsibility. For jobs with AID, contact:

U.S. Agency for International Development
Office of Human Resources
Personnel Operations Division
Room 208, RRB
Washington, DC 20523-2808
Phone: 202-712-0000
Web site: www.usaid.gov

Department of Defense (DoD)

Did you know that the ninth-largest American school system lies entirely outside the continental United States? Schools in nearly 30 foreign countries are set up by the DoD to provide education for children of overseas military and civilian personnel. Jobs in the DoD schools correspond to those in any large American school system, including positions such as administrators, counselors, classroom teachers, teachers of the physically and mentally challenged, teachers of special subjects, and librarians. Teaching experience is required.

Working with the DoD school system offers the chance to live and travel in a foreign country while pursuing a career. For jobs with the DoD Overseas Dependents Schools, contact your local U.S. Employment Service office.

Federal Correctional Institutions

Far from the hardened master-criminal stereotype, the average inmate in a federal prison is under 30 years old, has a fifth-grade education, and is serving time for auto theft. Educational programs within the system are aimed at helping inmates succeed at a second chance at useful citizenship. Academic programs range from remedial reading for functional illiterates to instruction at the high school level. Vocational training is aimed at providing marketable skills, including work as dental technicians, computer training, welding, masonry, small engine repair, and auto repair. The Bureau of Prisons also employs educators in these fields:

- arts and crafts
- guidance
- library work
- occupational therapy
- recreation
- research and development
- supervisory and administrative work

Department of Education (DOE)

The DOE links federal education programs with state and local agencies, colleges and universities, international education organizations, and professional associations. Its role has many facets, ranging from school desegregation under the Civil Rights Act of 1964 to administering funds for library construction, from researching education for physically and/or mentally challenged children to compiling statistics, from consulting services to adult and vocational education programs. Although the DOE is involved in so many phases of education, it has virtually no opportunities for classroom teachers as such. The need is for experienced professionals, including:

- administrators
- college and university presidents and deans
- counseling and testing experts
- curriculum specialists
- department heads
- research scholars
- staff assistants
- vocational and technical specialists

If you meet these qualifications, you will find the broad scale of DOE programs interesting and stimulating.

Public Health Educator

The public health educator specializes in getting health facts accepted and used. The work represents a rare blend of specific training and the ingenuity needed to communicate and work with a wide variety of groups of people. These specialists help to improve education policies in accordance with national objectives. For those few who meet the professional standards, it is a challenging, relatively new field for educators in government.

Education Research and Program Specialist

These specialists may perform any of the following duties:

- appraising educational practices in the United States and abroad
- planning, conducting, and evaluating surveys and research
- publishing educational articles and bulletins
- consulting with local, state, national, or international bodies
- planning and administering grants in aid

Fields of specialization include elementary, vocational, school administration, guidance, and international education.

Applicants must have a college degree in education and extensive experience in administration, research, or other activities in the field of education. For jobs at the GS-14 and higher grades, the applicant must have made significant contributions to education and earned outstanding recognition in his or her field. No written exam is required; rather, candidates are judged on background and experience. Salaries range from grades GS-9 to GS-15.

Librarian

The work of librarians involves acquisitions, cataloging, classification, reference, and bibliography in federal libraries. As many of the libraries are highly specialized, the work often lies in one field. At the higher levels, librarians may assume complete charge of a large library, organize and direct the activities of a division in a large library, or serve as consulting specialists to research personnel.

Depending upon the grade of the position, applicants must have a bachelor's degree with significant study in library science, a higher degree in library science, and/or equivalent experience. Some applicants are required to take a written test. Salaries range from grades GS-5 through GS-15.

Library Assistant

The duties of the library assistant include:

- arranging interlibrary loans
- answering reference questions

- book and bindery preparation
- checking in and routing periodicals
- circulation work
- compiling lists of books
- making additions to serial, shelf-list, and catalog records
- stack maintenance

GS-5 positions involve supervising library assistants in lower grades. Depending on the grade applied for, from one to three years' experience and/or undergraduate study is required. Two thirds of this experience must have been specialized. A written exam is administered consisting of alphabetizing, arithmetic, and verbal ability questions. Competitors for grade GS-5 positions are also required to take a test of supervisory judgment. Salaries start at grades GS-3 to GS-5.

Archives Assistant

Archives assistants work in:

- receiving, sorting, filing, classifying, and indexing noncurrent records and documents
- searching for, charging out, and providing information as requested
- packing, sorting, and preserving noncurrent records

This work requires the application of archival methods, procedures, and techniques. In some assignments, the work also requires a knowledge of the administrative history of specific Federal organizations, past or present. At the GS-5 level, many positions involve supervisory duties. Depending on the grade applied for, from one to three years of experience and/or undergraduate study in history, government, political science, sociology, economics, or public administration is required. The basis of rating and salary range is similar to that for library assistants.

SOCIAL WORK

In recent times, a new grouping of government activities built around certain basic needs of the people (i.e., Social Security, elderly, unemployment insurance, and various welfare projects) has become prevalent. The federal government takes a hand in disseminating nutrition and health information, publishes cookbooks, and advises on proper infant and child care. It grants aid to states for dealing with people suffering from emotional and psychological problems, and to some extent it aids these people directly. Much of this work is performed by trained social workers.

Social Worker—Corrections

Social workers work in correctional institutions to develop personal histories of new inmates; prepare progress reports on their adjustment both within the institution and in the outside environment; explain rules, policies, and decisions to prisoners; plan with them regarding parole and release; and advise them about personal and family problems. They make recommendations to prison administration regarding prisoners' special needs and requests, and they are responsible for the detention of prisoners assigned to them. Social workers at grade GS-7 work as trainees, whereas those at grade GS-9 work with a large degree of independence.

Applicants for GS-7 positions must have had five years of experience in social casework, including one year of correctional work or an equivalent bachelor's degree. Applicants with a master's degree in social work are eligible for GS-9 positions. No written test is required. Applicants are rated on the extent and quality of their experience. Salaries range from grades GS-7 to GS-9.

SCIENCE AND ENGINEERING POSITIONS

Scientific research and development is carried out in 25 federal departments and agencies, principally in the laboratories of the following:

- the Army, Navy, and Air Force
- NASA
- Department of Agriculture
- National Bureau of Standards
- Department of the Interior
- the FAA
- the NIH
- the VA

Recently, employment conditions in the federal service for scientists have radically improved. There are now more than 70,000 federal employees in science and nearly 120,000 in engineering.

Within the framework of government-wide personnel laws and policies, agency and laboratory directors maintain a creative environment by providing privileges and recognition for their scientific personnel, such as the following: encouraging staff members to attend meetings of professional societies and to publish in professional journals, giving them credit lines on official publications of the laboratory, giving them the freedom to teach and serve as consultants on the outside and to write books, maintaining a liberal patent policy, providing reasonable flexibility of working hours, establishing meaningful professional titles, and encouraging coworkers of different grades to consider themselves colleagues, not bosses and subordinates.

The scientific and engineering jobs listed in this section comprise only a sample of the many occupations available.

Chemical Engineer

Chemical Engineer is the authorized title for positions classified to this series. Supervisory Chemical Engineer is the authorized title for positions that require supervisory qualifications. To determine the specific criteria for various grade-level positions, consult the OPM's Position Classification Standard for Chemical Engineering (GS-0839). Criteria are very specialized and depend on the position's individual grade level.

Physicist

Physicists work in one or more of the branches of physical science, conducting or assisting in technical projects and applying scientific knowledge to the solution of problems. For GS-5 positions, a bachelor's degree with a concentration in physics is required. For grades GS-7 through GS-15, applicants must meet additional experience requirements. Applicants' qualifications are judged from a review of their experience, education, and training. Salaries start at grades GS-5 through GS-15.

Engineer

Engineering fields include agricultural, civil, electrical, electronic, mining, and others. All applicants must have a bachelor's degree in engineering or an equivalent combination of engineering education and experience. They must also have passed the Engineer-in-Training Examination, participated in certain specialized courses, or have demonstrable professional stature. Superior academic achievement, creative research or development, or extensive graduate work may qualify applicants for higher positions. All applicants are rated on experience, education, and training. Starting salaries range from grades GS-5 to GS-15.

Engineering Drafter

Engineering drafters use calculations and drafting instruments to make working drawings, assemblies, and layouts of various types of equipment. Engineering drafters are included in positions that involve portraying engineering ideas through drawings. The positions require a practical knowledge of drafting methods and procedures.

For all grades, applicants must meet specific experience and/or education requirements. Experience may be in working as a cartographic, engineering, or statistical drafter, or experience in skilled and mechanical trades and related scientific and engineering technician occupations. Competitors for GS-2 and GS-3 positions are rated on a written test. Competitors for GS-4, GS-5, and GS-7 positions are rated on the extent and quality of their education, experience, and training relevant to the position. The rating is based on the application and sample engineering drafting work.

Engineering Aide—Highway

Engineering aides assist with highway location surveys, highway construction, and minor inspection of highway or bridge construction. Applicants must have had one-and-a-half years' total experience or equivalent education in engineering, drafting, mathematics, and/or the physical sciences. Competitors are rated on the extent and quality of their education, experience, and training. Salaries start at the GS-3 level.

Geologist

Geologists utilize the principles of geology to collect and analyze information about the composition of the earth. They apply their knowledge to solve a variety of scientific problems. Typical duties of geologists involve:

- compiling and interpreting data
- collecting samples for laboratory analysis
- geological mapping
- identifying and studying samples
- making and recording field observations
- making special studies
- preparing professional scientific and economic reports for publication

Applicants must have a bachelor's degree with a concentration in geology and related sciences or an equivalent combination of education and professional experience. A graduate degree, superior academic achievement, professional work experience combined with this education, or creative investigation or research contributions may qualify the applicant for higher grades. No written test is required. All ratings are based on an evaluation of experience, education, and training. Salaries range from GS-9 to GS-15.

Metallurgist

Metallurgy is a domain of materials science that studies the physical and chemical behavior of metallic elements and compounds. For GS-5 positions, a four-year college course including metallurgy study is required. For GS-7 positions, additional professional experience or graduate study is required. Applicants are rated based on an evaluation of their education and experience. Salaries start at grades GS-5 and GS-7.

Research Psychologist

The types of work covered under this heading include experimental and physiological psychology, personnel measurement and evaluation, social psychology, and engineering psychology. Depending on the grade applied for, applicants must have had professional experience and/or graduate study. No written exam is required. Applicants are rated on an evaluation of their personal and professional qualifications. Starting salaries range from grades GS-9 to GS-15.

Forestry, Agriculture, and Conservation Positions

The Departments of Agriculture and the Interior employ experts on soil, forestry, and water resources. Although the work they do is often difficult and sometimes dangerous, those who hold these positions express a real love for the tasks they perform. The pay is not always high, but it has been increasing gradually. As the nation learns how vital it is to conserve and improve its natural resources, these jobs should grow in importance. Occupational experts believe that jobs in forestry, agriculture, and conservation are "good bets" in coming years.

The tasks performed by government workers in agriculture, horticulture, soil science, conservation, and farming include the following:

- developing agriculture techniques and products
- inspecting farm products
- care of trees
- experimental landscape gardening
- soil research
- testing fruits, vegetables, trees, and shrubs
- dairy sanitation and efficiency studies
- determining the mineral, water, and agricultural resources of public lands
- controlling and preventing soil erosion
- moisture conservation
- research on rapid reforestation
- experimental farming
- research on animal grazing
- care, breeding, and feeding of farm and dairy animals
- research on forest conservation and use of forest products
- calculating the economic costs of each project

Agricultural Manager

Agricultural managers perform a broad range of functions in carrying out credit and technical assistance programs for rural communities. The work involves:

- crop and livestock production
- preparation and marketing of products
- support of financial, management, rural housing, and community resource development activities

A bachelor's degree in farm, livestock, or ranch management; agricultural economics; agricultural education; agronomy; husbandry; agricultural engineering; general agriculture; horticulture; or other related area is required.

Agronomist

Agronomists perform research on the fundamental principles of plant, soil, and related sciences, as they apply this information to:

- crop breeding and production
- conservation
- propagation and seed production
- ground maintenance
- plant adaptation and varietal testing

A bachelor's degree in the basic plant sciences (botany, plant taxonomy, plant ecology, plant breeding or genetics, microbiology, or soil science) and/or in agronomic subjects (plant breeding, crop production, or soil and crop management) is required.

Forestry Specialist

These specialists work to develop, conserve, and protect natural forest resources. They also manage those resources, including timber, forage, watersheds, wildlife, and land, to meet present and future public needs. Forestry specialists fulfill positions that require professional knowledge and competence in forestry science. Research work involves development of new, improved, or more economic scientific instruments and the techniques necessary to perform such work. A diversified college degree in forestry is required. Supplemental professional experience may also be required for some administrative positions.

Husbandry Specialist

These specialists develop and improve methods of breeding, feeding, nutrition, and management of poultry and livestock and the quality of meat, poultry, and dairy products. A college degree in the basic biological and agricultural sciences is required, with a concentration in animal sciences.

Plant Quarantine and Pest Control Specialist

These specialists apply knowledge of the biological and plant sciences, the transportation and shipping industries, and quarantine techniques to the establishment and enforcement of plant quarantines, the government of the movement of injurious plant pests, or to the survey, detection, identification, control, or eradication of plant pests. College coursework in any combination of the following (or in closely related fields) is required:

- botany
- entomology
- horticulture
- invertebrate zoology
- nematology
- mycology
- plant pathology

Range Conservationist

Range conservationists take inventory of, improve, protect, and manage rangelands and related grazing lands. They also perform the following tasks:

- regulate grazing on public rangelands
- develop cooperative relationships with range users
- assist landowners with planning and applying range conservation programs
- develop technical standards and specifications
- conduct research on the principles underlying rangeland management
- develop new-and-improved instruments and techniques

College coursework in the plant, animal, and soil sciences and natural resources management is required.

Soil Conservationist and Soil Science Specialist

Soil conservationists coordinate work in soil, water, and resource conservation programs to bring about sound land use and improve the quality of the environment. A bachelor's degree in soil conservation or closely related agricultural or natural resource sciences is required.

Soil science specialists study soils from the standpoint of their morphology, genesis, and distribution; their interrelated physical, chemical, and biological properties and processes; their relationships to climactic, physiographic, and vegetative influence; and their adaptation to use and management in agriculture.

Wildlife Biologist and Wildlife Refuge Manager

Wildlife biologists work to conserve and manage wildlife and to establish and apply the biological principles and techniques necessary for the conservation and management of wildlife.

Wildlife refuge managers develop management and operation plans for bird and game refuges; see that the wildlife is properly protected; and work with individuals, organizations, and the general public on refuge and related wildlife management programs. College coursework in zoology, mammalogy, ornithology, animal ecology, or wildlife management and/or botany is required.

Zoologist

Zoologists research the following:

- parasitic and nonparasitic organisms affecting plants and domestic and wild animals
- pathology
- epidemiology
- immunology

- physiology
- host relationships
- biological, physical, and chemical control

A college degree in biological science, including coursework in zoology and the related animal sciences, is required.

Selected State and Municipal Positions

Nearly all states and municipalities use trained business, technical, and professional employees in a variety of fields. College graduates who have prepared for such positions are encouraged to step directly from the classroom into state and municipal service at the bottom rung of any one of the many career ladders in its numerous departments, institutions, and agencies. This appendix describes some of these entry-level positions, which are generally filled competitively by civil service exams.

In addition to the requirements described below, additional testing or continuing education may be required for those who serve in high-security facilities such as penal institutions. Many state and municipal jobs have been affected by the Department of Homeland Security's rules and regulations concerning detection and prevention of terrorist activity.

CLERICAL POSITIONS

Clerical support staff is employed through state and municipal government. Clerks perform a variety of administrative and clerical duties necessary to run state and local government. Often, applicants must pass a written clerical and verbal abilities test to become eligible for these positions. For more advanced positions, a typing or stenography test, higher education, or professional experience may also be required.

Here are some examples of clerical jobs in state and local government:

- Messengers sort and carry mail, documents, and other materials among government offices and buildings.

- Clerks perform basic clerical duties such as gathering and providing information, sorting, filing, and checking materials.

- Clerk-typists perform typing and clerical duties such as providing information, composing short letters and memos, sorting, filing, and checking materials.

- Clerk-stenographers take dictation and transcribe notes. Other duties may include typing, providing information, composing letters and memos, sorting, and filing materials.

- Secretary-typists perform secretarial duties, which usually involve typing correspondence, reports, and statistical material while acting as a secretary to one or more employees.

- Executive secretaries perform highly responsible secretarial work as staff assistants to executive directors. They may also supervise a small clerical staff.

appendix e

- Library assistants perform clerical work in a library, such as maintaining files and records, sorting and shelving books, and checking materials for accuracy.

COMPUTER-RELATED POSITIONS

Computers are steadily becoming more important in all branches of the civil service, and for many functions of state and municipal governments, they are now essential. The duties of computer personnel vary with the size of the installation, the type of equipment used, and the policies of the employer. As computer usage grows in government organizations, so will the need for computer professionals and related occupations. Computer-related positions often require related experience, vocational training, and/or a college degree in computer science, in addition to passing the civil service exam. Applicants for some positions may also be given a performance test, or the written test may include computer-related questions to ascertain applicants' technical knowledge.

Here are some representative computer-related jobs in state and local government:

- Data-entry machine operators operate a variety of data-entry equipment, entering information from various source documents onto magnetic tape, disks, or into a computer. They may also verify information, operate auxiliary equipment, and perform editing and coding tasks.

- Computer operator trainees are trained to monitor and control the operation of data-processing equipment in conformance with programmed instructions. They may also operate peripheral equipment, such as disk and tape drives and printers.

- Computer operators monitor and control computers in compliance with instructions describing each computer application. They also operate magnetic tape and disk drives, printers, and other peripheral devices. In some installations, they may confer with programmers or system analysts on procedural matters and problems.

- Computer specialists in applied programming have highly complex technical or supervisory responsibilities involved in the development and maintenance of applications and systems for use in the operation of a large or medium-sized computer installation. They conduct feasibility studies, write reports, prepare specifications for systems and programs, evaluate the work of subordinates, and perform related duties.

- Computer specialists in database administration have technical or supervisory responsibilities for the design, implementation, enhancement, and maintenance of database management systems. They have a wide range of duties that can include maintaining software, providing on-the-job training, and ensuring data security.

- Computer programmers prepare detailed instructions to adapt various operations to data processing, prepare input and output layouts and block diagrams to show the sequence of computations for the solution of problems on computers and peripheral equipment, and use programming languages to develop machine instructions for data manipulations.

FINANCIAL POSITIONS

Officials in government must have updated financial information to make important decisions. Accountants and auditors prepare, analyze, and verify financial reports that furnish that kind of information. In addition, government accountants and auditors maintain and examine the records of government agencies and audit private businesses and individuals whose dealings are subject to government regulations.

These positions often require higher education in accounting, economics, finance, banking, or related subjects, as well as professional experience or a valid CPA license. The written test may include questions about accounting principles and practices, reviewing financial records, interpreting financial written material, analyzing accounting systems, and related areas. Some higher-level positions are judged based on education and experience and do not require a written exam.

LAW ENFORCEMENT POSITIONS

Law enforcement in America is fragmented and specialized. There are approximately 40,000 separate law enforcement agencies representing municipal, county, state, and federal governments. Highly trained police officers are found in both large and small cities. Of the law enforcement units at the state level, two of the best-known are the state police and the highway patrol. State police engage in a full range of law enforcement activities, including criminal investigation. Highway patrol units are concerned almost entirely with traffic control and enforcement and have limited general police authority.

Municipal Police Officer

Police officers work in partnership with the public and are in the front line in the fight against crime and the fear of crime. They are citizen focused, responding to the needs of individuals and communities. Using the latest technology, police officers are trained to manage information and intelligence in order to secure successful court prosecutions. Major priorities include: tackling antisocial behavior; reducing theft, robbery, and street-related crime; combating organized crime; countering terrorism; supporting victims; and providing a reassuring presence in the community.

Applicants typically must meet age and medical requirements, have a high school diploma or have served in the armed forces, and have a character suited for police work. Applicants must pass a written exam that tests for the abilities required for success as a police officer. The questions on the exam test mental abilities, such as interpreting rules and regulations, verbal reasoning, number series, table interpretation, and reading comprehension. Some positions may require unique skills, such as an Emergency Medical Technician certificate or fluency in a foreign language.

State Trooper

The essential functions and tasks required for the position of state police trooper include, but are not limited to: qualification and use of firearms, providing emergency assistance, conducting investigations, report writing, and presenting testimony in a court of law. State troopers are often required to work on a rotating shift basis, be available for duty 24 hours a day, work on holidays, and work in inclement weather. They can be transferred anywhere in the state. Applicants must be able to use a firearm and perform strenuous tasks.

The basic requirements include U.S. citizenship, state residency, passing a background investigation, meeting age limits, possessing a high school diploma, passing a medical exam, and meeting vision and hearing standards. Conviction of a felony, an unsatisfactory driving record, or conviction of driving while under the influence of alcohol or drugs can serve as a basis for disqualification. Applicants must also pass a written test pertaining to accuracy of observation and memory and ability to read and comprehend reports, manuals, and laws. They must also pass an oral appraisal exam assessing communication skills and a physical performance test.

First-year employees are trained to function independently as law enforcement officers. They must complete a basic police training curriculum of law enforcement coursework and physical training. During the training period, they accompany experienced troopers on patrols to detect or prevent traffic and criminal law violations, investigate complaints, and provide related services to the public.

Corrections Officer

Corrections officers are charged with the safekeeping of people who have been arrested and are awaiting trial or who have been convicted of a crime and are sentenced to serve time in a correctional institution. They maintain order within the prison, enforce rules and regulations, and often supplement the counseling that inmates receive from mental-health professionals.

Entry-level correctional work is of a training nature. Trainees participate in formal courses to develop the skills and techniques for the proper supervision and custody of inmates. Training covers areas like law, sociology, psychology, counseling, firearms, and crisis prevention and intervention. Work assignments are routinely performed under senior officer supervision and include maintaining security and order, monitoring inmate movement, inspecting grounds and buildings, and searching for contraband.

Candidates must be state residents, meet age limits, and pass written and oral tests, an employment interview, a physical fitness test, a medical exam, and psychological tests. The written exam tests observation and memory, associative memory, and reading comprehension. The oral test determines job interest, poise and self-confidence, the ability to organize and express thoughts, and problem-solving abilities.

Firefighter

Every year, fires take thousands of lives and destroy property worth billions of dollars. Firefighters help protect the public against this danger.

During duty hours, firefighters must be prepared to respond to a fire and handle any emergency that arises. Because firefighting is dangerous and complicated, it requires organization and teamwork. At every fire, firefighters perform specific duties assigned by an officer. They may connect hose lines to hydrants, operate a pump, or position ladders. Their duties may change several times while the team is in action. They may rescue victims and administer emergency medical aid, ventilate smoke-filled areas, operate equipment, and salvage the contents of buildings. Some firefighters operate fire apparatus, ambulances, emergency rescue vehicles, and fireboats. Between alarms, they have classroom training, and they clean and maintain equipment, conduct practice drills, and participate in physical-fitness exercises.

Most fire departments are also responsible for fire prevention. They provide specially trained personnel to inspect public buildings for conditions that might cause a fire. They may check building plans, the number and working condition of fire escapes and fire doors, the storage of flammable materials, and other possible hazards. In addition, firefighters educate the public about fire prevention and safety measures. They frequently speak on the subject before school assemblies and civic groups.

Basic requirements include a high school diploma, a valid state motor vehicle driver's license, age and height limits, vision standards, and proof of good character. Applicants must take a written exam that tests ability to learn and perform the work of a firefighter. The exam may include questions on understanding job information; applying laws, rules, and regulations to job situations; recognizing appropriate behavior; understanding mechanical devices; and remembering the details of a floor layout. In addition, there is a physical test.

INVESTIGATIVE POSITIONS

The range of activities performed by modern state and municipal authorities means that they have a great need for information—hence the need for investigators. Investigators have a wide variety of functions: to examine claims for benefits or compensation to ensure that they are valid and conform with regulations, to gather evidence of fraud and other wrongdoing to be used in legal actions, and to discover violations of rules and regulations.

Investigative positions often require related experience, such as police work, insurance investigation, private investigation, or federal or military investigation. Higher education may be substituted for experience. Applicants must also take a written exam that tests for knowledge, skills, and abilities in areas like reasoning, interviewing and investigative techniques, evaluating information and evidence, understanding and interpreting written material, and preparing written material. Higher-level positions may not require a written exam; rather, those applicants are judged on education and experience alone.

Here are some typical investigative positions:

- Investigators examine violations of tax-liability laws and violations of miscellaneous rules and regulations of various state or local agencies. They may also determine applicants' qualifications for civil service employment.

- Compensation claims investigators investigate workers' compensation and disability benefits claims.
- Unemployment insurance investigators investigate fraud by claimants or employers and cases of employee misconduct, determine employee status and claimant eligibility, and investigate related employment cases. Trainees in this position receive on-the-job training while performing the duties of the job.

LEGAL POSITIONS

The legal activities of many government departments require the services of attorneys of various grades. Lawyers in the office of the Attorney General handle a great deal of important state legal work. In addition to these are many legal positions, some under specialized titles, that are filled from open-competitive civil service lists. The state offers opportunities for legally trained employees to rise to highly responsible, well-paid positions.

In state and municipal government, legal assistants, under the direction of staff attorneys, are responsible for compiling and organizing documentation, preparing legal documents and forms, logging information, and preparing correspondence and subpoenas. They respond to inquiries and complaints, track cases, ensure that deadlines are met, and maintain calendars. They also conduct research into legal matters, analyze materials, prepare and maintain files, record and monitor the status of legislation, and gather materials and summaries of legislation pertinent to the agency.

Legal assistant positions require a degree in paralegal studies or legal specialty training. Written exams for legal assistants test abilities in areas like record-keeping and preparing written material in a legal context, understanding and interpreting legal material, and conducting research into legal matters.

SOCIAL WELFARE POSITIONS

Those involved in the social welfare field are community troubleshooters. Through direct counseling, referral to other services, or policymaking and advocacy, they help individuals, families, and groups cope with their problems. Those in planning and policy help people understand how social systems operate and propose ways to bring about needed change in institutions such as health services, housing, and education. Among the major helping professions, a tradition of concern for the poor and disadvantaged characterizes and distinguishes social work.

Often, a higher degree is required for these positions, such as a bachelor's or master's degree in social work, social sciences, health sciences, or psychology. Related professional experience also counts heavily. When working with inmates, applicants may have to pass an investigative screening, be trained in using firearms, and meet physical and medical standards. Written exams, when given, test for understanding of social issues; effective interviewing skills; development and maintenance of client records; characteristics, behavior, and problems of human behavior and the disabled; methods of investigating child abuse; understanding laws and regulations; preparing written material; and the principles and practices of social casework.

HEALTH-CARE POSITIONS

With the continuing growth of social services, state and local governments increasingly need physicians, medical researchers, nurses, and similar workers. The growth of psychiatric concepts, the development of occupational therapy, and the increasing demands that an aging population will place on society in general and the health-care industry in particular—all of these factors demand a force of health-care practitioners working for the government at the state and local levels, as well as at the federal level.

Nurses, physician's assistants, physical therapists, occupational therapists, pharmacists, and dental hygienists in the employ of the government must have a current license to practice. Additional experience or a higher degree may be required for some positions. For many positions, no written exam is given; instead, candidates are judged on experience and training. For lower-level positions, the written exam may test abilities to read medical charts, complete forms, write reports, record data, work with patients, know laboratory principles and practices, and to recognize basic principles of health care, biology, or chemistry.

ENGINEERING POSITIONS

Engineers design machines, processes, systems, and structures. They apply scientific and mathematical theories and principles to solve practical technical problems. In state and local governments, most work in one of the more than twenty-five specialties recognized by professional societies. Electrical, mechanical, civil, industrial, chemical, and aerospace engineering are the largest specialties. Although many engineers work in design and development, others work in testing, production, operations, and maintenance.

In addition to specialized higher education and related experience, mathematical skills, drawing skills, and familiarity with architectural design and drafting may be required. For many positions, no written test is needed; rather, candidates are judged on their educational backgrounds and professional experiences. Written tests, when given, generally measure mechanical knowledge and ability, shop, safety, and conservation practices.

MECHANICAL POSITIONS

Most mechanics acquire their skills on the job under the supervision of experienced workers. Increasingly, formal mechanic training acquired in high school, vocational or technical school, community or junior college, or in the armed forces is an asset to those entering mechanical or repair careers. Often, experience is required. The civil service exam tests mechanical knowledge related to the vacant position.

CUSTODIAL AND SERVICE POSITIONS

Many of these positions require no formal education, qualification, or experience, but applicants must pass a written exam testing their ability to understand instructions, their arithmetic skills, and their mechanical knowledge. Physical exams may be required for some positions.

Glossary of Civil Service Hiring Terminology

Career Appointment—Competitive service permanent appointment given to an employee who has completed three substantially continuous, creditable years of federal service. In special cases (such as Administrative Law Judges), a career appointment may be given to a person at the time he or she is hired from a civil service register.

Certificate—A list of eligibles taken from a register and submitted to an appointing officer for employment consideration, or an agency office with delegated examining authority that submits certificates to appointing officers.

Change to Lower Grade—Personnel action that moves an employee, while serving continuously in the same agency, to (1) a position at a lower grade when both the old and new positions are under the General Schedule or under the same type graded wage schedule, or (2) to a position with a lower rate of basic pay when both the old and the new positions are under the same type upgraded wage schedule or in a different pay-method category.

Civilian Position—A civilian office or position (including a temporary, part-time, or intermittent position), appointed or elective, in the legislative, executive, or judicial branch of the federal government. This includes each corporation owned or controlled by the federal government or in the government of the District of Columbia, and it includes no appropriated fund instrumentalities under the jurisdiction of the Armed Forces.

Competitive Position—A position in the competitive service.

Competitive Service—All civilian positions in the federal government that are not specifically excepted from the civil service laws by or pursuant to statute, by the president or by the OPM under Rule VI, and that are not in the Senior Executive Service.

Competitive Status—A federal employee's basic eligibility for assignment (e.g., by transfer, promotion, reassignment, demotion, or reinstatement) to a position in the competitive service without having to participate with members of the general public in an open competitive examination. When a vacancy announcement indicates that status candidates are eligible to apply, career employees and career-conditional employees who have served at least 90 days after competitive appointment may apply. Once acquired, status belongs to the individual, not to a position.

Creditable Military Service—Total number of years and months of military service that are creditable for annual leave accrual purposes.

Creditable Service—Federal government employment (civilian or uniformed service) that meets requirements for a particular type of appointment or benefit, such as leave accrual or reduction in force retention.

Delegated Examining—Applies to external hiring, refers to the U.S. Citizenship and Immigration Services's efforts to recruit applicants outside of the current federal workforce.

Duty Station—The city/town, county, and state in which an employee works. For most employees, this will be the location of the employee's work site.

Effective Date—The date on which a personnel action takes place and on which the employee's official assignment begins.

EOD (Entry on Duty)—The process by which a person completes the necessary paperwork and is sworn in as an employee.

Ex-Serviceperson—A person who was separated from active duty performed in peacetime or wartime. (A person on active duty may be an ex-serviceperson because of separation from previous active duty.)

Excepted Position—A position in the excepted service.

Excepted Service—Unclassified service, unclassified civil service or positions outside the competitive service and the senior executive service. Excepted service positions have been excepted from the requirements of the competitive service by law.

Grade—A level of work or range of difficulty, responsibility, and qualification requirements.

Merit Staffing Program—A system under which agencies consider an employee for vacant positions on the basis of personal merit. Vacant positions are usually filled through competition, with applicants being evaluated and ranked for the position on the basis of their experience, education, skills, and performance records.

Pay Plan—The pay system or schedule under which the employee's rate of basic pay is determined; for example, General Schedule, Executive Schedule, or Leader under the Federal Wage System.

Preference (Veterans' Preference)—A category of employee entitlement to a preference in federal service employment based on active military service that was terminated honorably:

- a 5-point preference is granted to a preference-eligible veteran who does not meet the criteria for one of the types of 10-point preferences listed below. Ten-point (disability) preference is the preference to which a disabled veteran is entitled.

- a 10-point (10% compensable disability) preference is the preference to which a disabled veteran is entitled if he or she has a compensable service-connected disability rating of 10 percent or more.

- a 10-point (30% compensable disability) preference is the preference to which a disabled veteran is entitled if he or she is entitled to a 10-point preference due to a compensable service-connected disability of 30 percent or more.

- a 10-point (other) preference is the preference granted to the widow/widower or mother of a deceased veteran or to the spouse or mother of a disabled veteran. It is called "derived preference" because it is derived from the military service of someone else—a veteran who is not using it for preference. When the disabled veteran does use the service for preference, then the spouse or mother is no longer entitled to preference.

Preference Eligible—Veterans, spouses, widows, or mothers who meet the definition of "preference eligible" in 5 U.S.C. 2108. Preference eligibles are entitled to have 5 or 10 points added to their earned score on a civil service examination (see 5 U.S.C. 3309), and are accorded a higher retention standing in the event of a reduction in force (see 5 U.S.C. 3502). Preference does not apply to in-service placement actions such as promotions.

Probationary Period—The first year of service of an employee who receives a career or career-conditional appointment under 5 CFR part 315. During this period, the agency determines the fitness of the employee, and the employee has no appeal rights.

Special Hiring Authority—Used to fill a position by seeking potential applicants of a specific type. Examples include the Veterans Employment Opportunities Act, the Veterans' Recruitment Act, the Federal Career Intern Program, Schedule A, Schedule B, and Schedule C.

Status Employee—An employee who has completed the probationary period under the career-conditional employment system. Also known as an employee with competitive status.

Temporary Appointment—An appointment made for a limited period of time and with a specific not-to-exceed date determined by the authority under which the appointment is made.

Tenure—The time during which an employee may reasonably expect to serve under his or her current appointment. Tenure is governed by the type of appointment under which an employee is currently serving, without regard to whether the employee has competitive status or his or her appointment is a competitive service position or an excepted service position.

Tenure Groups—Categories of employees ranked in priority for retention during reduction in force.

Term Appointment—Appointment to a position that will last more than one year but not more than four years, and which is of a project nature whereby the job will terminate upon completion of the project.

Time-After-Competitive-Appointment Restriction—The provision that states that three months must elapse after an employee's latest non-temporary competitive appointment before he or she may be (1) promoted, reassigned, or transferred to a different line of work or to a different geographical area, or (2) transferred to or reinstated to a higher grade or different line of work in the competitive service.

Tour of Duty—The hours of a day (daily tour of duty) and the days of an administrative workweek (weekly tour of duty) that are scheduled in advance, and during which an employee is required to perform work on a regularly recurring basis.

Veteran—A person who was separated from the military with an honorable discharge or under honorable conditions from active duty in the Armed Forces performed during one of the periods described in 5 U.S.C. 2108.

Work Schedule—The time basis on which an employee is paid. A work schedule may be full-time, part-time, or intermittent.

Peterson's
Book Satisfaction Survey

Give Us Your Feedback

Thank you for choosing Peterson's as your source for personalized solutions for your education and career achievement. Please take a few minutes to answer the following questions. Your answers will go a long way in helping us to produce the most user-friendly and comprehensive resources to meet your individual needs.

When completed, please tear out this page and mail it to us at:

> Publishing Department
> Peterson's, a Nelnet company
> 2000 Lenox Drive
> Lawrenceville, NJ 08648

You can also complete this survey online at **www.petersons.com/booksurvey**.

1. **What is the ISBN of the book you have purchased? (The ISBN can be found on the book's back cover in the lower right-hand corner.)** _____

2. **Where did you purchase this book?**
   - ❑ Retailer, such as Barnes & Noble
   - ❑ Online reseller, such as Amazon.com
   - ❑ Petersons.com
   - ❑ Other (please specify) _____

3. **If you purchased this book on Petersons.com, please rate the following aspects of your online purchasing experience on a scale of 4 to 1 (4 = Excellent and 1 = Poor).**

	4	3	2	1
Comprehensiveness of Peterson's Online Bookstore page	❑	❑	❑	❑
Overall online customer experience	❑	❑	❑	❑

4. **Which category best describes you?**
   - ❑ High school student
   - ❑ Parent of high school student
   - ❑ College student
   - ❑ Graduate/professional student
   - ❑ Returning adult student
   - ❑ Teacher
   - ❑ Counselor
   - ❑ Working professional/military
   - ❑ Other (please specify) _____

5. **Rate your overall satisfaction with this book.**

Extremely Satisfied	Satisfied	Not Satisfied
❑	❑	❑

6. Rate each of the following aspects of this book on a scale of 4 to 1 (4 = Excellent and 1 = Poor).

	4	3	2	1
Comprehensiveness of the information	❑	❑	❑	❑
Accuracy of the information	❑	❑	❑	❑
Usability	❑	❑	❑	❑
Cover design	❑	❑	❑	❑
Book layout	❑	❑	❑	❑
Special features *(e.g., CD, flashcards, charts, etc.)*	❑	❑	❑	❑
Value for the money	❑	❑	❑	❑

7. This book was recommended by:
- ❑ Guidance counselor
- ❑ Parent/guardian
- ❑ Family member/relative
- ❑ Friend
- ❑ Teacher
- ❑ Not recommended by anyone—I found the book on my own
- ❑ Other (please specify) _____

8. Would you recommend this book to others?

Yes	Not Sure	No
❑	❑	❑

9. Please provide any additional comments.

_____

_____

_____

_____

_____

Remember, you can tear out this page and mail it to us at:

Publishing Department
Peterson's, a Nelnet company
2000 Lenox Drive
Lawrenceville, NJ 08648

or you can complete the survey online at **www.petersons.com/booksurvey**.

Your feedback is important to us at Peterson's, and we thank you for your time!

If you would like us to keep in touch with you about new products and services, please include your e-mail address here: _____

NOTES

NOTES

NOTES

NOTES

NOTES

NOTES

NOTES

NOTES

NOTES